Norway 1940

Also by Bernard Ash

FICTION

Silence for His Worship
Omega Street
Three Men Went to War
Fitchett's Inn
Burning Glass
Too Deep the Sea

NON-FICTION

Someone Had Blundered
  (*The sinking of* Prince of Wales
                      and Repulse)

NORWAY
1940

by
BERNARD ASH

CASSELL · LONDON

CASSELL & COMPANY LTD
35 Red Lion Square · London WC1

and at

MELBOURNE · SYDNEY · TORONTO
JOHANNESBURG · CAPE TOWN · AUCKLAND

Set in 156–11 on 12 Garamond Type
and printed in Great Britain by
Cox and Wyman Ltd
London, Fakenham and Reading
F. 1163

FOREWORD

THIS book owes much to many people—especially to some busy people who gave up precious time to delve into their memories of the past, with no other end than that a writer might set down at second-hand things they knew and suffered in person. I am immensely grateful to them all and hope they may not consider their pains in vain; for they have helped to clothe the narrative with whatever authority it may be held to possess.

In some respects the Norwegian Campaign—simple in structure but complex in detail—is remarkably well documented, although the documents are sometimes at variance; in other respects it throws up mysteries which defy explanation, such as Auchinleck's treatment of Lieutenant-Colonel Trappes-Lomax, and circumstances—such as the state of things aboard *Glorious* immediately before her sinking—of which it is difficult to establish the truth because insufficient people survived to give a complete picture.

In fairness to all who have helped me, both in personal and official capacities, I must make it clear that where there are conflicting accounts of events, the onus of selection is upon me, and I take full responsibility for my decisions. Likewise, where reconstruction has been called for, the reconstruction is to be laid at my door. Finally, any conclusions drawn from established facts, or expressions of opinion arising out of them, are mine and mine only.

Specific acknowledgements are due to the following:

Major-General Johan Beichmann of the Royal Norwegian Army for great personal labour in straightening out for me the confused pattern of events in Southern and Central Norway in the earlier part of the campaign; Captain S. Östervold of the Royal Norwegian Navy and Major-General Trygve Sandvik of the Norwegian War Historical Department.

My Lords Commissioners of the Admiralty for permission to examine unpublished records; the staffs of the Admiralty Historical Section and Library for the ready help they gave me and the kindliness with which they received me on this, as on other occasions.

The friendly and enthusiastic people at the War Office, whose encouragement meant much at the outset of a difficult project; in particular, Major-General R. A. Fyffe, as Director of Public Relations, and

Major 'Buster' Wilson-Brown, whose aid in tracking down contacts was invaluable; Mr. King, War Office Librarian, and his able staff for their active interest and assistance.

Individual survivors of the campaign to whom I owe a special word of thanks for help and in some cases hospitality are Lieutenant-Colonel the Rev. E. J. C. King-Salter (who has also allowed me to reproduce his personal account of the action at Tretten, page 163), General Sir Cameron Nicholson, Major-General A. E. Robinson ('Robbie' of the Green Howards); Brigadier S. H. Kent and Lieutenant-Colonel W. Ambrose for the loan of photographs; Colonel Robert Thomson, who suggested some most fruitful lines of thought and investigation. Several of these also read the typescript.

Air Marshal Sir Kenneth Cross, C-in-C Bomber Command, and Air Marshal Sir Richard Atcherley were particularly helpful in sorting out air operations.

I apologize for the amount of top brass there appears to be in these acknowledgements: the fact is that partly because the Norwegian Campaign was early in the war and partly because ability in command was thrown up very sharply by the shortcomings and disasters of the British forces, an unusually high number of officers emerged from it who afterwards attained distinction in their careers.

General Ruge's description of his army on pages 85 to 86 is reproduced from *I Saw it Happen in Norway* by Carl J. Hambro by permission of Hodder and Stoughton Ltd, Theodor Broch's farewell to Norway on page 313 from his book *The Mountains Wait* by permission of Michael Joseph Ltd, and extracts from published official reports by permission of the Lords Commissioners of the Admiralty and H.M. Stationery Office.

CONTENTS

CONTENTS

ILLUSTRATIONS

* By kind permission of the Imperial War Museum

MAPS

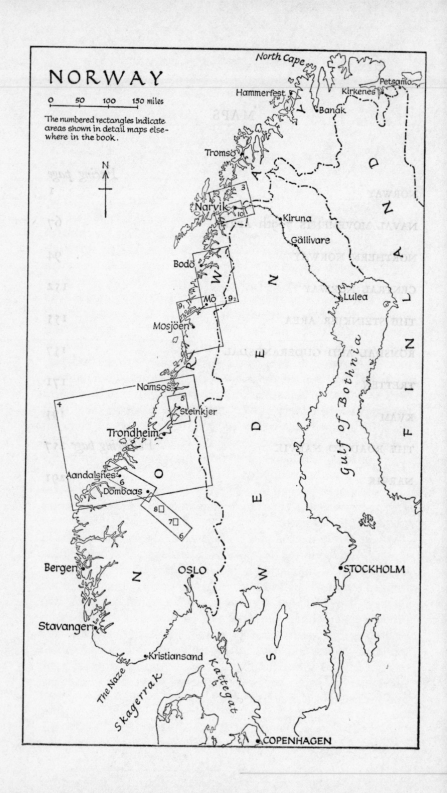

NORWAY

0   50   100   150 miles

The numbered rectangles indicate areas shown in detail maps elsewhere in the book.

N

North Cape

Hammerfest
Banak
Kirkenes
Petsamo

Tromsö

3
Narvik
10
Kiruna
Gällivare

Bodö
Mö
9₁   9₂

Mosjöen
Lulea

Namsos
5
Steinkjer
Trondheim
4

Aandalsnes
6
Dombaas
8
7
6

Bergen
OSLO
STOCKHOLM

Stavanger

Kristiansand

The Naze

Skagerrak
Kattegat

Gulf of Bothnia

COPENHAGEN

CHAPTER I

THE GORGE AT TRETTEN

THE troops looked south-eastwards down the valley to the
bend which the Germans would come round, in front of
which they had placed their improvised roadblock. They shivered:
from being overburdened with far more clothing and kit than
they could carry, they had had to jettison so much in the hasty
retreat which had brought them here that many of them were even
without greatcoats. They were hungry; they had eaten little and
rested not at all for a day and a half. They had nothing but their
rifles for defence and not very many rounds for them at that, no
tools for digging in, even if the frozen, rocky ground had permitted it; but the enemy would come with artillery, mortars,
machine-guns and tanks, and his aircraft would spy out their every
position and their every move. They had no transport they could
count on bar their own weary feet, but the enemy would come on
wheels and his ski-runners would be moving swiftly behind the
frozen hills on their flanks, where the snow was knee-deep with a
crust that would not support a man in boots. They were beyond
hope and almost beyond fear. In this evil dream from which there
was no awakening they were beginning to know the crazy
courage of the damned.

A year before they had been Territorials—week-end soldiers in
the burgeoning spring of a peaceful England. They had hardly
known their weapons: some of them had never so much as
handled a Bren. They had been called up in the September of the
Phoney War, and the blacked-out winter that followed had
brought many chores but little real training—so that when, in
February, they were suddenly warned for active service, they
were half-soldiers and half-civilians still; none of them had known
or pictured this iron-bound land of snow and ice where a hard,
late winter had barely yet given the merest suggestion of thawing
into spring. Into it they had been flung hastily and half-equipped

with many vacillations and changes of plan involving embarkations, disembarkations and re-embarkations, to be the saviours of Norway against hardened, well-equipped troops, who seemed to move with ease amid these clogging snows, efficiently directed and full of confidence and purpose. And now they were on the run with the exhausted Norwegian forces, who had been at war for nearly a fortnight longer than they had but were scarcely now in worse condition.

For all the Press and public knew at home they were still pressing triumphantly and rapidly overland towards Oslo, to drive the German invaders into the Baltic. 'Landings at a number of points in Norway' had been trumpeted to the world before they were even ashore at Aadanalsnes, now already bombed to pieces behind them. 'Substantial British forces' they had been dubbed by General Ruge,* the Norwegian Commander-in-Chief, in desperate encouragement to his improvised, half-mobilized army. They had never reached Oslo. They had never been within striking distance of Oslo. They had known only the rapid rail and road journey to Lillehammer and beyond, and the long, bitter road back. And many of them would leave their bones here, in these grim hills where they were to fight another desperate delaying action.

Both sides of the valley were precipitous. Across the river, where the rock face was almost sheer, the railway line ran precariously on a snow-clad ledge towards Lillehammer and Oslo— the same railway down which these men of the Sherwood Foresters had rumbled hastily southwards less than four days before, stretching their lines of communication to breaking point. Behind them, the glistening hills rose to a snowy shoulder more than fifteen hundred feet above. Somewhere behind it were the remains of the Norwegian dragoons, covering their flanks in makeshift fashion against the German ski-runners, with a handful of Vickers guns and a single mortar; between these and themselves was a company of the Leicesters, who were equipped with nothing but their small arms and a couple of ·5-inch anti-tank rifles—although they had once had a few mortars but nothing but smoke bombs to fire from them.

Below, on their other flank, the road, following the River

* Pronounced 'Rooga'.

2

Laagen along the valley floor, turned sharply northwards towards the village of Tretten and the bridge that must be held. The road itself was a narrow defile cut between deep walls of snow: along it some of them might be lucky enough to retreat again. The other bend, where road, river and railway turned southwards out of sight altogether, was the one which the Germans would come round. . . .

Throughout the morning the two companies of Sherwood Foresters and the company of Leicesters above them waited, their hunger gnawing at them and the cold in the marrow of their bones. There was little sound, little movement in the flat-bottomed valley. From time to time above them came the drone and throb of Ju 88s that would one day be familiar to Londoners in the blitz. These aircraft were on other business—they were ferrying troops and supplies to build up the German base at Trondheim away behind them, which was already strengthened beyond hope of recapture—although the men did not know this or for that matter, most of them, where Trondheim was. The regular morning air reconnaissance had been made and the Luftwaffe was for the moment far too busy on other matters to bother itself about a few companies of troops whom the land forces would easily brush aside, as they had repeatedly brushed them aside on their advance from the south.

The morning wore on. It warmed a little. There was the faintest suggestion of the thaw that in a bare few weeks would come with the sudden Norwegian spring, softening the icy hills, setting the rivers roaring and for a short space making the country impassable altogether. There was little to talk about, little room for speculation, for they already knew the inevitability of what was coming to them, and their tired brains could not compass much more than that. Numbly, desperately, as the hours passed there came an unreal hope that perhaps the Germans would not come.

When the sun was high, past midday, they came. Suddenly, there was a group of tanks at the bend in the road—the memories of survivors are vague and some say that there were three, some five. There was only a handful of infantry with them at first—so that it seemed that they might be picked off in the confined space. The rifle-fire echoed across the valley and told those in the village and on the other side of the river that the long suspense of waiting was over. But the enemy had more than rifles, they had mortars and machine-guns; and they grew rapidly on the ground so that rifle-fire could not pick them off fast enough or hold them back. The first tank charged the roadblock and at first failed to get through; but two others did, and immediately the tanks were in command of the road. They passed on towards the village, leaving behind them the confused fighting where the Foresters and the Leicesters on the hill behind them strove, in spite of heavy casualties, to hold off the Germans at close quarters. Thus the forward companies were already cut off from the village: they were fighting an isolated little war in an isolated little pocket of their own. To the German advance they were no longer of any importance.

Battalion headquarters and the troops posted in the village and around the bridge were still listening to their comrades' rifle-fire and wondering how long they could hold when the tanks were upon them and they were in the battle themselves. Mortars, machine-guns and 5·9s had come up on the railway shelf on the other side of the river, driving in the company that was posted there and shooting them up at close range. There was no defence against these weapons, there was no defence against the tanks, on which the big soft-nosed bullets of the anti-tank rifles made no more impression than peas from a pea-shooter.

Yet they held, they would not leave their forward companies lightly: in the intervals of their own battle they could still hear the small-arms fire over the hill, though it was diminished now because many were already dead and others were out of ammunition. Desperate things were done. Captain Ramsden of the Leicesters led a bayonet charge to silence a machine-gun post. Platoon Sergeant-Major Simpson covered the withdrawal of his men with a single Bren. For three bitter hours they held on in the village, hoping that the remnants of the forward troops would come back to them, but there was no road back and by now the ski-troops had come over the hills on their other flank and in the rear, sniping and mortaring, and they could hold on no longer.

They left a small rearguard a little to the north of the village: in the dusk and into the shortening northern night this last remnant of the retreating forces strove to keep the road open for their comrades. In the growing darkness a handful of the Foresters came in over the hill along the track by which the Norwegian dragoons had already retreated. No more came. With night the last echoes of the small-arms fire died away. The battle was over and those who had fought it were either dead, in captivity or making a last desperate effort to get away over the mountains to their base or into Sweden. And what was left of 148 Brigade was in full flight down the river towards the Heidal Valley.

It had never been a full brigade. It had never mustered more than two battalions, or had heavier weapons than rifle, anti-tank rifle and Bren, and was wholly dependent on Norwegian civilian transport: such little artillery and transport as had been belatedly sent them had been sunk on the way. The following day it would muster less than four hundred men without a single officer of the rank of company commander or above. The much publicized saviours of Norway in this vital sector had been reduced to a bedraggled remnant.

What brought these men here in such small numbers, so ill-trained, poorly armed and lacking the essential tools of battle against a well-organized and determined foe? Was this the might of Britain that had held a world in thrall and boasted the greatest empire in the history of the human race? Were these the same people that had burned the Spanish Armada, vanquished Napoleon, and driven the Kaiser's armies to surrender little more than twenty years ago?

It is already far away and long ago and children unborn when the Sherwood Foresters and Leicesters were making their last stand in Tretten Gorge have already grown to manhood.

Anger dies with the years, just as questions seem less urgent. But it never quite dies, and history at least will ask the questions—without the means of answering them unless something of the story is told while there are still those alive who remember it. Sparse credit has been given to the hard-pressed men of Norway for what they tried with great bravery to do without the means of accomplishing it: the world at large has never realized how very little it was that they had—or what they could have done with only a trifle more. It is time they had the credit—time they took their place with the men who played their part either in more glorious battles or in failures on a grander scale.

This, then, is the sorry tale of the Norwegian Campaign of 1940. It was a campaign unprepared for by the Norwegians—by the Allies conceived in folly, beset with delusions and conditioned by an apparently complete lack of appreciation of the kind of war they were going to have to fight. In many of its aspects it was almost comic, but it was a comedy of a grim kind relieved only by acts of outstanding heroism and by the sardonic humour of fighting men. In a few short weeks of fighting it laid bare Britain's disastrous deficiencies to a shocked and unbelieving world and gave birth to the short-lived legend of German invincibility. It was by the merest luck that it did not end with the complete elimination of the forces that had taken part in it. It was speedily overshadowed by the still more disastrous events that followed it —defeat in the Low Countries and in France, and the evacuation from Dunkirk—but it was not without its effect on them and has its place in history.

CHAPTER 2

'PHONEY' WAR

THE prelude to the vain stand at Tretten Gorge and the six-week battle for Norway of which it was a part was what the Americans had very aptly dubbed the Phoney War.

It is necessary to take a look back very quickly at this Phoney War because in the course of it two things in particular were demonstrated—first, the kind of campaign Hitler was likely to wage against smaller nations who got in his way; and second, the kind of help Britain and France appeared likely to give to small nations so attacked. Both these demonstrations were well noted by the neutral nations of Europe although they would appear to have been quite quickly forgotten by France and ourselves. The first certainly accounts for the fact that both Norway and Sweden were desperately anxious to avoid giving Hitler any cause to attack them. The second accounts for our own odd and quite unjustifiable assumption that if we wished to forestall a German attack on Norway by occupying key points in that country ourselves, the Norwegians would welcome us with open arms. And it accounts, incidentally, for some of the shortcomings in the equipment of the forces we sent to Norway—because the equipment of these forces was planned in the first place, before Norway was invaded by the Germans, on the assumption that they would be effecting unopposed landings in a friendly country.

In March 1939, Britain and France—following Hitler's tearing up of the Munich agreement by annexing the whole of Czecho-Slovakia—had given guarantees to Poland. On 1st September Hitler, having secured himself by a neutrality pact against intervention by Russia, invaded Poland. France and Britain thereon declared war against Germany. France mobilized her army of a hundred divisions and manned the Maginot Line, and Britain sent an expeditionary force to France—initially of four and ultimately of eleven divisions. Neither made (nor could they have made) any attempt to send direct help to Poland, which was being speedily obliterated with unparalleled ferocity and ruthlessness by a combined assault both on land and from the air—a demonstration of the long-awaited *blitzkreig* or lightning war.

In a little over three weeks Poland capitulated in the face of appalling slaughter and the destruction of most of her major cities: Germany and Russia thereupon divided the country between them. Britain and France continued to sit on the Maginot Line, demonstrating the truth of an old Polish epigram, that heaven was high and France far off. Was it any wonder that other small nations would thereafter hesitate to invite a similar fate, or to call upon the assistance of the Western Allies? And Germany had liquidated her greatest risk, that of having to wage war on two fronts at once.

Britain and France, on the other hand, now found themselves confronted with a victorious Germany, whose resources had been immeasurably increased in the previous twelve months and whom they were now pledged somehow or other to defeat. Both had gone reluctantly to war in a spirit very different from the flag-waving and cheering of 1914. Britain was still immensely rich and strong, but her resources were nothing like so great as they had been at the opening of the Kaiser's war: moreover both her vital industries and the morale of her people had been weakened by economic chaos and the long periods of unemployment and depression between the wars. France was a sick nation—sick not merely at the thought of her territory becoming a battleground yet again, but also through years of decay, social unrest, ideological strife and political corruption. Though her armed forces were large on paper—very much larger than Britain's—they were ill-equipped and much of their equipment had been in store since the end of the previous war: their morale was low and was to become still lower. They were suffering from a disease known in their own language as *le cafard*.

Neither of the Allies had an air force anything like the size of Germany's. The latest types of British fighters were to prove themselves superior in performance to their German counterparts but their numbers were woefully few, while there was a complete absence of bombers of really long range. Only on the sea could the Allies outmatch the Germans. Many of Britain's ships—especially the capital ships—were old, and there was an appalling shortage of smaller vessels, particularly of destroyers and escort craft; but between them the Allies could hold the Mediterranean and the Atlantic and spare some sort of token forces for the rest of the oceans. The command of the sea was the only real weapon we had.

Under these circumstances the only possible strategy seemed to be to hold Germany at bay on the fabulous Maginot Line (although this could be turned at any time if Hitler invaded the Low Countries as he ultimately did) and in the meantime hope to strangle the life out of her by the blockade. Should the process of strangulation be too long drawn out it was hoped in the course of three years or so to build up a substantial striking force which would arise, as the Guards arose in the final phase of the Battle of Waterloo, and deal a shattering final blow against an undermined and tottering enemy. It appears to have been assumed that German strength would remain static throughout all this period. It also appears to have been assumed that the Germans for their part would sit tight and leave us to take the initiative at any time that suited us and put up with the slow strangulation of the blockade without any attempt at breaking out of it by military action. This particular kind of wishful thinking, glaring though its lack of logic may seem, was characteristic of this period of the war: it will be seen in the preparations for our own invasion of Norway. Our strategy was forced on us by circumstances, by the resources at our disposal: to delude ourselves that we would be allowed to pursue it without any interference was highly dangerous and in the event turned out to be disastrous.

Moreover, however good the reasons for our defensive and static strategy, the outside world could not be expected to see or appreciate them and it is essential to give the picture from the outside world's point of view. For that matter the ordinary people of Britain—both civilian and in uniform—saw the picture in a very different way and had very little idea either of how things were with us or what policy the government was following. These people were still ignorant of the poverty of our resources, the inadequacies of our equipment and the smallness of our forces. They were to remain ignorant till Churchill laid bare to them the naked, appalling truth after Dunkirk. They visualized us holding the seas in our traditional naval supremacy, demonstrating with leaflets what our bomber forces could do with more lethal loads if necessary and, above all, building up our armies in France for the spring push that would roll the Nazis all the way back to Berlin. No one had told them that there was going to be a spring push and there was not the slightest justification for any assumption of one. But there had always been a spring push in the First World War and in all other wars since the beginning of time: it was part of the thinking and part of the language of war—the spring push was taken for granted.

So the civilians put up with the perils of the blackout, in which a very large number of people were killed on the roads, assaulted, robbed and suffered accidents of varying degrees of pain and inconvenience—these being in a very real sense the first casualties of the war. Troops in Britain trained as best they could in the face of a universal famine of the weapons in which they were supposed to be becoming skilled—the greater proportion of them Territorials whose peacetime training had amounted to very little. The age limit for conscription was twenty-six and it was practically impossible to volunteer. The R.A.F. patiently waited for the delivery of sufficient aircraft to make either air defence of Britain a possibility or operations of any weight against Germany a practical proposition. Civilians, soldiers and airmen alike sang 'We'll Hang Out the Washing on the Siegfried Line', which events proved to be the most inane popular hit of all time: later, played in a minor key, it made sardonic background music for the German film of the retreat of the B.E.F. on Dunkirk.

The other thing of which there was little appreciation in Britain (though once more it was well noted by the neutrals as well as by the enemy) was that the winning of the war had fallen for the most part into the hands of the selfsame men who had lost the peace. The mere fact of declaring war on Germany had wrought no spectacular transformation in these men. 'Old, decayed serving men,' Leo Amery was to call them, using Cromwell's words about the Long Parliament, in the cataclysmic debate which, in the awakening of the following spring, was to rock Chamberlain in his seat and be the prelude to his resignation. These men fought a war by a system of committees—a policy which fostered indecision and grievously hampered those in charge of the service departments: the service chiefs, as Churchill has told us, spent so much time in committee that they were left too little for their proper work and they were in any case handicapped in their ordinary day's work by lack of staff. The indecisiveness of this system, still more the habit of indecision and vacillation which it fathered, will again be evident not merely in the preparation for the Norwegian Campaign but in its actual conduct.

Only at the Admiralty, Churchill, brooding and restless, chafed at the committees and itched for power to command the action for which he craved. His destiny was not yet upon him and the spirit of Britain which he was to arouse was still unawakened; but it was appropriate that he should be there. For only the Navy was really at war.

The Navy had been at sea and at battle stations around the ports from which the enemy might break out two days before war was declared. Within hours of the declaration of war the torpedoing of the defenceless and unescorted *Athenia* made it clear that Hitler proposed to wage total and unrestricted warfare at sea. There were ships all over the oceans carrying supplies vital to Britain's survival, let alone to any sort of war effort, to be rounded up and brought home as safely as might be. Thereafter there were immediately convoys to be organized and conducted, watch to be kept for the German Navy's more powerful battle units breaking out into the Atlantic to savage defenceless merchant shipping, minefields to be laid, coastal waters to be patrolled and endless other tasks which arise in the defence of an island at war. As we have already seen, its ships of all sizes were inadequate in numbers alone for the tasks demanded of them. The areas of the sea they had to cover were vast and the advantage was always with the enemy, however much smaller the enemy's forces, for in war at sea the attacker can always choose the time, place and route of his breaking out while the defender must strive to watch all points of the compass and every square mile of sea and try to divine his opponent's intentions; moreover, naval intelligence had not been able to build up into a working system and was often both faulty and incomplete.

The seas in which the Navy had principally to operate at this time were the English Channel, the treacherous North Sea, the sub-arctic and Arctic Oceans as far as the iceline and the wintry

North Atlantic itself. These seas were beset by storms and shrouded with fog, rain and snow. Conditions were bitter, the demands on endurance immense. It was not given to every ship to sink a U-boat or sight a surface raider: for the majority there was only monotonous and unremitting vigilance in biting cold, in snow or driving rain, in wreathing fog or drenching seas; a vista of pitiless and unrelenting ocean that had to be watched without deviation or relief. But in the face of these hardships and dangers the Navy showed itself tenacious in its watch, bold and bloody-minded when the chance for action came. *Rawalpindi*, out-gunned and ablaze from stem to stern, steaming hard for the enemy with her guns still in action; *Exeter, Achilles* and *Ajax* weighing in with their six-inch and eight-inch guns against the eleven-inch guns of *Graf Spee* and battering her into submission—these stirred the hearts of a nation whose hearts some thought to be beyond all stirring. The boarding of *Altmark*, the heroic tale of Warburton-Lee, the last fights of *Acasta* and *Ardent* in the campaign that was to come, were to show an offensive spirit in the face of great odds that was totally lacking from the conduct of operations at home.

These men of this Navy were not different men from those of the Army and the R.A.F. The half-trained Territorials, fighting their first and last battles in the Gudbrandsdal, the handful of Gladiator and Hurricane pilots and a host of others were to show the guts that were needed to win a war. But the Navy's biggest advantage was that it was still virtually a force of regulars, trained to the last degree in the use of its weapons and the handling of its ships. In the land and air operations in Norway lack of training proved as disastrous as lack of equipment and in the end it was a small element of regular troops who carried out the only operations which were not completely catastrophic.

The Navy's patience and boldness brought results. By the end of 1939 probably half Germany's original U-boat forces—which were nothing like so large as the world imagined at that stage of the war—had been sunk. The volume of supplies reaching Britain was up to two-thirds of peacetime figures. Axis merchant shipping had been fairly effectively driven from the high seas and a quarter of a million tons of it sunk. When challenged, major units of the small German fleet showed a strange lack of inclination to fight things out, and the *Graf Spee* had so far been the only successful surface commerce raider.

But there was a back door to the blockade which it was extremely difficult to close; and that back door led to a covered passage down the coast of Norway. A glance at the map will show that the western coast of Norway is broken and scarred and tapers off into the sea through a belt of innumerable islands. It looks as though some giant, putting this corner of Europe in its appointed place, had set it down with a bang. Or, to put it another way, this coast has the appearance of a very complicated jig-saw puzzle which has had a bad shake-up, causing the pieces to separate and some of them to go adrift altogether. Inside this belt of islands runs a continuous series of deep-water passages known to Norwegians as the Indreled and to British mariners as the Leads. Through these, large ships could navigate from Narvik in the Arctic Ocean right round to the southern tip of Norway and so through the Kattegat to the safety of the Baltic. German ships, sneaking homewards by the northabout passage through the Arctic sea, could slip in through this back door and thence navigate inside not merely the islands but also Norwegian territorial waters where we were powerless to interfere.

Repeated protests had been made to the Norwegian government since the outbreak of war, against its condoning the use of its waters by enemy shipping; but Norway was not at war with Germany any more than she was at war with us. She not only refused to take any action against German shipping but maintained a neutrality patrol to ensure that her rights over her own territorial waters were not infringed by Allied ships of war. Moreover while Germany had shown scant regard for international law we were obliged to respect it; not only because we had proclaimed that we were fighting for the rule of law among nations but also because neutral opinion all over the world and especially in the United States would have reacted to any violation of neutrality by us, however justified the results might have shown it to be.

Norway was bitterly attacked at the time and has been soundly berated since for insisting on her neutral rights and the inviolability of her waters. We were naturally prejudiced in this matter and still are today. Certainly in the light of later events it is easy to say that Norway was very foolish to follow any course of action which would help build up German strength. But all this is after-thinking: the Norwegians were no more prophets than we were, and though the duplicity of the Nazis and the falseness of Hitler's promises and avowals had already been demonstrated more than once, they had not been demonstrated nearly often enough to influence the thinking of people who had been brought up in a fairly straightforward world.

There were strong cultural and human links between the Norwegians and the Germans. In the famines of the 1920s thousands of children from southern Germany and Austria had been cared for in Norway: *Wiener-barn* (Vienna children) they were called, and they had lived with Norwegian families, been to school in Norway, learned the Norwegian language. In the 1930s the *Wandervögel* had tramped and sung their way through the hospitable country—indeed it was in imitation of these, the first of the hikers, that the youth hostel movement grew in our own land. Later it was said that 'their love of nature was of a peculiar variety and the sketches they were making were the sketches of bridges and cross-roads, of strategically important points . . .' but this again is after-thinking. The Germans had invited a great many Norwegians to special meetings and events in Germany and they themselves had sent to Norway artists, singers, scientists, literary men and lecturers. There seemed not the slightest reason or excuse for German hostility to Norway; while on the other side the ruins of the Polish cities, their ashes yet barely cold, continued to give their appalling object-lesson of the possible results of getting in Germany's way.

So even when neutral shipping—for that matter even Norwegian shipping—was sunk by German action in the Leads, and in spite of all the representations and protests, Norway continued to hang on stubbornly to her neutrality. Time and time again Churchill, with the unanimous support of the Admiralty, had pleaded for the mining of the Leads or for other action to close them to German ships. He was denied as often as he pleaded. He was opposed by the Foreign Office—who throughout the war seem to have exercised an unjustifiable and quite wrong-headed influence on military affairs, and who were concerned with the possible effect of such actions on the Italians and Japanese. He was opposed by tired old men, who were afraid of anything that might precipitate action. He was opposed by the French. He was opposed by the Americans—or at least by such of them as did not want the war to spread. The Leads remained open, the Norwegians uncompromising. The Navy continued its endless, stormy vigil. The troops in Britain continued their guard duties, chores and discomforts. And civilians and servicemen alike continued to sing about the washing on the Siegfried Line.

CHAPTER 3

THE IRON ROAD

I F the use of the Leads by German shipping had merely been a
matter of inconvenience to the Navy, it would probably have
never become an issue of importance. But it was not merely an
inconvenience to the Navy—it was a matter of great importance
in the economic blockade. It was a vital channel for iron ore
imports into Germany, and the economic experts believed that
Germany's two most serious industrial weaknesses were her need
to import oil and her need to import iron ore. It is now fairly
clear that we had got both these issues out of proportion—the
issue of Swedish iron ore in particular. But if we were to strangle
the life out of Germany by blockade quite clearly that blockade
had to be as effective as possible.

Swedish iron ore is among the richest in the world, and both
the Germans and ourselves were anxious to import as much of it
as possible. The experts assessed Germany's 1938 iron ore imports at about twenty-two million tons, of which at least nine
million tons came from Sweden. We were believed already to
have cut off nine and a half million tons of her imports from other
sources by the blockade: if by design or miracle the Swedish
imports could be cut off too, Germany's war industries could not
last a twelvemonth. So, at any rate, the argument ran, although
like all arguments on paper it was far from foolproof.

The most important of the ore fields are in the north of
Sweden in the area of Gällivare. For eight months of the year the
ore is railed to the port of Lulea at the north of the Gulf of
Bothnia and shipped down to Germany's Baltic ports; but for
four months of the year the Gulf is frozen, and in the period
between the wars a railway had been built through the mountains, across the Norwegian border and the very narrow strip
of Norway which at this point lies between Sweden and the
North Sea. Here, at the head of a series of deep fiords, the little

port of Narvik had grown up, well above the Arctic Circle and a good seven hundred miles from Norway's capital, Oslo. During the winter months the ore could be shipped from here down the ice-free and comparatively sheltered coastal waters behind the islands, round the Naze, the tip of Norway and so to Germany once more. And because of Norway's refusal to allow any interference with German traffic through the Leads, the shipping of this ore was continuing uninterrupted through the winter of the Phoney War. How much ore would be lost to Germany if it had been possible to stop this traffic was a matter of argument on both sides at the time, has continued to be a matter of argument and has never been precisely determined; but obviously it would be considerable, and not less than one million tons a year.

The Ministry of Economic Warfare urgently desired to stop this traffic but it could clearly not be stopped unless some sort of interruption could be caused to traffic down the Leads, and the Ministry of Economic Warfare was up against precisely the same obstacles as the Navy.

This question of Swedish iron ore somehow assumed a position of tremendous importance. It was discussed and debated so much that it became out of all proportion to its actual weight. It is safe to say that the War Cabinet became curiously mesmerized by the iron ore question in general and by Narvik in particular. In consequence, the importance of the Narvik area bulked so large in the minds of people responsible for policy and strategy that some curious decisions were made when the invasion of Norway broke. In fact, for the easier understanding of our moves in the earliest days in particular of the German invasion, we must bear two things in mind: that the naval chiefs of staff and the naval commanders at sea were obsessed with the containing of German raiders trying to break out into the North Atlantic, while the War Cabinet was obsessed with Narvik and iron ore.

The Germans themselves were also concerned about their iron ore imports; though it would hardly be true to say that they were obsessed with them to the same extent as we were. None the less, while the British War Cabinet argued the Germans acted. As early as October 1939, Grand Admiral Raeder had put to Hitler a scheme for the invasion of Norway which would not only secure the iron ore route but also give Germany effective bases for operations in the northern ocean. By December he had been able to produce for Hitler's personal inspection a gentleman called Vidkun Quisling, whose name has now become a dirty word in the dictionary and of whom we shall hear more later. In mid-December Hitler issued orders for the planning of the Norwegian operation in detail under Field Marshal Keitel. Early in the new year plans were completed and on 20th February General von Falkenhorst was appointed to command it. The original date fixed for the invasion was 20th March: it was later postponed to early April.

While this planning was going on and troops, supplies, aircraft, merchant shipping, naval units and all other necessary elements were being organized and planned, the British War Cabinet and its committees continued their deliberations—but did no planning. They might have gone on deliberating for ever but for two things —one of which appeared to open a door for the War Cabinet, while the other opened the eyes of people in Britain to the German traffic through Norwegian coastal waters.

The first of these was that on 30th November 1939, Russia invaded Finland. We were not at war with Russia and had no particular desire to be, having quite enough on our plate by being at war with Germany. But sympathies were very much with the Finns, not only in this country but in the neutral countries, including America, and there was great anxiety to get both supplies and men to help her. The latter would have to be 'volunteers', which was after all no different from the guise under which Germans and Italians had fought in Spain; and at least it was more than had been done to help our Allies, the Poles, when they were invaded by Germany.

How to get volunteers and supplies into Finland? The Baltic and the Gulf of Bothnia were closed to us and were, moreover, ice-bound. There was a route that was not ice-bound and which might not be closed to us; and that, by an extraordinary coincidence, was the route through the port of Narvik, over the railway into Sweden and through Sweden's iron ore fields. If the Norwegians and the Swedes would allow us to use this route it would have to be guarded and protected, and this would involve occupying the objects of our greatest longing, the selfsame port of Narvik and the selfsame ore fields. The only fly in the ointment was that neither Norway nor Sweden would give their permission for these measures and they refused their permission for precisely the same reasons that had led the Norwegians to refuse to allow us to apply our contraband control to their coastal waters. Both avowed the greatest sympathy with the Finns but they also considered that they had a responsibility to themselves; and although Sweden had a reasonable army and air force and a small but efficient navy, while Norway had virtually no military forces at all, both of them were quite squarely, and fairly, convinced of the folly of getting on the wrong side of Germany.

There was never the slightest possibility of our being allowed to send supplies and troops (volunteer or otherwise) through Norway and Sweden, still less to have any bases there. The whole thing was a pipe dream.

None the less, the planning of this pipe dream progressed by degrees into practical realities while the Finns, with great tenacity, continued to hold the Russians at bay. Out of the very considerable force which emerged from the dream, two brigades only were intended as actual assistance to the Finns: the remainder would be responsible not merely for occupying the north of Norway and Sweden but also for seizing three southern ports in Norway, denying them to the Germans and protecting the north. Thus the ore fields would be ours—and, almost incidentally, the route to Finland. About 100,000 British troops were involved in this, including two whole divisions held back from France, and some 50,000 French. An important element in the latter were the Chasseurs Alpins, equipped to operate in snow-bound country. There were no equivalent troops available in Britain but a considerable number of experienced skiers were got together, equipped and formed into a battalion—the 5th Scots Guards. Aircraft—both fighters and bombers—were earmarked for this force and provisional allocations made of escort craft from the fleet. The operation was planned for mid-March.

But the Norwegians still refused to countenance any proposal that forces should be allowed to pass through their country or garrison any part of their territory, and eventually the War Cabinet—egged on by the French, who had increasingly been viewing this operation as a large-scale diversion of the war from their own territory—was driven to debate whether the plans might not be put into operation against Norwegian opposition. It would have been a particularly difficult decision to take under any circumstances, but it was particularly difficult under the conditions of procrastination and indecision then prevailing. It was not, in fact, until three days after the Finns had at last been driven to start armistice negotiations that the War Cabinet gave a very modified approval, still demanding assurance that the Norwegian and Swedish governments would acquiesce in the operation even if they did not agree to it. There was no more likelihood of them acquiescing than there had been of them agreeing—but, in any case, on 12th March the Finns finally surrendered and signed armistice terms with Russia. At this Britain dispersed the forces which had been held in readiness and the volunteer ski battalion was actually disbanded. These troops would have been of immense value in the campaign shortly to be forced upon us, but they could not be reassembled at the short notice required. The French forces, however, still remained available, although their transport to Norway would now be complicated and dangerous.

Outside the War Cabinet and the service departments no one was aware of the great struggle that had been going on over the Finnish project. Nor was anyone (least of all the War Cabinet) aware of the equivalent German plans now nearing completion. But the second of the two events of importance which occurred at this time was enacted—deservedly—in the full limelight of publicity, and served to make ordinary people aware, for the first time, of what was going on along the coast of Norway.

A few months previously, when *Graf Spee* was raiding Allied shipping in the South Atlantic and before she had been brought to account by Commodore Harwood's squadron, she had been attended by a fleet auxiliary called *Altmark*. This ship was in effect a floating, temporary prisoner-of-war camp and survivors from the raiders' victims were transferred to her as their ships were sunk, until she was believed to have at least three hundred Merchant Navy prisoners aboard.

She escaped during the action, and subsequent search failed to disclose her whereabouts—for what we now know to be the simple reason that she wisely remained in the South Atlantic until late in January, instead of making directly for home and almost certain capture on the way. Eventually, however, she made

Aboard S.S. *Sobieski* the ship's officers talk to British troops.

Troops aboard S.S. *Oronsay*, off the Norwegian coast.

Disembarkation—Aandalsnes.

course for Germany by the usual northabout route and in bad weather with very poor visibility passed between the Faeröes and Iceland and made her way into the protection of the Leads. On 14th February she was off Trondheim, on the 15th off Bergen, and a successful end to her voyage seemed to be in sight.

Late on the 15th, however, she was spotted with two Norwegian gunboats in close attendance by a Hudson aircraft of Coastal Command, and her whereabouts were promptly signalled to the 4th Destroyer Flotilla, commanded by Captain Vian in *Cossack*, which together with the cruiser *Arethusa* was carrying out a sweep in that area. Captain Vian was promptly ordered to intercept her, which he did. She took refuge in Jossingfiord.* The Norwegians, who were on neutrality patrol, protested that they had examined the ship and that she had neither contraband nor prisoners aboard; but Vian insisted that they should accompany him with *Altmark* into Bergen for further examination. This they refused to do.

Vian withdrew; but that night, on direct orders from the Admiralty, he re-entered the fiord with searchlights ablaze. *Altmark* attempted to ram him but merely succeeded in running herself aground; and *Cossack* was laid alongside her and she was boarded with gusto in the traditional fashion—probably the last time this time-hallowed operation was ever to be carried out in war at sea. A brief hand-to-hand struggle followed in which several Germans were killed and the rest finally fled ashore. The prisoners, battened down below decks, listened to the rumpus with some apprehension; but their fears rapidly gave way to joy as a great banging was set up on doors and hatches and the cry was heard, 'The Navy's here!'

With lightning speed the story spread over Britain and the world. 'The Navy's here!' became a catchphrase which threatened the supremacy of the washing on the Siegfried Line—and indeed it was a much more realistic and appropriate one, for in the years to come and especially in the months immediately to follow, hard-pressed men, driven to the end of their tether in more than one theatre of war, were to find that the Navy was there and to thank God for it.

Two other consequences followed. One was that virtually every

* Pronounced 'Yursingfure'.

troopship on which the British Army sailed in campaigns to come was dubbed *Altmark* by its unfortunate passengers. The other—much more important—was that once everyone had been awakened to the problems and implications of the Norwegian coast, public opinion surged up in a demand that something should be done about it.

The outcome was Operation Wilfred.

CHAPTER 4

APRIL FOLLY

M R. CHURCHILL was obviously a reader of the *Daily Mirror*; his own explanation of the title 'Operation Wilfred' was that by itself it was minor and innocent—and Wilfred was the youngest and most innocent of three animal characters in a children's strip in that newspaper, highly popular in those days. It also, one suspects, alluded to the smallness of the operation in relation to the amount of discussion that had taken place on it over a period of months, for it had been before the service departments heaven knows how many times, before the War Cabinet quite a number of times, and before the Allied Supreme War Council at least twice: in common with all war operations at this period it had been subjected to approval, cancellation, reappraisal and reapproval. Its execution was finally fixed for 5th April.

Wilfred itself amounted to the laying of two small belts of mines off the Norwegian coast and the simulated laying of another: the first two of these were in the approaches to Narvik and between Aalesund and Bergen farther south, while the fictitious one was off Molde. Their object was quite simply to stop traffic down the Leads. The mines were to be laid whether the Norwegians agreed or not.

Even the War Cabinet could not but be aware of the possible consequences of Wilfred—either that the Norwegians would make some sort of move in protest, that the Germans would react strongly by moving into Norway, or both. There was to be a 'pause to assess the reactions of Germany and Norway',* after

---

* This phrase was used in the briefing given to the C.O.s of the Army units involved at the War Office on 2nd April and at the same meeting the policy that we would not move these units until Norwegian neutrality was violated was also clearly stated. The official history of the campaign, however, declares that the units were timed to sail immediately on the heels of the mine-laying expedition. The discrepancy does not affect the ultimate outcome, but it well illustrates the confusion that was a 'built-in' element of the whole operation. It is not unlikely that the Navy and the Army were given quite different impressions of what was intended to happen.

which we would proceed to develop our own counter-measures to these reactions: everything, apparently, was going to move in slow motion for the convenience of all concerned.

The instrument of our counter-measures was Plan R.4. Under this an expeditionary force was to be held ready for Norway, but was on no account to sail until the enemy was clearly about to violate Norwegian territory. It would then sail in four cruisers from Rosyth and transports from the Clyde escorted by the cruiser *Aurora* and six destroyers. It would occupy Narvik and the railway to Sweden, together with Bergen and Trondheim; and a small detachment of it was to raid Stavanger, where the only really sizeable airfield in central Norway was situated.

So far, so good—on paper. But of what, in fact, did this force consist and how was it equipped to keep the Germans out of Norway? Something extraordinary had happened since the planning of the Finnish campaign with its strong core of regular troops, its full equipment for attack and defence, its air support and all the rest. There had been a complete change of thinking— or perhaps one should say that there had been a complete cessation of thinking—about the kind of operation that was going to be necessary to keep the Germans out of Norway. Even allowing for after-knowledge of the sort of of campaign Norway was going to be, it is absolutely impossible to guess what was in the minds of the people who laid out Plan R.4. The official history declares that the forces allocated to Plan R.4 were all that could be spared from our commitments in France, the Middle East and elsewhere; but if larger and better-equipped forces could have been spared for Finland, why had they suddenly ceased to be available for Plan R.4?

For as against the 100,000 men who had been earmarked for Finland, Plan R.4 was to be carried out by one incomplete infantry division—49—augmented by 24 (Guards) Brigade, only one battalion of which was actually embarked in readiness.

The Narvik portion of the force, for which the Guards Brigade was intended, was indeed to be strengthened later by French troops; but these were not ready to move immediately following on Wilfred and could at this stage be counted out of the picture. 49 Division itself was wholly made up of Territorial troops: it was a brigade short and one of its brigades was a battalion under strength. The units were to take with them no transport and virtually no artillery. There were no arrangements whatsoever for air support. They were visualized as carrying out garrison duties, and, therefore, their lack of more essential stores and supporting arms was counterbalanced by a wealth of office equipment: normal regimental accounting procedures were to be followed. To counterbalance this in turn one battalion at least was short of the most elementary cooking equipment. In the series of embarkations, disembarkations and re-embarkations the inadequate stores vouchsafed to the units (including such vital things as signal equipment) were to be so confused, depleted and generally bedevilled that all had some difficulty in knowing what they had and what they had not. Generally speaking, both in actual manpower and in what they had to fight with, they would have been just about adequate to occupy Southend Pier.

To round off the picture, there was an acute shortage of maps, and those that were issued were forty years old and lacking in detail; there had been apparently not the slightest attempt to assess the physical conditions the troops would have to face on the landing in Norway or the extent to which their missing items could be made good from local sources; and very definitely there had been no thought of, nor attempt at, forewarning the troops of the conditions they would meet, or preparing them in any way for them.

Anyone who served in a Territorial unit at home in the first winter of the war will know what sort of training these troops had had. Some of them, scattered in detachments about their areas on guard duties, had hardly been together as battalions at all, let alone as brigades. Those that had not been so scattered had had their training badly restricted by the severe winter, by the lack of equipment with which to train and the shortage of experienced officers and instructors: neither their health nor their fitness were outstanding and the 1/4th Lincolnshires had suffered from an epidemic of measles. All of them with the exception of the Hallamshire Battalion of the York and Lancaster Regiment had been carved in twain in the reorganization of Territorial battalions in the summer of 1939—which by this splitting process was supposed to make two battalions grow where only one had been before but which, in fact, produced double the number of inefficient battalions in place of the original number of battalions with some degree of training at least.

A very detailed account exists of the history during this period of one of the battalions concerned—the 1/4th King's Own Yorkshire Light Infantry. The original 4th Battalion, recruited in south Yorkshire, had been an enthusiastic Territorial unit and prided itself on its standard of training. In the summer of 1939 it was completely ruined by being cut in two, the halves of the two new units so created being filled up with completely untrained men. In the early months of the war it was split up not merely into companies but into platoons detached at some distance from each other on guard duties. It had received little or no new equipment. By January 1940 it had had no commanding officer for several months and was in a very low state of training and discipline, with a large number of officers and other ranks physically unfit.

Early in February 1940 the battalion was concentrated—for many of its personnel, both officers and men, the first time they had been together as a battalion at all. In what sort of state it would finally have embarked for active service overseas can hardly be imagined, had there not appeared on the scene a new commanding officer, Lieutenant-Colonel H. B. Hibbert. A resolute and efficient regular officer, he looked upon his new command and was appalled by what he saw—particularly since he had been told that the unit must be ready for active service in less than two months. Training of the most elementary sort was necessary (not to speak of the training of specialists) and he discovered a need to make it clear to his officers as well as to their men that orders were intended to be obeyed and not discussed. To start off with, the medical officer down-graded no less than thirty per cent of the men, but the War Office rejected his down-grading: fortunately the situation was partly made good later by a good draft from the 2/4th Battalion—including a new M.O. Thereafter Hibbert determined on a policy of 'blood, sweat and tears' and for a brief space the 1/4th Battalion did not quite know what had hit them, except that they disliked it exceedingly and disapproved of it even more. They were to change their minds about this later, for in the two months allotted to him, Hibbert accomplished the apparently impossible task of drumming into them the basic essentials of military training and making them hard and fit; to this, as well as to the resource and leadership of an outstanding officer, his men were to owe their lives in the disaster that followed. Not all the troops in Norway were so fortunate.

There is nothing in all this that impugns either the character or the essential qualities of the men of 49 Division. There was absolutely nothing wrong with the men: faced with fighting conditions of which they had never so much as dreamed and had certainly not been forewarned, under relentless pressure by a stronger enemy backed by all the equipment of total war, they showed steadiness and strength that could not have been expected of them. But this was not to be an amateurs' war. There was no longer any place in the scheme of things for amateurs at war, and the difference in sheer training and conditioning between the British and German troops was as important as the differences in equipment on the ground and support in the air which were the two other deciding factors in this campaign.

By contrast it is surprising to learn from German sources that they for their part had misgivings about the quality of the troops available for *Weserübung*, as their operation was called. In practically every British account of the campaign the German forces are spoken of as hardened regular troops. But this was not so. Only the mountain divisions were regulars—the remainder were recently embodied units. But the military training and indoctrination of the German youth in the years of hate and preparation which preceded the war were such that what they regarded as comparatively raw units were far more advanced in training and in the use of their weapons (quite apart from having the right weapons for the job) than any Territorial division in this country could hope to be. Furthermore they had been carefully chosen and included a very high proportion of men who had been in Norway either as children or adults, knew something of the country, its climate, its conditions and even its language—whereas many of the British troops had never seen a mountain in their lives. Organized command and planning gave them confidence and success made them more confident still. In central Norway it was only when, after a long pursuit and continuous victory, they came up against the magnificent regular troops of 15 Brigade that their comparative rawness was revealed: then they recoiled rapidly and hesitated to re-engage. The same reaction was seen farther north for a very brief period against the Guards and when two solitary Gladiators were able to operate for a short time against German positions.

So much for the contrast between the types of units we had ready on our side for the occupation of Norway and the types of units the Germans had for their invasion. What is even more striking is the sheer contrast between their size and equipment. While we held ready one ill-trained and incomplete Territorial division with a few regulars tacked on, the Germans held six army divisions. Where our troops lacked even their normal mechanized transport, the Germans had at their disposal soft-skinned transport, armoured cars and tanks, and two hundred transport planes. Where we had no plans for fighter or bomber cover, eight hundred operational aircraft (in addition to the transport aircraft) were allotted to the German forces. And every unit of the German Navy that could swim was allocated to one or other of the six groups into which their force was divided. It was a complete combined operation of a kind which was as yet utterly unknown in British military planning.

Finally, the Germans possessed another force which was, in fact, already in Norway. It was not the Fifth Column—certainly it was not the miserable pro-German party of Vidkun Quisling, which his German masters were speedily to find was a puny and contemptible thing. It was assumed at the time and has often been assumed since that the Fifth Column played as big a part in the conquest of Norway as it did in the conquest of France; but this is not so, and facts now at our disposal make it quite clear that the proportion of Norwegians who helped the Germans either actively or passively was probably lower than in any of the other occupied countries. But virtually every member of the German diplomatic and consular organizations in Norway was either a spy or had his or her allotted functions against the time when the German invaders should come. The same was true of the members of the many German business organizations—both real and fictitious—which had staffs in Norway. The same was even true of the apparently innocent and sociable wives of German business executives who happened, apparently fortuitously, to be staying with their husbands in hotels in Oslo and elswhere. These were far more effective and far more deadly than any Fifth Column could possibly have been and both they and their functions were part of the planning for the campaign.

Quisling would come out into the open when the time came, but had the Germans depended solely on Quisling and his followers to pave the way for them they would not have got very far.

There were postponements in the starting dates planned by both sides, which had the effect of neatly synchronizing the operations. On our side the interminable discussions and vacillations of the committee-ridden war caused the putting-off of Operation Wilfred from 6th April to the 8th. On the 5th, however, notes were handed to the Norwegian and Swedish governments which, in effect, warned them of some sort of impending action, and the Press in both those countries immediately headlined speculations about the date of an impending Allied invasion of Scandinavia. In any case the Allies were telegraphing their punches to such an extent that German Intelligence would have had to be both blind and deaf not to have picked up an abundance of hints, which were duly reported: afterwards they claimed to have known of our minelaying plans on 25th March.

Wesurübung, the German plan, was originally schemed for 20th March. Various reasons, including the slow clearing of winter ice from the Baltic, caused it to be put off till 9th April. This meant that the movement of the main forces would begin in the moonless night of the 6th/7th, though certain of the disguised invasion ships, whose place in the plan we shall see presently, would be under way on the 2nd. And here again prior warning to the outside world had not been lacking. From the beginning of the year persistent reports had been coming in from both Sweden and France that some sort of German operation was in the wind against either Norway, Sweden or both. Aircraft reconnaissance had spotted troop concentrations in North Germany and ship concentrations in Kiel. As late as 6th April information came from Copenhagen that a German division would land at Narvik on the 8th. In all fairness too much can be made of the fact that these reports were not heeded. For the whole of the winter, while the opposing forces faced each other futilely across the Maginot Line, London and Paris had been inundated with rumours and reports of every degree from the fantastic to the apparently factual. Those which (by luck or knowledge) presaged things which actually happened survive in the records—the remainder of the vast mass of froth is lost to history, though no doubt it survives in dusty archives somewhere. It is easy, in the light of after-knowledge, to point to those to which heed should have been paid: it was well nigh impossible, at the time, to sort the one from the other. And some of those which foretold fact appeared, in the light of imperfect understanding or wishful thinking, to be the most improbable: a German landing at Narvik, for instance, sounded and looked like an utterly foolhardy project for the German High Command in face of the Allied mastery of the sea.

So much, then, for plans, ambitions and circumstances—a great deal of detail and a great mass of words without any action. There will be action enough before long, but before the action breaks, one more word of explanation will be of great help to the reader. The six-week campaign in Norway is made up of many engagements on land and at sea—in the air the pattern is, deplorably, very much simpler. These are often actions involving small units—brigades, companies, even platoons—and at first sight the web of events is complicated in the extreme. But the overall pattern is extremely simple. We laid our minefields. At the same time the Germans invaded Norway and successfully occupied key points from Narvik in the north to Oslo in the south. It was several days before our own land forces could be got on their way and those days were occupied by a rapid build-up of the German forces, by a heroic though hopeless stand by the Norwegians themselves and by a number of clashes between units at sea. Thereafter we landed forces at three main points in Norway, which the Germans inexorably proceeded to roll up with a speed which not only surprised the Nazis themselves but also staggered British opinion at home—as well as such people outside the sphere of conflict who still believed that Britain and France were two first-class imperial powers capable of waging war on a grand scale. From the moment when the first German units put to sea and successfully evaded the masters of the oceans, a sense of steadily marching doom hangs over events in Norway and builds up to a climax with the advancing days.

Here, then, is 7th April 1940, a day of earliest spring in Britain and Western Europe, though in the Baltic the winter ice has barely cleared, while even Southern Norway is still deep in snow and its Arctic North in the grip of ice, albeit the nights are shortening and the thaw will soon come: the northern seas are likewise still prey to tempest, rain, snowstorm and treacherous fog. It is the last day of the Europe that a whole generation has known and the last day of their lives, or near it, for many brave men.

Off Rosyth are four cruisers—*Devonshire, Berwick, York* and *Glasgow*; at the Tail o' the Bank in the Clyde estuary is a group of troop transports (not long since luxury liners) with the cruiser *Aurora* and six destroyers. In *Devonshire* is the 1/5th Battalion of the Royal Leicestershire Regiment, in *Berwick* the 1/4th Battalion of the Royal Lincolnshire Regiment, in *York* the 1/4th King's Own Yorkshire Light Infantry with its redoubtable Colonel Hibbert, in *Glasgow* the 1/8th Battalion Sherwood Foresters—all these shoe-horned somehow into ships already stuffed with their wartime complement, but the Navy is being as hospitable as circumstances will allow and their stores (such as they are) are stowed tactically and in good order. In the Clyde, in much greater spaciousness and comfort, are the Hallamshire Battalion of the York and Lancaster Regiment in the Polish liner *Chrobry* and the 1st Battalion Scots Guards in *Batory*: the first, an eleven-thousand-ton ship with eight hundred bunks, makes a troopship to dream about and the second, even larger, is still haunted by the perfumed ghosts of film stars, though the Guards are kept busy humping and re-arranging stores, with P.T. to fill in idle moments, and there is a route march ashore ordered for the morrow. None of these troops have the slightest idea what they are there for and rumour has destined them for anything from the Arctic Circle to Singapore. The Home Fleet is at Scapa Flow, only recently re-occupied after the 'flap' following the sinking there of *Royal Oak*. Various other units of the Navy are disposed at their monotonous and dangerous tasks about the stormy oceans; among them nearly a score of submarines are watching the approach routes to Norway. These have strict instructions to abide by the conventions for submarine warfare signed in the 1930s—which, among other things, oblige them before sinking anything other than an obvious ship of war, to surface, give warning and allow those aboard to get clear. Far to the north four destroyers and another four for escort are at last about their minelaying job in the approaches to Narvik, the minelayer *Teviot Bank* and four more destroyers are on the way to their similar mission farther south which in the press of events that followed was not carried out. Two destroyers are about to simulate the non-existent mine-field off Molde by appearing to guard it. Vice-Admiral Whitworth in the battle cruiser *Renown*, with destroyers *Greyhound, Glowworm, Hyperion* and *Hero*, is in attendance on the northerly force, to protect it against Norwegian coast defence ships, of which four are said to be at Narvik. It is filthy weather for the destroyers, which have had to battle their way to their destination through heavy seas in bad visibility.

The Germans are at sea likewise, in the six groups which have been carefully organized for their initial landings—no pause here to assess reactions in Norway or anywhere else: their whole plan, by land, sea and air is in operation. Steaming hell-for-leather for Narvik are the battle cruisers *Scharnhorst* and *Gneisenau* with ten large, modern destroyers: their task is to cover the whole opera-tion, draw off any British naval forces and land 2,000 troops. The heavy cruiser *Hipper* and four destroyers are similarly bound for Trondheim with 1,700 troops. The cruisers *Köln, Königsberg* and *Bremse* (the latter a vessel of great antiquity) with an E-boat flotilla, two torpedo-boats and the depot ship *Karl Peters* have 900 men for Bergen, while *Karlsruhe* and the depot ship *Tsingtau* with three torpedo boats and an E-boat flotilla have 1,100 for Kristian-sand and Arendal. *Blücher* and *Emden*, with the pocket battleship *Lützow*, three torpedo boats and some smaller vessels are making course for Norway's capital, Oslo, with 2,000 men; and lastly a small force of minesweepers have a detachment for the cable station at Egersund. (See Map 2, page 66.)

There is another important difference between the German troops and ours, apart from the fact that theirs are at sea while ours are sitting aboard troopships anchored in home ports. While ours are speculating on what they are there for, the Germans have no doubt about their destinations. They are going to Norway and they are going to Norway to save it from the British and the French. They have been well rehearsed, they know what the country is like and indeed many of them have been there, they have the kit and the equipment for the conditions they are likely to meet. Every German soldier has a phrase book (although many of them speak Norwegian) and a bundle of proclamations. Their officers have good maps and their units have precise orders.

But some of the German troops are not at sea. They are already at their destinations, because the little armada now under way cannot carry all the troops that will be required and there is a need to allow for accidents on the way. Germany has been buying fish from Norway as part of the price for her iron ore shipment facilities, and big German refrigerator ships are in Narvik—a surprising number of big German ships with a surprising number of men on board, explained away by the need for a double shift for continuous loading. There are German ships in Bergen and German ships in Trondheim and in the bowels of these ships there are German troops hidden—not to speak of ammunition and other supplies. At Narvik again is the German whaling factory ship *Jan Wellem*, just in from the Arctic and wearing the American flag: it has not merely troops, ammunition and supplies aboard, but also a full-blown general, Dietl by name, who is to be German commander in that area. These and others are what have been very aptly termed the 'Trojan Horse' ships, ready to open up their apparently innocent hulls and disgorge their attackers before the Norwegians have time to suspect. And all of them left Germany a good week in advance of the main invading force. These are the only troops on the German side who are sitting aboard ships at anchor, but they are sitting with a difference.

What of the Norwegians? The Norwegians enter all too little into British and French calculations and will continue to do so throughout the brief campaign. They have not entered much into German calculations, except that they are to be taken care of and, it is hoped, not give too much trouble. Neither side has paid overmuch heed to the fact that it is the Norwegians' land that is being trifled with.

The Norwegians are at peace. They have been at peace for many years and have used that peace, after a hard struggle, to achieve in their tiny country a standard of life which greater powers might envy. Once upon a time they feared the Swedes and some at least of such fortifications as they have, equipped with ancient guns—some serviceable, some not—point towards the Swedish border rather than towards the sea, which has been friend rather than enemy. There are a few destroyers and a few coastal defence vessels, some of them no more than whalers armed with pop-guns. There are forts guarding some of their larger harbours, minefields that can be electrically detonated from the shore and torpedo tubes also shore-mounted: some of these are ready for use and some not. There is no standing army bar a permanent cadre of less than two thousand officers and N.C.O.s, whose job it is to give elementary training to the twelve and a half thousand men who are called up annually for eighty-four days' army service. One of the six divisions into which this citizen army is organized has been mobilized during the Finnish war and is still mobilized around Narvik under General Fleischer. Based on the remaining centres there are three or four mobilized battalions which are keeping a not very exacting guard on the Swedish frontier, manning the forts and elsewhere. There is virtually no air force—roughly a hundred machines in all, many of them Moth biplanes and similar.

In the big centres of population and government—Oslo, Trondheim and so on—there is knowledge and even apprehension of the state of Europe and the world. Only a matter of days ago the German ambassador has invited a selected audience to see a horror film of the German *blitzkrieg* in Poland, *Baptism of Fire*, from which the audience have emerged bewildered and shaking their heads, but most of them convinced that this is no more than an exhibition of bad taste on the part of their hosts. Even these and even those most closely concerned with the business of government, aware though they are of the rumours and counter-rumours seething and bubbling in the witches' cauldron of the Phoney War, still cannot convince themselves that war will come to Norway. Still less—very much less—convinced are those isolated in the peaceful villages in the long valleys, the hamlets in the narrow fiords—cut off from their capital and from the world by the poor communications and great distances of a mountainous and sea-rent land, where their very isolation has been a part of their happiness.

Much has been said about the obstinacy with which the Norwegians clung to their neutrality until it was too late to send them effective help. Much has been made of the fact that if only they had allowed us, we could have occupied their country and made them safe against German invasion. To read some of the books of reference one would think that the Norwegians and their government were a race of moronic idealists, trying to live in a world utterly divorced from the realities of total war. Indeed they were so living—indeed they impeded us and indeed they did not accept help until it was too late. Was not this precisely what we had done ourselves with far less excuse, as the irresolute 1930s drifted inevitably towards war? Who were we and who are we still to criticize the Norwegians for doing precisely what we had done? Of course the Norwegians were fools: so were we. Of course they ought to have known better: we ought to have known better likewise, and if there had been any inclination among them to take sides with Britain and France against Germany, they may well be forgiven for not wishing to draw upon themselves the fate of Poland while France and Britain sat behind the Maginot Line, or of Finland while the Supreme Allied War Council argued the toss.

So much for the picture.

At twenty past eleven on the morning of the 7th the uneasy peace of Scapa Flow was broken by the news that Coastal Command Hudsons on patrol had sighted a cruiser and six destroyers with fighter aircraft in attendance steering northwards in the Skagerrak. The report was somewhat belated because the sighting had been made more than three hours previously, and by the time it reached Scapa a squadron of Blenheim bombers was on its way to attack these ships, which were pretty well at the bombers' extreme range. The Blenheims found their quarry but failed to score a single hit, and others which followed shortly afterwards were equally unlucky. When they returned many hours later they reported that the German force consisted of a pocket battleship, two cruisers and ten destroyers and we therefore are able to identify it as the force detailed for the attack on Oslo. Admiral Forbes had not the advantage of the knowledge we possess more than twenty years later and he immediately jumped to the very understandable conclusion that what was happening was the thing that was always uppermost in his mind—a breakout by enemy surface raiders into the North Atlantic, where the vital convoy lines converged on British ports. Shortly after one o'clock a report from a Sunderland flying-boat, which had caught a brief glimpse through scudding clouds of three German destroyers steering south well below the tip of Norway, offered no enlightenment. He also now received from the Admiralty, for the first time, the reports which had arrived in the previous few days describing obvious activity in the ports of North Germany: to help him still further he was told that the reports were of doubtful value and probably only another move in the war of nerves. It is not, therefore, surprising that he continued to think in terms of enemy forces breaking out into the North Atlantic, which was undoubtedly the most important danger at sea which faced us at this time. The naval records of the early months of the war abound with fruitless sorties based on poor intelligence against enemy units bound for the northabout passage, which were either not where they were said to be or not there at all, and yet none of these reports could ever be disregarded: we had a vast area of stormy sea to guard and the enemy, although their forces were much inferior, could always choose the time and place in their attempts to break out.

At half past five Forbes ordered every available unit of the Home Fleet to raise steam and at quarter past eight he put to sea in very bad weather, steering north-east at high speed. He himself had two battleships and a battle cruiser, two cruisers and ten destroyers: two cruisers and eleven destroyers sailed an hour later from Rosyth and two more cruisers which were escorting a convoy were ordered back. This was a force which could have made mincemeat of the whole of the German forces bound for Norway (although the author of the official history rightly and ruefully points out that the last time the Home Fleet had gone to sea on a similar chase twenty-two years previously it had mustered thirty-five battleships and battle cruisers, twenty-six cruisers and eighty-five destroyers) but unfortunately it was on a course which was taking it farther away from the German fleet with every revolution of its screws. This was the most vulnerable moment of the whole invasion, the moment which Hitler and his admirals feared more than any other. A mortal blow against the German forces would have scuppered the whole invasion, shown conclusively both to the Norwegians and the world that it was Germany who was the aggressor, and sent the prestige of the Allies rocketing sky-high. It was missed. It was not Admiral Forbes's fault that it was missed because his preoccupation with the North Atlantic is perfectly understandable; though it is impossible not to feel that if the intelligence that had been coming in in previous days had been passed to him more smartly, the true situation might have dawned on him then instead of more than twenty-four hours later. Mr. Churchill described the Commander-in-Chief's dilemma very accurately in the debate which followed a few days later in the House of Commons in these words:

'. . . when you get out on the sea, with its vast distances, its storms and mists, and with night coming on and all the uncertainties which exist, you cannot possibly expect that the kind of conditions which would be appropriate to consider in respect of the movements of armies have any application to the chance and haphazard conditions of collisions by ships of war at sea. . . . Anything, I say, more foolish than to suppose that the life and strength of the Royal Navy should have been expended in ceaselessly patrolling up and down the Norwegian and Danish coasts, a target for the U-boats, wearing out their crews and machinery on the chance that Hitler would launch a blow like this—anything more foolish than that nobody can imagine.'

Throughout the night Admiral Forbes's ships pressed furiously on northwards, but dawn brought them no sighting in the wrack of the storm. At eight o'clock, however, there came a sudden cry for help from the destroyer *Glowworm*, three hundred miles to the south, reporting herself engaged with superior enemy forces. Before nine her signals faded out and no more was heard of her.

Glowworm was in fact at the bottom of the sea and she had fought the first action in the battle for Norway. Two nights previously, battling northward through tempestuous seas in poor visibility with Admiral Whitworth's force covering the mine-layers, she had lost a man overboard and stayed to search for him. Conditions were so bad that she was unable to regain contact with the force. In the early morning of the 8th she was a little north of the latitude of Trondheim when her look-outs sighted two German destroyers: these were actually two of the ten bound for Narvik, who had lost contact with *Scharnhorst*, *Gneisenau* and the other destroyers just as *Glowworm* had lost touch with *Renown*. Without hesitation and in true destroyer fashion Lieutenant-Commander Broadmead-Roope attacked this superior force—one of whom fled while the other received considerable damage in the running fight which followed. The Germans' call for help was picked up by *Hipper* which was now waiting off Trondheim with her destroyers; and shortly after eight o'clock *Glowworm*, pursuing her fleeing antagonist, was suddenly confronted with the great German cruiser, looming out of the heavy weather. *Hipper* opened fire—accurately as the Germans nearly always did with their first salvoes—and in a matter of minutes Broadmead-Roope's little ship was heavily damaged and ablaze. He fired a salvo of torpedoes at *Hipper* but she was able to 'comb' them; while she was doing so *Glowworm* made smoke and appeared to turn away from the unequal action. Broadmead-Roope knew he could not out-steam the heavier ship in those high seas. He had not even the chance of getting out of range of *Hipper*'s great guns; and in a moment of time he made a decision which earned him the Victoria Cross and a place in the long and glorious saga of the Navy's fighting men. *Hipper* charged into the smoke screen and after a brief, choking interval emerged on the other side—to find *Glowworm*, not still in flight but steering straight for her on a ramming course as fast as her turbines could drive her. If she was going to sink, she was going to do as much damage as she could before she went. The ships were too close for *Hipper* to avoid the destroyer, which tore her way into the cruiser's hull with a great jarring, grinding crash and, sliding along it, savaged her until she finally lost way altogether. No less than one hundred and thirty feet of *Hipper*'s armour belt was torn away and her starboard torpedo tubes were wrenched out of her. Then *Glowworm* fell away, a burning, mangled hulk tossing in the tempestuous sea. Her strength was spent. The guns were silent. She was not worth another shot. Presently she turned over and slowly sank. With greater chivalry than was shown in some actions soon to come, *Hipper* rescued such of her crew as she could from the icy water. Among them was Broadmead-Roope, but this brave man was not to live to fight another day: at the moment of being hauled aboard, his numbed fingers lost their grip, he fell back into the water and was seen no more.

Hipper was left to carry on with her task, which the sacrifice of *Glowworm* could not prevent, and she was able to keep the sea for the remainder of the Norway campaign. Thereafter, however, her damage repairs kept her in dock for many months, together with most of the major units of the German navy which survived the Norway battles: so that indeed the heroism of Broadmead-Roope and his men paid a real dividend in the desperate months that were to follow.

Glowworm's fading signals had caused Admiral Whitworth, now nearly one hundred and fifty miles away, to turn south, but it was a hopeless mission in the heavy seas which reduced his speed and made it practically impossible for his destroyers to keep company. The mine-laying destroyers in the north had completed their task at four-thirty a.m., and the Admiralty, intervening directly, as it was to do a number of times in the forthcoming days, ordered them to join Whitworth's force: he therefore turned north to make rendezvous with them. The Vestfiord was thus left unguarded and it was soon to be realized that the Admiralty had played completely into the hands of the Germans, for the field was clear for their forces to slip into Narvik without opposition— which they promptly did.

At the same time, from farther north, Admiral Forbes detached the battle cruiser *Repulse*, the cruiser *Penelope* and four destroyers in a vain effort to help. It was the same story: a hopeless battle with mountainous seas. Long before they could make good more than a fraction of the three hundred miles that separated them from *Glowworm*'s last reported position, *Hipper* and her destroyers were in Trondheim with their mission accomplished.

In the meantime the laying of the minefields had been announced officially to the world. All over Britain people felt good. This was in the spirit of the *Altmark* episode, and once more we had shown we would stand no more nonsense. The Norwegian and Swedish governments protested strongly: Britain, collectively, curled its lip, wondering when the neutrals would see reason and realize that we could not tolerate their being Hitler's virtual allies for ever. The government waited for the expected 'reactions', which would cause them to press the button on Plan R.4. The reactions (or what for the moment looked like the reactions, owing to the remarkable coincidence in time between the Allied and German operations) were, in fact, already under way, and advance news of them was not long in coming.

On this same morning, the 8th, the Polish submarine *Orzel* was on patrol in the Skagerrak—one of the submarines detailed to watch the approaches to Norway. About midday and in thick weather (which fortunately protected her from air reconnaissance in that death's alley) she sighted a large German transport, *Rio de Janiero*: this, correctly surfacing and challenging, she sank, and some hundreds of those who had been aboard her were rescued by Norwegian fishing-boats in precisely the way in which the submarine warfare conventions intended they should be. Hauling them out of the sea the astonished Norwegians found them to be German soldiers in uniform—who, on being brought ashore and questioned, declared that they were on their way 'to protect Bergen against the British and French'. They admitted to having transport, guns and ammunition and supplies in the ship which had been sunk. There were no security regulations in operation in Norway and all this was duly reported by the Norwegian Press. It was, however, late afternoon before the reports reached the Admiralty and nearly eleven o'clock at night before they reached Admiral Forbes—who, after sending *Repulse* and *Penelope* chasing south in vain quest of the forces that had destroyed *Glowworm*, had continued on to the north-east. He still felt obliged to make quite sure that there was no breakout into the Atlantic afoot; but he was becoming more and more convinced that what was actually happening was the German invasion of Norway, so long heralded in the war of nerves.

Now it was just for the countering of this same invasion of Norway—one of the possible 'reactions' to Operation Wilfred—that troops were ready embarked in cruisers at Rosyth and troop-ships in the Clyde. The moment was at hand when they were to be needed, and needed in a hurry; and the genius for confusion which brooded over Britain's affairs at this time imediately took steps to see that they would not be available. In the 'flap' that followed the Home Fleet's hasty departure from Scapa and the further hurry and scurry that followed *Glowworm*'s action reports, the Admiralty decided that every ship that could be laid hands on was needed at sea to reinforce Admiral Forbes. *Aurora* and her six destroyers were therefore ordered to sea from the Clyde and the cruisers at Rosyth to 'march their troops ashore', in Sir Winston's words, and do likewise. The words 'march ashore' give an orderly sound to what was, in fact, a very disorderly operation which was to have its consequences. The Lincolnshires were already ashore, exercising on the football ground: they were left there with what they stood up in and as much of their stores, supplies and kit as could be unloaded in the short time available were dumped in any sort of order on the quayside for them to sort out as best they might. The Leicestershires were disembarked at an hour's notice and their stores (which, with great care, had been loaded 'tactically'—in other words as ready for action as possible) suffered a like fate. The Sherwood Foresters were only partly embarked, and so their confusion was a little less, but not much. As for the K.O.Y.L.I., their records give a vivid description of the chaotic scenes that followed the order to 'march them ashore' from *York*. Six hundred men struggled to get off the ship with their baggage while the crew struggled to clear the decks for action. Stores and equipment were literally hurled bodily on to the quay without any regard for damage, let alone for good order. In the wild hurry soldiers and sailors jostled, shoved each other, shouted and swore: the German High Command would have held their sides with laughter had they been able to see it all. In the end *York* put to sea in just over an hour, carrying with her, among sundry items left aboard, most of the K.O.Y.L.I.'s signals equipment and both their three-inch mortars—in other words their most valuable weapons and all their means of communication in the field, which they would feel the want of very bitterly in the days to come, when the only means of passing messages to hard-pressed companies and platoons was by runners floundering desperately up to their waists in snow.

In the Clyde the Hallamshires and the Scots Guards were luckier. The Guards had a narrow escape because the previous day it had been decided to transfer B Company's baggage and kit, together with one platoon of men, to *Aurora*, but later both the baggage and the men had been transferred back. They and the Hallamshires, therefore, had the chagrin of seeing their escorts depart at high speed, leaving them behind inside the boom: for all they were worth, sitting in two troopships without any escort, they might as well have been back where they started, at Thirsk and Chelsea Barracks respectively. However, the Scots Guards had the consolation of their route march being cancelled— they would have to content themselves with P.T. on the decks instead.

It does not need a very vivid imagination to picture the morale of the troops dumped with so little ceremony on the dockside at Rosyth like so much useless ballast—sundered in some cases from their kit and the small, cherished possessions which mean so much to soldiers. For platoon and company commanders and above all for quartermasters, the thing was a nightmare. In the preceding days and weeks they had gloatingly beheld the issue of all the things they had lacked and given up all hope of having in an army apparently doomed for ever to make do and make believe. They had been about to go on active service, fully equipped beyond their wildest dreams. They had supervised the loading and stowage of their new acquisitions with loving care. Now much of it was bucketing across the high seas beyond hope of recovery: what was left them was piled higgledy-piggledy and would entail an agony of sorting out, and undoubtedly much of it would be damaged.

They sorted things out for the time being, disconsolately and in a temporary sort of way: they were then ordered to march on foot to the transit camp at Dunfermline, twelve miles away. In this desolate place the troops made themselves as comfortable as circumstances permitted, while the quartermasters set about the heartbreaking task of assessing their losses and then of begging, borrowing or acquiring by any other means stores to make them good under circumstances which no army regulations appeared to allow for. They were greatly helped by the fact that there was not so much as a single telephone in the camp. The K.O.Y.L.I.'s quartermaster went without sleep for sixty hours but got only part of what he sought. Later, after the unit's hurried disembarkation in Norway, the three-inch mortars and signals equipment he had begged for without apparent success were discovered in the hold of the ship that had carried them there, but too late to unload: no one had told him that his prayers had been granted.

All these movements, says Sir Winston Churchill in his war memoirs, were concerted with the Commander-in-Chief, Admiral

Forbes. The Navy's official history, on the contrary, declares that Admiral Forbes knew nothing about them. With his growing realization that the invasion of Norway was afoot, it is at least doubtful whether he would have agreed with them; for as this day, 8th April, drew to a close, information about enemy movements came pouring in from all directions, so that a skeleton picture of the German operation began to take shape. This was one of the two moments in their campaign so feared by German military and naval planners—the moment when their forces were upon their objectives but as yet had no foothold, when the superior sea power of the Allies had been alerted, when the trifling resistance the Norwegians would be able to make might just swing the balance between success and failure. It is futile to argue that the troops allotted to Plan R.4 were not adequately equipped for the job. We know that they were not adequately equipped, but they were going to be flung into the battle even worse equipped against an enemy who had already established himself. It is even futile to argue that German air power would in any case have proved to be the decisive factor, for even German air power could be of little avail if their troops failed to occupy Norway on the ground. And although they rapidly showed their ability to move troops in by air, a little determined and organized resistance might have been effective against these—operating, as they were, under very different conditions from those which brought them success in Crete and elsewhere. On no sort of argument does it make sense that the troops allocated for coping with the 'reactions' to Wilfred should have been disorganized and rendered impotent at the very moment when they were needed most.

In the face of the situation rapidly becoming clear the War Cabinet took no further action than the naval movements and the few air attacks which had already been set in train. The Norwegian parliament met but took no action either, beyond alerting the coastal forces. No order was given to lay mines in the shore-controlled minefields which protected the key ports for which the Germans were heading—nor was any mobilization order issued to the Army, although mobilization would take several days.

CHAPTER 5

INVASION

B Y eight o'clock on the evening of the 8th, Admiral Forbes
became convinced that the German invasion of Norway was
on and that he must take a risk of allowing raiders to break out
into the Atlantic. This risk was more real than some of the critics
have imagined, because the battle cruisers *Scharnhorst* and *Gneisenau* had orders that, once they had seen the invasion forces safely
in, they were to go off on a foray to the north. The moment after
the troops had been deposited at their destinations was the other
moment the Germans feared—because now their naval vessels
would have to make their way home through waters which the
Royal Navy would be quartering with a lust for vengeance: a
sortie by the two battle cruisers would keep them out of harm's
way for a couple of days and might yield other dividends into the
bargain. In fact, as we shall see, the Germans did not get away
scot-free, and their fears in general were justified because the
losses of their small fleet were very severe indeed. The Home
Fleet, therefore, turned south, and the additional cruiser forces
that were coming up to support it were given areas to sweep, but
it was already much too late to catch the invasion fleet. The
nearest point any of our ships got to the Germans was off Bergen,
where Rear-Admiral Edward-Collins's cruisers from the Clyde
passed within sixty miles of them: for all he could know of it and
for what use it was, the sixty miles might have been six hundred.

When we see the damage that the almost trifling Norwegian
resistance was able to inflict on the Germans, particularly in the
approaches to Oslo, it is hardly bearable to think of how different
the Norwegian campaign and indeed the whole course of the war
in the west might have been if our own Navy had caught only a
part of the invading force at sea. It is no use harping on it because
it did not happen that way, and it is certainly no use blaming
Admiral Forbes.

The weather was still unhelpful. To the north, in the approaches to Narvik, very heavy seas were still running, with poor visibility and heavy snowstorms, although later in the night there was something of a lull. Farther south the weather was calmer, but around central Norway there was intermittent fog. There was no moon: the Germans had in fact chosen this period for its moonlessness and if the weather conditions did not help them much, they certainly hindered us more.

By midnight *Blücher*, *Lützow* and *Emden* with their escorts were well inside Oslo fiord—a moving dagger thrust at the heart of Norway. Far down the fiord, Wielding Olsen, in command of a cockleshell of a patrol boat, *Pol III*, mounting a single gun, saw the darkly moving shapes of the big ships and challenged them. Getting no satisfaction and without any regard for neutrality or anything else he promptly went into action with his single gun and rammed the German torpedo boat *Albatross*. He and his ship were promptly annihilated, and her complement became the first of the Norwegians who in coming days were to wipe out by their outstanding heroism any misconceptions that might have been entertained about them. His sacrifice was in vain except for the fact that he raised the alarm, and the little armada continued onwards. There were several points at which the fiord was defended: the first of these were the two islands of Rauöy and Bolaerne, not far from the naval base of Horten on the west shore. After these came the Drobak Narrows guarded by the century-old forts of Oscarsborg: shortly after the latter the fiord widens out again and if they could pass these points the Germans had a clear run to Oslo. Between Rauöy and Bolaerne there was one of the shore-controlled minefields—minus its mines and therefore useless. The forts did no more than illuminate their searchlights and fire warning shots across the bows of the Germans, who steamed by unharmed. They then stopped and landed troops to take the forts from the rear and attend to the naval base at the same time: Rauöy fell easily but Bolaerne held out in hopeless siege for two whole days after the Germans were in possession of Oslo. Off Horten they encountered their second Norwegian naval vessel, named after Norway's first Christian king, the warrior Olav Tryggvason—larger than *Pol III*, with four 4·7-inch guns. She in her turn opened fire without hesitation and drew first blood.

One of the German torpedo boats was sunk and *Albatross*, in trouble for the second time, retired before this onslaught. The big ships then blew *Olav Tryggvason* to pieces and once more the force moved on towards the six-hundred-yard-wide passage, where the two forts of Oscarsborg were now thoroughly alerted. These forts had teeth, albeit teeth best part of fifty years old—eight-inch guns at Drobak on the one side and eleven-inch guns at Kaholm on the other, with shore-mounted torpedo tubes. The range was short and they rapidly scored hits on *Blücher* which first set fire to petrol in her aircraft hangar, then damaged her stern gear and put her out of control. While the Germans were struggling to keep her off the rocky shore she came into the field of fire of the torpedo tubes, which got home twice on a sitting target, and the brand-new ship blew up and sank—taking with her best part of a thousand Germans including virtually all the headquarters personnel destined for Oslo.

At the same time *Lützow* was hit three times in rapid succession and had her fore turret put out of action. Together with *Emden* and the rest of the force she then slipped back into the mist and darkness and retired down the fiord to put her troops ashore there with still ten miles to march on their objective. The city of Oslo was, in fact, taken by airborne troops the following morning, not without casualties, and while Drobak was captured the same afternoon Kaholm held out till the 10th, when the bombers and airborne troops were able to get into action in daylight. Therefore Oslo hung in the balance until the first effects of German air supremacy began to show themselves, and the German Navy had acquired a bloody nose.

Elsewhere also the invasion faltered, though there were no checks so serious as those in Oslo fiord. At Kristiansand *Karlsruhe* found herself faced with two adversaries—the dense, intermittent fog and the highly belligerent defenders of the fortress of Odderöy. The welcome from the latter was sufficiently warm for the Germans to beat a retreat twice and on her third attempt the cruiser all but ran herself ashore in the fog. It was not until eleven o'clock in the morning that the defenders received a message in Norwegian code—whether it was a decoy message sent by the Germans or whether it had come from their own people as a result of earlier happenings is not clear—which gave them the impression that British and French naval forces were on their way and should not be fired on. The weather now came to the Germans' rescue, because next time they appeared the Norwegians had difficulty in making out their ensigns, which were first reported as French. While they hesitated the Germans shot past into the harbour out of the field of fire of the defending guns, rapidly put their troops ashore and all was soon over. *Karlsruhe* herself was not to escape, for she was torpedoed by the British submarine *Truant* on her way home the same evening but this could do nothing to save Kristiansand and its little airfield.

Stavanger and its much more important airfield were scheduled for occupation by airborne troops, but one of the 'Trojan Horse' ships carried their anti-aircraft guns and heavy artillery, together with ammunition and supplies. She appeared in the port, to be challenged by the Norwegian destroyer *Sleipner*, which had received news of the alarm raised by *Pol III*. In spite of a circumstantial story about the ship being on passage from Murmansk it was sunk; but Nazi-troop carriers arrived over the airfield shortly after eight o'clock in the morning. The airfield defences consisted of no more than a couple of machine-gun emplacements and there were but a few Norwegian aircraft there. Two of them were destroyed by German Messerschmitts and the rest got away: hard on the heels of the Messerschmitts came the first ten Junkers transports. Troops piled out of these and took possession of the airfield, where further transports were soon arriving with clockwork regularity until by the end of the day one hundred and eighty of them had touched down. At this very early stage of the campaign air power was beginning to make itself felt.

At Bergen things were precarious at first because the slowness of the ancient *Bremse* and some of the transports held the convoy back: when they arrived, in darkness, they were met by searchlights and a challenge from a patrol vessel, to which *Köln* identified herself as the British cruiser *Cairo*. None the less the forts opened fire as the ships steamed by and scored hits on *Köln* and *Bremse*, but the troops were got ashore and Norway's second largest city was occupied without any further trouble.

At Trondheim, *Hipper* and her destroyers stormed their way up the fiord at top speed although the forts of Brettingen and Hysnes, which guarded the passage, had received the alarm. A lucky shot from the heavy cruiser in answer to the fire cut the power cable on which their electric supply depended and doused their search-lights. One of the destroyers was mauled and beached, and the forts themselves held out until the 11th; but the town was taken by surprise and occupied without much difficulty, and here also the Germans commenced a rapid build-up by air transport.

At Narvik the Germans had all the luck. General Dietl's troops had had a most depressing and uncomfortable voyage up the coast of Norway, crammed like sardines in the overcrowded destroyers and woefully seasick in the rough weather; there is no more disgusting and unpleasant fate that can befall troops in such circumstances. They were well north of the Arctic Circle and although the nights were shortening, sea and land were still in the grip of winter. There were a number of hazards—known to them and otherwise—which they should have met, and any one of these could have proved their undoing. In the first place their track took them straight through the area where the British destroyers should have been guarding their minefield. In the second place there were extreme navigational hazards in the long passage through the complex system of islands and ever-narrowing fiords running deep into this narrow strip of Norway till it reaches Narvik itself, which is much nearer to the Swedish border than it is to the sea; Narvik harbour was packed with merchant shipping swinging at anchor in the darkness and snow—there were more than twenty-five ore-ships alone there that very night. In the third place the only mobilized and effective military force in Norway, Major-General Fleischer's* 6th Division, was in these parts, guarding the northern provinces of Nordland, Troms and Finmark, and had, moreover, been recently reinforced by two infantry battalions from the south. A company of one of these, the 13th Infantry Regiment, was in Narvik itself and the re-mainder of the unit was that very night on the way to reinforce it. There was also an ack-ack battery with four 40-mm. Bofors guns. Finally, the people of these regions, used to hard climate, hard times and hard work, were the sturdiest, most independent and most resourceful of a sturdy, independent and resourceful nation.

But as the malodorous and sea-wracked little ships rolled and plunged their way inside the tip of the Lofoten Islands, where the

* Pronounced 'Flaysher'.

approach to Narvik begins, they gained a measure of shelter and
the worst agony of the troops was over: there were no British
destroyers to greet them, because the destroyers had been withdrawn on direct orders from London to join Admiral Whitworth's hunting force—so short a time before that the crooked
destiny of Nazi Germany itself might seem to have had a hand
in it. Many of the navigation lights were still burning, so that
even in the snow and poor visibility the tricky passage was
made without accident. The snow which caused the navigating
officers of the invaders' ships so much apprehension also stopped
the infantry reinforcements from getting into Narvik on time; and
as for the rest, virtually the only fifth columnist in Narvik happened to be the military commandant of the town, Colonel
Sundlo.

At three in the morning they were off the pilot station at
Tranöy, where Warburton-Lee was to stop for news of them the
following morning. An hour later they were off the island of
Baröy and swinging round into the Ofotfiord, which gives access
to Narvik, and here two patrol boats spotted them and gave the
alarm. They stopped off Ramnes and put ashore a few troops to
look after some forts which were supposed to be there, but these
forts were non-existent except in the misinformed mind of Major
Quisling. The second lot of troops they put ashore farther on,
however, in the Herjangsfiord, shared in the luck of the whole
operation: their job was to capture the Norwegian infantry depot
at Elvegaardsmoen, which contained the stores and reserve
ammunition and arms for four whole battalions, as well as all
General Fleischer's bridging and engineering equipment and
much else of importance. It was unoccupied save for a token
guard, and the battalion that was already hurrying back to it
was held up by the same snowstorm which frustrated the reinforcements for Narvik; the Germans gained possession of it
without a shot. By five o'clock the destroyers were picking their
way through the packed shipping in Narvik Harbour itself.

Now in the harbour were the only two warships of any considerable size which Norway possessed, the four-thousand-ton
Eidsvold and her sister ship *Norge*. They were more fitted to be in a
maritime museum than in a battle, for they had both been built in
1900, but they did mount 8·2-inch and 5·9-inch guns—the former,

at least, very much larger than anything even the modern German destroyers carried—and they had every intention of using them, being alert from the alarm that had been raised by the patrol boats. *Eidsvold*, therefore, fired a warning shot across the bows of the German flotilla leader, which stopped, lowered a boat and sent an officer across for a supposed parley with the Norwegians. He got no change out of them—nor did he need to, for as he left *Eidsvold* and while the Norwegians were still humanely holding their fire, he fired a Very light to show he was clear, whereupon the German *Heidkamp* slammed a salvo of torpedoes into the old ironclad at a range of barely a hundred yards and literally blew her to pieces. The tremendous explosion awoke the whole town, but it was already too late. *Norge* was able to fire seventeen rounds at the Germans before she in turn was blasted to bits by torpedoes; while the bewildered citizens were still rubbing the sleep from their eyes, German troops were ashore and the traitor Sundlo had already ordered his men to lay down their arms. The wildest gamble in the whole German game had come off.

Similarly, in all the key cities of Norway, people awoke to find the Germans already in possession. Among the very few who had followed the events of the night in any sort of coherent way were the members of the Norwegian cabinet, which had been late in session on the business of Britain's violation of their country's neutrality by Operation Wilfred and had stayed in session as the news of the German approaches had begun to come in from one point after another. At half-past four in the morning the German Ambassador, Dr. Brauer, called upon the Norwegian Foreign Minister with a long and carefully prepared document, which began by asserting that the German Reich had taken over the protection of Norway against the British and the French. The German Reich, it declared, expected the Norwegian people to accept the German action in an understanding way and not offer any kind of resistance: resistance would be crushed with every means. There were phrases about 'the most terrifying aspects of war'—as to the nature of which Dr. Brauer's film entertainment of a few days previously had left no doubt. And there followed thirteen points to which the Norwegian government was expected to agree, which included the issue of a proclamation forbidding all resistance, the handing over intact of all military installations, means of communication, pilotage and weather services, the submission of Press and radio to German censorship and arrangements for the control by the Germans of the armed forces. The Foreign Minister took this document to the cabinet, which rejected it without hesitation, and King Haakon gave his support to the decision with similar decisiveness. Norway was at war with Germany.

But with what was Norway to fight? Even General Fleischer's Division in the north had been caught out: the other divisions were not even mobilized, and although the order for mobilization was now made it would be two days before the troops would begin to report to the depots. Long before then the depots themselves and all their stores of equipment, together with the couple of small-arms and ammunition factories, would be in German hands—as would all the means of communication in this mountainous and difficult land. The British War Cabinet, meeting a few hours later, would immediately offer assistance to Norway without being asked; but the very troops that had been got ready to give this assistance were either ashore at Dunfermline in a high state of disorganization, or swinging at anchor in troopships in the Clyde without so much as a rowing-boat to escort them. With a sounder instinct for the realities of the situation than might have been expected from a government which had not expected in the slightest to find itself involved in a total war at a moment's notice, the Norwegian Cabinet now took a series of decisions which were to keep the government in being although in appalling difficulty. It decided to evacuate its Parliament, such of the government staff, records and equipment as could be made mobile, the King and the country's gold reserves to Hamar, seventy miles up the valley at the mouth of which Oslo stands, and declare the capital an open city. By half past seven all were on their way by road and rail and the Nazi puppet Quisling was in control. He promptly declared himself Prime Minister and appointed a cabinet—most of whom refused to serve. Norway was lacking in many things: an effective Fifth Column was one of them.

So far the events of the night of 8th to 9th April can be clearly traced. There is one element that is more elusive. Many Norwegians were convinced, and are still convinced to this day, that

German troops came over the Swedish border that night, especially into southern Norway. When one tries to get at the facts one keeps on grasping phantoms. One is told of Swedish frontier guards who delayed their challenge until armed figures in the night had technically crossed the border, but who actually saw this happen, where, what time and so on? It is always a question of someone else having passed on the story, of the time and place and details being vague. Is it merely another product of the unease that still survives from Norway's separation from Sweden in the early years of this century and of the fear that persisted, all too slow to fade, that Sweden would seek to control Norway again? Does the principle that there is some foundation of fact to the most improbable legends apply here? There is no doubt whatsoever—it is admitted by the Swedes themselves—that German reinforcements and supplies got over the Swedish border, particularly on the northern front, in the subsequent part of the campaign: reinforcements came, for instance, as Red Cross personnel, although they seemed large and beefy men for hospital orderlies. Ammunition came in cases marked 'Fish', but they were fish of remarkable weight. German troops were allowed passage back through Sweden, sick or on leave without their arms. All these things the Swedes admit, and there is something to be said for the claim that they either had no means of stopping them or no right to under international convention. Our own fighter pilots around Narvik were convinced that if they chased a Nazi plane across the border the Nazi got away scot-free and the British both the flak and the formal protest: but how much of this is imagination in the heat of battle, how much of it thinking conditioned by what was said to have already taken place?

The Swedes appear to have shown no active hostility to Norway. They allowed Norwegian civilians to come and go, impartially they interned personnel in uniform of both sides who crossed their border. In northern Norway towards the end, when the Germans were well nigh defeated, some people confidently expected that Sweden would declare war on Germany. No German claim, nor any confession for that matter, has been made that the Swedes assisted them. The truth will never be known, but the rumour persists and the speculation is almost idle because whether or not Germans came in through Sweden, Germans were

Dombaas village after German bombing.

Anti-tank guns on improvised transport on the road to the front.

H.M.S. *Eskimo*, torpedoed in the second attack at Narvik.

undoubtedly in Oslo, in Bergen, in Trondheim and all the places they had chosen for their landings, and Norway awoke to find them there.

The first reaction was a shocked unbelief and a curious numbness, a sense of unreality—which in itself helped to tide the Germans over this still precarious time when they were thin on the ground and still depended on the impression of force rather than on force itself. The reaction was exactly the same from Narvik in the north to the capital in the south. A *Daily Telegraph* correspondent was in Oslo at this time. He described later how at a quarter to eight, while the population were still in doubt, confusion and ignorance of exactly what had happened, five German bombers came thundering low over the house-tops—how for a couple of hours thereafter small groups, and small groups only, of planes continued to feint and fly, dropping no bombs but keeping alive the fear that at any moment they would: while this was going on, of course, airborne troops were being landed at the city's airfield to take over the objective which those landed contrary to intention farther down the fiord had as yet failed to reach.

'Thousands of Osloans gazed at them curiously and fearfully,' he wrote, 'but there was no panic. None of us dreamed that German warships were in the inner harbour and that Oslo was already doomed. . . . The same madness of incomprehensible events continued all day long. . . . Tens of thousands of persons clustered in the streets and on the pavements, waiting, utterly baffled. We all asked where the British were, but where also were the Germans?'

It was not until the middle of the afternoon that the Germans appeared—first of all two lorries filled with troops, followed at a short interval by a marching column headed by General Falkenhorst himself. It was a short column, it took only a few minutes to march by. The men marched with detachment, grim bearing and beautiful precision; a city of a quarter of a million inhabitants crowded to watch this tiny column go by and, still numbed, were possessed by it. Guards were presently posted on the government offices and other principal buildings. A group of German soldiers was seen carefully posed in one of the windows of the Parliament building singing lustily while one played an accordion. The parades and counter-marchings continued. It was the most fantastic army that had ever captured a city in modern war, because it was a stage army, a comic opera army—something mighty and unending but in fact composed of the same few groups of actors marching backwards and forwards behind the set and seen through door or window. There was no substance to it at all and in this period the Germans were hanging on by their eyebrows, using every stratagem and every psychological trick to convince the people of the invaded country that they were in the grip of a great army—whereas in fact until the build-up began the Norwegians could almost have overwhelmed them by sheer force of numbers with hardly a weapon in any man's hand.

It was a brief moment. The build-up was even now under way, by air to the cities of central and southern Norway and by the short sea passage across the Skagerrak. This was the moment at which the Allied powers should have struck their blow in defence of Norway; yet they were powerless to strike.

One of Quisling's first actions when he assumed authority in Oslo was to cancel the mobilization order. The legal Norwegian government had no means to deny the cancellation, because at Hamar to which they had retreated there were no national broadcasting facilities and the Germans were in control of the telephone system. But it so happened that in a speech over the radio just before the government was evacuated the Foreign Minister, Dr. Koht, had mentioned that mobilization had been ordered, and men of military age all over Norway took this as an actual order to report for duty. In most cases they found this impossible because one of the first objectives of the Germans in every region where they landed were the mobilization depots, and because the communications system of the country was disrupted and for all sorts of other reasons. Nevertheless, as the stupefaction of the day began to wear off—and it wore off more or less as the German Army's comic opera act quietly faded itself out—they became determined to fight where they could and with whom they could find to join them. Some of them were rusty in their training and some of them had had very little training at all. But it so happens that marksmanship is a national sport of Norway and it also happens, of course, that most Norwegians of active age are able to get about on skis—not unnatural in a country which for much of the year is covered by snow. If they could not fight as an army, they could fight as guerrillas in the mountains and the valleys, as long as they could find fellow Norwegians to fight by their sides. In quite a short time, therefore, the southern part of the country at least was quietly alive with moving men—crowded would be the wrong word because Norway is a large country with a small population. In small groups, in twos and threes, sometimes at first singly, men had left their homes, their families, everything they had and set out to find some sort of focus around which they could group themselves. The groups would grow into larger groups and presently, although what was happening bore no relation at all to the paper establishment on which the Norwegian Army should have been mobilized—an army of sorts came into being; an army that was to be built against all rhyme and reason to hang on in desperate delaying actions until help should be forthcoming.

At the same time such planes as Norway possessed—unsuitable most of them for use as fighters or bombers—were got into the air and used in any sort of way that could be devised to distract and trouble the Junkers and the Messerschmitts. Some of them hurled out by hand what few light bombs they had, others merely dived, feinted and straffed the ground forces in make-believe. They speedily ran out of aviation fuel and most of them in the end out of any sort of petrol. Some faced the impossible and got themselves over to Scotland—at least preserving their pilots to fight on as free men, for the planes were, without exception, promptly condemned as unserviceable.

As to the Norwegian Navy, there was little left of it after the hopeless battles in the fiords bar a couple of destroyers and a handful of torpedo boats and smaller craft. These made up their minds about their duty as unhesitatingly as they had challenged and attacked the invaders, paying no heed whatsoever to any orders from Quisling. All of them set sail for British ports or for wherever they might expect to join up with the British Navy. The destroyer *Sleipner*, which we have already seen making her first kill, set off across the sea, chivvying with her a large German transport whose captain protested vainly that he had no troops or war materials aboard; but half-way across this unwilling companion succeeded in scuttling herself. *Sleipner* received a tremendous ovation when she arrived in the Shetlands and another when she steamed into Scapa Flow: she was back on the job with the Royal Navy off the Norwegian coast barely a week later and her First Lieutenant was serving as liaison officer to the naval forces there. Others followed the same pattern and Norwegian ships, including new ones paid for out of the gold reserve whisked away from under the Germans' noses or by the earnings of Norway's merchant ships, played their full part in the war at sea through the years to come.

But it was undoubtedly the merchant ships that were Norway's greatest gift to the free world. This country had the third largest merchant marine in the world—it mustered two hundred and seventy-two modern oil tankers alone and oil tankers were worth their weight in gold, as well as being the most dangerous of all merchant ships to serve on. Altogether twenty-five thousand seamen and a thousand ships went on to serve in the desperate battle of the Atlantic and all over the world—ships whose home ports were forever in a strange land, seamen who often did not know whether their families were alive or dead, well or starving, free or in a German concentration camp. Their work was magnificent and their contribution to the Allied victory indispensable, though now seldom remembered or spoken of.

Thus in the course of a day that started with numbed unbelief and apathy, Norway found her soul. Britain had still to find hers and would not do so until faced with the similar shock of her own disastrous defeats in the west. When news of the invasion of Denmark and Norway broke on the radio and in the newspapers on the morning of 9th April it was confidently assumed that the mightiest Navy in the world, the Army which over the generations had fought victoriously all over the globe and an Air Force that was technically superior to anything the Germans possessed would together descend on Norway in retribution and drive the presumptuous Germans into the sea. A thousand newspaper cuttings perpetuate the legend that the German Air Force was already out of date, the belief that attack by air on ships of war was ineffective, and much more that was partly illusion, partly wishful thinking. After all, had not the Prime Minister himself said, not many days since, that Hitler had missed the 'bus? Even in the matter of what appeared to have happened in Norway the amount of wishful thinking that hung over Britain like a cloud of self-deception was incredible—not least over the government of old men and the war of committees: so that even on the day following the invasion Mr. Chamberlain could blandly tell the House of Commons that reports that the Germans had landed at Narvik seemed open to question, that there was a place on the southern tip of Norway called Larvik and that this was probably where they had landed. There is no trace of any of the reports having mentioned Larvik.

None the less the War Cabinet (to which incidentally responsibility for operations in Scandinavia had been delegated by the Allied Supreme War Council and which therefore could not shelve its responsibilities elsewhere) had promised full and immediate aid to the Norwegian people: it now had to make this promise good. How was it to do so? Every ship the Navy could spare was already on the job and units were at this moment in battle or about to go into battle. The Air Force would try to reach targets in Norway; but as we have already seen the weather was bad, some of the targets at extreme range for the machines we then possessed and some out of range altogether. Moreover the Air Force, like the other forces, was bound at this time by strict instructions to bomb only when military targets could be segregated and clearly identified. As to the army which would have to be landed in Norway, we are already familiar with the forces available in the camp at Dunfermline and in the transports on the Clyde and what state some of them were in. They were presently to be rescued from their enforced quarantine and be put on the way once more, destined now to fight instead of merely to land, occupy and carry out garrison duties: but there seems to have been no rethinking at all as to what changes in their arms or equipment this involved or to appreciate the country where the landing and fighting were to be done.

Norway is a long narrow strip of land bounded, except in the extreme south-east, by the North Sea and the Arctic Ocean. Its southernmost tip lies roughly in the same latitude as the Orkney Islands and more than half the length of it lies within the Arctic Circle. It is for the most part a barren, mountainous land: though its mountains rarely reach any tremendous heights, they are continuous, and the long fiords which are one of the country's most famous characteristics pierce deeply into the land, joining forces with the mountains in making communications extremely difficult: measure the complicated configurations of the coastline itself and it comes out at something like seventeen hundred miles—but measure it around the fiords and the figure comes nearer twelve thousand. Communications across the country are restricted to the long valleys between the hills and in these roads and railways had been built. The roads are few in number, mostly narrow, while the railway routes were even fewer and at this time there was no railway communication with the northern part of the country at all. It was, in fact, the difficult character of their land that had long since made the Norwegians a race of sea-going men, their sheltered coastal waterways compensating for the difficulty of their routes overland.

A bare two and a half per cent of this country is cultivated and no more than a quarter of it will even support forests. It has a few large cities and ports separated by long distances and by the difficult terrain already described. The largest of these is Oslo, the capital, which at the time of the invasion housed no more than a quarter of a million people: the rest are much smaller and what are spoken of in this invasion story as towns and seaports are no more than villages and hamlets by our standards. Perhaps the nearest approach in this country to places like Namsos, Aandalsnes, Molde and so on, which were to be disembarkation ports in the coming campaign, is on the western coast of Scotland or, still more, on the coast of central Wales, where little towns with infinitesimal quays nestle at the tips of estuaries emerging from winding valleys through the rugged hills on whose steep slopes conifer trees climb row on row. But the climate of Norway was very different from the climate of Wales or even the climate of the Highlands of Scotland. The winter is hard, dark and long. For months on end virtually the whole country is covered by snow, with the exception of very small areas of low-lying coastland around some of the western ports. Both roads and railways are kept open only with difficulty, while off the roads movement is impossible—not only for wheeled traffic, but even for men without skis or snowshoes. The inland lakes are covered with thick ice even down the valley towards Oslo. Snowstorms and blizzards howl down these valleys and over the bare plateaux above them:

temperatures in the long nights are very low in the south and sometimes approach polar conditions in the north. The Norwegians themselves know how to live under these conditions but even so—in the campaign in the north particularly, when they were forced to sleep without shelter for days on end and ran short of fuel for cooking—they suffered severely.

While the land is still gripped by winter the days begin to lengthen. By the middle of April there are only a few hours of complete darkness and by the middle of June there is very little night at all: the midnight sun is one of Norway's tourist attractions and songs have been written and jokes made about it from time immemorial, but it was no joy to hard-pressed men on land or sea, aching with tiredness and willing to trade their souls for a few hours' cover from a foe with almost undisputed command of the air.

Sometime roughly between the end of April and the end of May —depending on whether spring comes early or hangs back—the thaw sets in, to melt the deep snow and ice over all but the highest parts of the country. Now the land becomes a quagmire, rivers roar in spate and roads are more often than not impassable. And then quite quickly and quite suddenly the land is green and beautiful.

In the whole of the British Army there had been but one solitary unit even remotely trained for conditions such as these. This was the 5th Scots Guards—the unit specially recruited for service in Finland. It was a remarkable unit because it had been got together from members of the Brigade of Guards all over the world, both serving and civilians. It had included on its nominal roll men like Gino Watkins, Lindsay, Spencer-Chapman, Wigram of the 1935 Everest Expedition, as well as no less than one hundred and sixty 'decommissioned' officers voluntarily serving in the ranks for the time being. Assembled, it had trained at Chamonix—but on 20th March, while the battalion was actually loading ship at Glasgow, its orders were cancelled as a result of the Finnish armistice, it was disbanded with almost unseemly haste and within a week its members were dispersing to the four quarters of the earth. The only other units which had any experience at all of being in the field in severe European winter conditions were the units of 15 Brigade who were to come upon the scene too late to take any part in the advance into central Norway, but who covered the retreat of the Territorials of 148 Brigade in a magnificent fighting withdrawal that temporarily rocked the Germans back on their heels. Units of this Brigade had each in turn spent a period in the snow-bound Saar, in front of the Maginot Line between France and Germany, and had benefited immensely from the experience.

There were other perils in Norway for troops of all arms. The very nature of the country makes airfields few and far between: the Germans had already laid hands upon every single one in the centre and the south and those farther north were still snow-bound. The same mountains which limit road and rail traffic to the deep valleys gave cover up to the last moment to aircraft swooping on unprotected troops. Precisely the same conditions apply in the fiords, where ships could have little visual warning of air attack. The high mountains blanketed detection devices; and in many places, more particularly in the north, the high iron content of the rock played tricks with them. The biggest ships could float in the fiords but their narrowness left no sea-room for manœuvre or evasive action under air attack.

All these conditions the Germans had studied and studied well. Many of the aspects of them which put British, French and even Norwegian troops into such desperate straits could be turned to their own advantage. Against them and in a country where the British Army had never fought in the whole of its history, the War Cabinet had now given a solemn pledge to put an army into the field. Under the threat of a German air force which had overwhelming superiority in numbers and airfields in Norway and well within range of their own country, this army would have to be transported, sustained and protected by a Navy with anti-aircraft defences far, far below the needs of modern war. The Air Force might help—if ever landing grounds could be found for it, or if it could ever get within range from landing grounds in Britain.

It would obviously take many days to get the promised army on its way. The units that had been disembarked in such haste and confusion would somehow have to be re-embarked—and somehow even approximately re-equipped. Two battalions of the Guards' Brigade were not even at the starting point. Landing points had to be determined, strategy to be worked out. Even the truth about the situation itself had to be determined with just a modicum of accuracy—and this was one of the most difficult things of all, because on the day following the invasion Intelligence was almost wholly dependent on Press reports from abroad. While all this was being done the war would not stand still, nor would the Germans wait for us to get both the situation and results sorted out.

The war was in fact going on: it would be fought for the time being by the Norwegians with their improvised forces on land and by the Navy at sea, below the sea and in the air. While the War Cabinet was actually debating the situation on the morning of 9th April the second action of the campaign at sea was being fought in the tempestuous weather of the Arctic Ocean to the seaward of the Lofoten Islands.

The lull that had fallen on the tempest towards midnight had been only a brief one. As the early morning hours grew, Admiral Whitworth's great battle cruiser, *Renown*, was being severely buffeted by tremendous seas and the destroyers astern of him were at times well nigh out of control. He did not yet know of the invasion of Norway—still less did he know that Commodore Bonte's ten destroyers had slipped into the Vestfiord almost under his nose. He was still thinking, as Forbes had been thinking, of enemy units bent on a northabout breakout into the Atlantic sea lanes. And in fact, having seen the destroyers safely on the last lap of their perilous voyage towards Narvik, *Scharnhorst* and *Gneisenau* had parted company with them and laid course for their brief sortie into the Arctic sea, where they were to wait until the time came for their dangerous dash home to Kiel and do whatever damage they might compass at the same time. They were, indeed, taking the route which commerce raiders bound for the Atlantic would have taken.

Shortly before four o'clock in the morning—while the Norwegian cabinet was in session and Dr. Brauer about to present his ultimatum—*Renown* sighted the two German battle cruisers. The look-outs were straining their eyes through the storm and through the flurries of snow, and at first reported them as a battle cruiser and a heavy cruiser: in the fire control the target could scarcely be made out in the dark, distance and storm. It was a dangerous situation for *Renown*: she was but lightly armoured and her six fifteen-inch guns were outmatched by the eighteen eleven-inch guns of the two German ships. Had they been alert and weighed up the situation rapidly, the Germans could have played the same game on Admiral Whitworth that the British cruisers played on *Graf Spee* in the Battle of the River Plate. But it was the British ship that was alert and Admiral Whitworth turned in to attack, increasing speed to close the target, with the same utter lack of hesitation that characterizes the actions of all the naval units in the history of these fateful days. The first the Germans knew of the presence of their enemy was the flash of *Renown*'s guns a good ten miles away: they were so taken by surprise that it was full six minutes before they themselves were able to open fire—by which time even Whitworth's destroyers, rolling and pitching in the impossible sea, were firing also—although their chances of doing any damage at that range under those conditions were very slight. But *Renown*, although she was almost taking water green over her fore turrets, had the range and the target and she very rapidly scored a vital hit on *Gneisenau*'s foretop, reducing her main gunnery control to a shambles and putting all her main armament out of action. She turned away; *Scharnhorst* steamed across her wake, laying a smoke screen, and both ships then made away to the north at top speed. *Renown* was now hit three times in rapid succession but with no effects that her damage-control parties could not take care of. As she altered course in her turn to pursue the fleeing enemy, her fire got home again on *Gneisenau*, wrecking one of her turrets and doing other damage aft.

The action now became a stern chase with the Germans cramming on every ounce of speed they could get to save themselves for the tasks dictated by their orders in the coming days, and although Admiral Whitworth raised his speed for a short space to something over twenty-nine knots, he took such a pounding from the sea at that speed that he had to ease down, while the destroyers could not possibly keep up with him and remain afloat. As he reduced speed a snow squall blotted everything out. When it cleared the Germans were far ahead of him and he had no choice but to let them go.

Before many hours had passed Whitworth was retracing his course back to the Vestfiord. Now that the German invasion of

Norway was established beyond dispute, the Admiralty had signalled him to keep watch and prevent the Germans from landing
at Narvik—thus effectively bolting a door through which the
enemy had already steamed without opposition.

At the same time, farther south, Admiral Forbes was planning
an attack on the German ships in Trondheim; he had barely made
this decision when the Admiralty intervened to add Bergen as a
target. Before midday they intervened again to cancel Trondheim
and left him with Bergen: two hours later Bergen was cancelled
also. And half an hour later came the first taste of an entirely new
element in the situation—the first of a series of German air
onslaughts which were for all practical purposes to deny the Navy
the sea off the southern coast of Norway.

Now it is wrong to suppose, as many writers have done, that
British naval thinking in the years before the war underestimated
the effect of aircraft on the new shape of war at sea. The naval
planners had been much concerned with the danger from the air,
but unfortunately they had come to the wrong conclusions about
it. They had become quite convinced that a massive anti-aircraft
barrage from ships' guns would keep the bombers at arm's length
or destroy them if they ventured too close; but the four-inch
high-angle guns with which they had equipped their ships (and
too few of them were fully equipped with these) could not put up
the volume of fire this policy called for and the two-pounder pom-
poms which supplemented them, although they made a glorious
amount of noise and commotion, were unreliable and subject to
frequent stoppages. They had thought almost purely in terms of
high-flying aircraft and not reckoned with the dive-bomber; and
the Oerlikons and Bofors guns which were needed to cope with
dive-bombers were at that time few and far between in the fleet.
Last of all, they had taken very little account of the fact that the
best of barrages can be kept up only as long as there is ammunition
to raise it: in the prolonged attacks which were now to begin the
rate at which ships used up their ack-ack ammunition was alarm-
ing, and before the campaign had got very far there was actually
a shortage in the main ammunition supply depots at home.

Fortunately in this first attack dive-bombers were not yet very
much in evidence. It began at half past two and it lasted roughly
three hours. The weather was clear this far south—too clear—but

the seas were still running very steep and the ships, taking evasive action at speed, found anti-aircraft gunnery very difficult. The two cruisers *Southampton* and *Glasgow* were damaged, the battle-ship *Rodney* got a direct hit from a thousand-pound bomb, but her heavy horizontal armour saved her from serious hurt. The destroyer *Ghurka* was sunk. By the time the attack was called off the cruisers had used up half the anti-aircraft shell in their magazines and some quick and serious re-thinking was obviously necessary about the tactics of the British Fleet in these waters. It was soon to become clear that aeroplanes were the only real defence against aeroplanes: out of the precious few aircraft carriers which we possessed at that time, *Furious* was at this moment on her way to join the Fleet. Typically of the hasty improvisations of these days which even the Navy was unable to escape completely, she had left in a great hurry with her torpedo bombers in her hangars but without her fighter squadron. There was therefore no possibility of fighter protection either for the Fleet or for troops when they should land. The whole of Norway was completely out of range of land-based fighter aircraft from Britain and with the Germans already in control of the few permanent airfields of any importance in Norway itself, prospects were not bright.

Nor were the prospects of counter-attack by our own bombers on the German naval units much better. Of the two-engined bombers the R.A.F. possessed, the Wellington alone was to survive the test of war: the others were the Blenheim (capable of standing in as a long-range fighter, but not very effectively), the Hampden and the Whitley. The Whitley had the longest operational range although even this was no more than 565 miles: it was moreover a most unsatisfactory aircraft. But even for the Whitley the Norwegian coast was at extreme range under good conditions—in other words the slightest delays and deviations caused by weather or other circumstances, or any delay in finding the target, would make the long and perilous flight out and home abortive. None the less on the evening of the 9th twelve Whitleys and twelve Hampdens were sent to bomb Bergen harbour where all the ships of the German Group 3 were still in port preparing for their dash home to safety. They found their target and reported several near misses but no damage at all was done and one aircraft was lost. Almost immediately after the air attack the cruiser *Köln* put to sea with two of the torpedo boats and got safely home.

'Every ship in the Skagerrak will be sunk,' cried Churchill that day. Many people have taken this to be either a vainglorious boast or a thunder of impotent determination. What it really meant was that that day the First Lord had scored at least one victory: he had got permission for the restrictions on submarine operations to be relaxed in the approaches to Norway. Now at last submarines would no longer have to go through the pantomime of surfacing and giving due warning under a hostile sky before they disposed of obvious German supply ships or troopships—or to be forced to let these ships steam tantalizingly past their periscope sights when it was quite obvious that surfacing meant instant annihilation. It so happened that the submarine *Sunfish* was watching such a target—the German ammunition ship *Amasis*—pass through the waters above her at the instant the signal was received and without further ado she torpedoed it. She was to find three more victims of the same kind. In the coming days a heavy toll was taken both of supply ships and troopships in this area: even more important, both the cruiser *Karlsruhe* and the pocket battleship *Lützow* were torpedoed. The first was so badly damaged that she was sent to the bottom by torpedoes of her own escort and the *Lützow* barely got home with her decks awash, to spend the next twelve months in the dockyard at Kiel. This further depleted the Germans' very small reserve of first-class ships and so had effects in the difficult months to come; but the Germans had taken a gamble with these ships, reconciling themselves to losses of up to fifty per cent—and whatever the future effects might be the gamble had got them into Norway.

But every ship in the Skagerrak could not be sunk. The watching of these waters even by submerged submarines was a business of enormous peril. For, short as the Germans might be of capital ships, cruisers and destroyers, they had plenty of fast motor patrol craft and the Skagerrak fairly hummed with their activity—the more so because the German High Command was more worried than we even suspected about their losses in men, supplies and horses. The submarines found themselves constantly hunted by surface craft obviously well equipped with listening devices, so that submarine crews had to be constantly on the alert for their

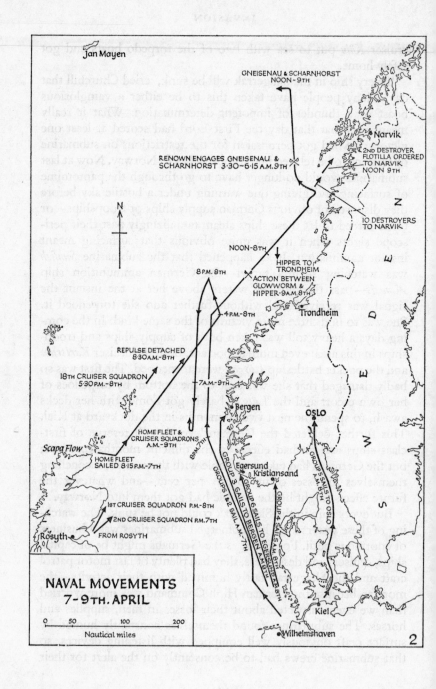

Jan Mayen

GNEISENAU & SCHARNHORST
NOON-9TH

Narvik

2ND DESTROYER
FLOTILLA ORDERED
TO NARVIK
NOON-9TH

RENOWN ENGAGES GNEISENAU &
SCHARNHORST 3·30—6·15 A.M. 9TH

IO DESTROYERS
TO NARVIK

NOON-8TH

HIPPER TO
TRONDHEIM

8 P.M. 8TH

ACTION BETWEEN
GLOWWORM &
HIPPER-9A.M. 8TH

Trondheim

4 P.M.-8TH

REPULSE DETACHED
8·30A.M.-8TH

7A.M.-9TH

18TH CRUISER SQUADRON
5·30P.M.-8TH

Bergen

OSLO

HOME FLEET &
CRUISER SQUADRONS
A.M.-9TH

8PM.7TH

Scapa Flow

HOME FLEET
SAILED 8·15P.M.-7TH

GROUP 3 SAILS TO BEERGEN A.M.8TH

GROUP 5 SAILS TO OSLO

Egersund

GROUPS 1&2 SAILS TO EGERSUND A.M.-7TH

GROUP 4 SAILS A.M.8TH

Kristiansand

1ST CRUISER SQUADRON P.M.-8TH

GROUP 6 SAILS TO EGERSUND A.M.-7TH

2ND CRUISER SQUADRON P.M.7TH

Rosyth

FROM ROSYTH

Kiel

NAVAL MOVEMENTS
7–9TH. APRIL

Wilhelmshaven

0   50   100   200

Nautical miles

2

comings and going; while an attack, successful or unsuccessful, was almost invariably followed by an avalanche of depth charging which could be escaped only by lying for long hours silent at the bottom of the sea while further targets passed by unharmed. At this time, moreover, the 'snort' device, which enables a submarine both to breathe and to use its diesel engines under the sea, had not been invented—they were compelled, therefore, to surface at night to recharge their batteries and replenish their air supply, and this left them wide open to attack. Several submarines were lost—the first on the Allied side to be sunk in this war. Their sacrifice was in vain because the campaign was lost. As in so many phases of the war in Norway, just a little more would have made so much difference; but the little was not there.

CHAPTER 6

ACTION IN THE NORTH

As 9th April wore on the War Cabinet were forced to admit to themselves that Plan R.4 had been forestalled and that the Germans were in Norway. The evidence was too weighty even for wishful thinking. None the less, there was a shortage of precise information about exactly what was going on, how much of Norway the Germans controlled, and about the size and composition of their forces. There was no British military attaché in Norway. There was no information to be got from the British Embassy in Norway, because although the speedy evacuation of the King and Government from Oslo saved them from falling into the hands of the Germans, it also cut them off from communication with the outside world. Radio, telephone and news service were in German hands. Any information came in a roundabout way through Sweden, partly from the British Legation in Stockholm but mostly in the form of newspaper reports. It is not much of an exaggeration to say that the bewildered troops incarcerated in the transit camp at Dunfermline were nearly as well informed, through what newspapers they could lay their hands on, as the Chiefs of Staff in Whitehall.

But however much the precise facts may have been in dispute, there was one thing that could not possibly be disputed—that action was urgent. And urgent action was precisely what a war conducted by committee meetings was least equipped to produce. In Germany an unopposed and ruthless dictatorship was able to make decisions for better or for worse at the drop of a hat: London gave a supreme demonstration of all the vices of democracy without any of its virtues. In the month following the invasion of Norway the Ministerial Committee on Military Co-ordination (the name itself has a ring of frustration) held no less than twenty-three meetings. The Chiefs of Staff Committee (in addition to the Chiefs themselves having to attend the Ministerial

Committee meetings) met forty-three times in April alone. There were, Mr. Churchill pointed out in a note to the Prime Minister, 'six Chiefs of Staff, three Ministers and General Ismay, who all have a voice in Norwegian operations'. Farther down the scale came the Joint Planning Sub-Committee, the Joint Intelligence Sub-Committee, the Inter-Services Planning Staff and so on. Inevitably, this kind of organization not merely failed to produce quick decisions and decisive action—it also failed to create any sort of co-ordination between the three Services, which remained separately and individually responsible for their own particular part in any operation which might arise. And this in itself was bound to result in errors and omissions, large and small, which played their disastrous part in every phase of the Allied campaign from the dispatch of the earliest forces to the last tragedy, the sinking of *Glorious*. Even naval operations—where, as we have already seen and will see again, quick and usually accurate assessments were produced when these were left to the commanders on the spot—were in danger of being confused. Admiral Whitworth was forced to protest that he had received three separate and differing directives within a matter of hours: the dithering over the attacks on Bergen and Trondheim was in glaring contrast to the single-minded decisions which would have led to the recapture of Narvik had they been promptly followed up and exploited. Where urgency was applied, it was applied at the wrong moment and to the wrong purpose: it was misguided panic from Whitehall that led to *Furious* putting to sea without her fighter aircraft—as a result of which ships and men were lost.

This was the climate in which the British War Cabinet, responsible for the Allied conduct of a rapid counter-stroke to the German invasion, sat down to consider what forces it had at its disposal, what it could do with them and where it should put them. Had the Germans had any inkling of it at all, they would have been less worried about their own situation—which, as they saw it, was by no means happy in some places and quite desperate in others. In the course of their landings they had suffered serious losses in ships, men and equipment, which had thrown their forces completely out of balance and upset their command structure. Quisling had misled them: the landings had not been unopposed, as he had confidently predicted, and his pro-Nazi organization had not produced a horde of supporters as he had led them to expect—he was even having difficulty in finding Norwegians to fill the posts in his puppet government. None the less, Oslo had been conceded them by the Norwegians, both to preserve the city and its population from destruction and to keep their government in being: through the short sea route and through Fornebu air-field, which was serviceable, they could replace their losses and build up. At Kristiansand, Bergen and Stavanger they were in control, though their forces were still relatively thin on the ground. Reinforcement here also was comparatively easy—especially at Stavanger, which possessed the best aerodrome in Norway. At Trondheim they were in difficulties: at this stage Norwegian strongpoints were holding out against all reason, and possession of the airfield at Vaernes (which in any case was not fully cleared of snow) was being hotly disputed. In spite of its vulnerability to air attack, now being demonstrated, the Royal Navy was strong this far north and active against German rein-forcements by sea. Narvik was a major headache. The Germans had their ten modern destroyers in the fiords (though they were not to have them there much longer) and they had their troops in the town, thanks to Colonel Sundlo. But General Fleischer's fully-mobilized 6th Norwegian Division was intact and menacing them, though they had captured his most important depot. There was no landing ground on the mainland: the only landing ground in the whole area of any importance, Bardufoss, was in any case completely snowbound, as was the airfield at Bodö farther south. Land communication with the other centres, hundreds of miles to the south, was virtually impossible, while the British fleet, out of range for the moment to the all-important dive-bombers, was angrily scouring the sea, had damaged *Hipper* in a David–Goliath action and given the powerful *Gneisenau* a drubbing.

Last but not least, an obstreperous and independent population with a rooted dislike for authority (even when it was native) was already making life most difficult for General Dietl and his troops: it is probably true to say that the familiar pattern of the Norwegian Reistance, of which there are so many tales that it has almost become a legend, first began to take shape among the sturdy northern folk of Narvik.

It was necessary for the Germans to make the maximum possible use of every moment, and they did so. Ju 52 transport planes they had in quantity: one writer describes these as converted airliners, but it would be truer to say that they were troop transports that had filled a temporary peacetime airliner rôle. Three-engined, ponderous, slow, they would have been an easy prey to fighters had there been any fighters to challenge them, but they were way out of enemy fighter range. From the first day of the invasion onwards they were touching down on Fornebu at the rate of fifty a day, and each carried thirty men with their weapons and equipment. At Stavanger operations were on the same scale; and from both Fornebu and Stavanger a further hop could be made to Trondheim as soon as Vaernes was got under control and made serviceable. Meanwhile seaplanes could get a limited number of men into Trondheim and at least thirty of these were counted in the fiord. Finally, as we have seen, every ship in the Skagerrak could not be sunk: before 13th April ten storeships and six transports had arrived in Oslo, carrying ten thousand men, and field guns, tanks and other heavy weapons, together with ammunition and supplies.

All in all, about twenty-four thousand German troops arrived in Norway in the week after *Pol III* had given the first alarm—and not merely troops, but all the arms and equipment necessary to fight a modern war. Once these were established, the chances of ousting them were slim—especially when the dithering War Cabinet in Britain had at its immediate disposal only the eight disorganized battalions of Plan R.4, for addition to which (though not immediately) there were six French battalions available, making a total of about 14,000 men with no tanks, light or heavy artillery or anti-aircraft guns.

Powerless to prevent the Germans from consolidating themselves ashore, the Navy at least did its best to keep them off the sea. The confusion in Whitehall might indeed spread far enough from time to time to impair the freedom of commanders on the spot—prevent, for instance, the naval attacks on Trondheim and Bergen, which involved acceptable risks and could, in the light of our later knowledge, have produced good effect. None the less, the men on the spot unavoidably had freedom of action, and they used it. The R.A.F. had failed with their high-level bombers against shipping in Bergen; but at Hatston in the Orkneys there were naval Skua dive-bombers which should have been on aircraft carriers, had there been enough aircraft carriers for them: for these the chance of action was welcome. They struck at Bergen—at the limit of endurance for them, as it had been for the R.A.F.—and were fortunate enough to find the harbour under a clear sky with the cruiser *Königsberg*, already superficially damaged on the way in, below them. Three bombs got home on her—the captain of an American merchantman in the harbour declared that he saw one bomb fall directly between her funnels—and she caught fire, blew up and sank. There were no more targets for them, for *Köln* and the torpedo boats had already left. *Karlsruhe*, as we already know, fell a victim to the hunting submarines, and the pocket battleship *Lützow* barely made her home port. At least a dozen of the supply ships were sent to the bottom, but the damaged *Hipper* and her destroyers got safely home from Trondheim and *Scharnhorst* and *Gneisenau* were also able to get back with no further damage. It was in the north that the Navy got its own back on the Germans in the greatest measure: this was to place Narvik, which still bulked larger than the rest of the whole of Norway in the minds of the War Cabinet, within our grasp for the taking—but the action of resolute men on the spot could still not compensate for indecision at home.

Few naval actions in the Second World War have been described as often as the 2nd Destroyer Flotilla's attack on Narvik led by Captain 'Wash' Warburton-Lee. Told without its background it is a story of dash, daring and great courage, true to all the traditions of destroyer service and to the traditions of naval men over the centuries. In fact it was something more: it was a considered operation calling for great skill, both in navigation, ship handling, tactics and gunnery, and carried out with great precision. It was a model of how decisions can be made by trained men and, once made, can be undeviatingly carried out in the face of great odds.

After *Scharnhorst* and *Gneisenau* had disappeared into the tempest and Admiral Whitworth had given up the chase, his patrol off the Vestfiord continued—still without knowledge that the forces against whom he was keeping watch had eluded him and made Narvik before the watch began. It became necessary to discover what was really going on at Narvik and the 2nd Flotilla, consisting of the destroyers *Hotspur, Hostile, Havoc, Hunter* and *Hardy*, was detached to go up the fiords. In more sheltered waters but still in blinding snowstorms and poor visibility, Warburton-Lee made up the Vestfiord through waters in which neither he nor any other officer in his flotilla had navigated a ship. In the late afternoon he stopped at the pilot station at Tranöy and there got his first positive news. There were, the Norwegians told him, six German destroyers at Narvik, much larger than his. We, of course, know that there were ten, but six was odds enough, for they were much larger than Warburton-Lee's vessels and mounted five-inch guns as against his 4·7s—the difference seems small until it is realized they fired a projectile roughly twice as heavy. The Norwegians roundly declared that he would need twice as many ships as he had.

But Warburton-Lee considered the risks against the plan he had in mind and—this factor of assessing the acceptability of risks comes up so often in the actions of these men at this time—accepted them. He made a signal reporting the information he had obtained and added to it the words, 'Intend attacking at dawn, high water'. The signal, which the senior surviving officer of the flotilla asked in his report to be given a place in the Admiralty's historical records, is dated 1751 hours, 9th April 1940.

Captain Roskill in his official history of the war at sea adds a timely footnote for the benefit of laymen about the meaning of that word 'intend'. By naval convention it signifies that a commander is reporting to his seniors an action he is determined upon taking. It does not ask for approval and calls for no reply unless this be a specific forbidding of the action concerned. The Admiralty (which had once more intervened directly in this matter) did in fact signal back that they would support any action Warburton-Lee had decided to take: Admiral Whitworth considered whether or not to reinforce him but quite rightly thought he should avoid delaying the operation by forcing him to wait for other ships.

The rest of the story is quite briefly told. There were still fifty miles to go from Tranöy to Narvik: the entire passage was made in almost continuous snowstorms. Ships, says the official report of the action, were twice separated owing to merchant vessels passing through them and on the solitary occasion that land was seen the whole flotilla nearly ran aground.

At a quarter past four the following morning the citizens of Narvik were awakened by gunfire in the fiord. They had passed the previous day in puzzled and by no means acquiescent contemplation of their German 'protectors' and now leapt from their beds to watch the spectacle of a firework display in which their protectors' ships were being sunk. The British, it was clear, were coming.

For Warburton-Lee, leaving *Hotspur* and *Hostile* outside to keep guard and cope with any shore batteries, had stormed into the anchorage with the other three destroyers and taken the Germans completely by surprise. Their first victim was the German Flotilla leader *Heidkamp*, which was torpedoed in the after-magazine and immediately blew up with an appalling explosion that echoed and re-echoed from the hills. Commodore Bonte himself died in her and there were few survivors. *Schmitt* broke in two and sank; *Roeder* was heavily damaged and on fire. All this happened before the German ships had so much as fired a shot. Of the remainder two more, *Künne* and *Hans Lüdemann* were disabled and put out of action. Two merchant ships had also been sunk. There had been some counter-attack from the German destroyers by torpedo but the torpedoes had either been avoided or were suffering from the curious defects to which the torpedoes of both sides seemed liable in these waters. There had been rifle and machine-gun fire from the shore but nothing heavier—the fact was that General Dietl's mountain guns had been washed overboard from the decks of the destroyers, where they had been lashed, and the supposed Norwegian gun positions had either not yet been manned by the Germans or did not exist. *Hotspur* and *Hostile* therefore steamed in and joined the rest of the flotilla in the attack.

All this has taken only a few sentences to tell but by now Warburton-Lee had been running riot in the harbour for a full hour. The results were most satisfying, and with five of the enemy's six destroyers either sunk or disabled there seemed little prospect of counter-attack. He stopped to make a quick assessment of the situation: mist was now coming down heavily over the fiord and the snow-covered shores—but on the other hand, with the exception of *Hunter*, all his ships had a few torpedoes left and it seemed a pity to take them away with them. So he formed up his ships again and made one final sweep round the harbour: in the poor visibility four more merchant ships went to the bottom— the sinkings now totted up to a good 40,000 tons—but the last destroyer eluded him. It was time to withdraw: it was more than time to withdraw, because whereas in the light of his incomplete information he thought there was only one destroyer left, there were in fact five. These ships had not been lying in the main anchorage by Narvik but had been up two of the side fiords which branch out of the Ofotfiord to north and south—Herjangs- fiord and Ballangenfiord: they had been late in getting the alarm and had thought at first that the whole commotion was an air raid. Now they were on their way to the rescue at top speed and, in contrast to their sister ships at the beginning of the attack, were very much on the alert. Just as Warburton-Lee commenced his withdrawal three of these destroyers appeared out of the mist on his starboard side and almost immediately two more ahead of him on his port bow. He promptly increased speed to thirty knots and engaged the new adversaries with his guns, but in a moment found himself under the accurate fire of their much heavier arma- ment. *Hardy* was hit and set on fire: *Hunter* and *Hotspur* were damaged and collided out of control. Immediately afterwards *Hardy* got a direct hit on her bridge which killed or seriously injured every soul about it, including Warburton-Lee himself. His last order was to abandon ship: while *Hotspur*, disentangling herself from the sinking *Hunter*, made off down the fiord with the two undamaged destroyers, the flotilla leader was beached with the Captain's secretary, Paymaster-Lieutenant Stanning, at the wheel and her survivors took to the icy waters of the fiord. The Germans did not press the pursuit: they were short both of ammunition and fuel and leaderless into the bargain. Although Warburton-Lee was desperately wounded and obviously dying his men would not leave him: they managed to get him on to an improvised raft and towed him ashore, but he died on the beach.

One last blow was struck by the three surviving ships as they sped away down the fiord making for the sea: they encountered the German ammunition ship *Rauenfels* coming in and sent her to the bottom: it was a loss the Germans were to feel severely. Although a terrible price had now been paid for it, nothing could undo the havoc that had been wrought among the German forces and their supply ships both in actual loss and in the shaking of morale. Had the extent of both been realized either by Admiral Whitworth, Admiral Forbes or in London, very different action would perhaps have been taken to follow it up. No attempt even was made to round up the one hundred and seventy survivors of *Hardy*, who struggled ashore to find themselves in snow six feet deep with their wet clothes freezing on their bodies. Shocked and shivering, they managed to make their way, taking their injured with them, to a Norwegian farmhouse, where the Norwegians took them in—they crammed eighty men into the five rooms of the farmhouse itself—half stripped themselves of their own clothing and tore up blankets, curtains and even carpets to serve as coverings and make bandages for the wounded. Thus fortified, those of the crew who were able to struggle on got themselves to the village of Ballangen, where the Norwegians once more turned out to make them as comfortable as they could; and here they met up with some British merchant seamen, who had also escaped from the Germans, and stayed without interference to be taken aboard Admiral Whitworth's ships a couple of days later, after the second attack on Narvik.

Hunter's survivors got ashore on the opposite side of the fiord and after many hardships made their way into Sweden: a German officer is said to have shown them the way.

Warburton-Lee was posthumously awarded the Victoria Cross —the first of the Second World War—and a letter to *The Times* quoted a passage from Southey's *Life of Nelson*:

'He has left us a name and an example which are at this hour inspiring thousands of the youth of England—a name which is our pride and an example which will continue to be our shield and our strength.'

To the survivors Mr. Churchill said:

'You are the vanguard of the army which we and our French Allies will use this summer to purge and cleanse the soil of the Vikings, the soil of Norway, from the filthy pollution of Nazi tyranny.'

It may be said that it was a pity that the War Cabinet were not so inspired by Warburton-Lee's example and that Mr. Churchill's prophecy was unfulfilled.

The next two days make a curious kind of lull in the story. Not a lull in fact but an absence of decisive action. In the extreme north Admiral Whitworth, prey to conflicting instructions from London, patrolled the approaches to Narvik. There was endless discussion about a second attack—confused by an impression the withdrawing destroyers had got that one of their final assailants had been a cruiser. It was thought that the cruiser *Penelope* and the other destroyer flotilla might be used for this purpose, but *Penelope* was sent rushing off to Bodö on a false alarm, failed to find herself a pilot and ran aground; so she had to be towed into the Skjelfiord, where a temporary repair depot had been established and where the damaged *Havoc* was already being patched up. Reinforcements came: the battle cruiser *Repulse* and the battleship *Warspite*. Admiral Forbes was also steaming north, and doing so got some little respite from the Luftwaffe, although the respite was not complete: his ships suffered further damage— mostly minor—and shot away still more of their anti-aircraft ammunition. *Furious*, still without her fighter squadron, was unable to provide any protection but on successive days her Swordfish torpedo bombers carried out two attacks on enemy-occupied harbours—first on Trondheim, where there were now only four German destroyers left, and then on Narvik. Both these attacks were utter failures. At Trondheim the target was found without difficulty but the torpedoes grounded in shallow water and exploded before reaching their objectives. The Narvik attack was in two waves, the first of which did no more damage than at Trondheim, while the second failed to find the target at all in the heavy overcast. There was a minor exchange of gunfire between a couple of destroyers and the Trondheim forts; farther south, in the area already denied to surface vessels by the omnipotent and watchful German air arm, the submarines continued to keep their perilous watch in the Skagerrak.

In London the interminable discussions still went on. Where were we to counter-attack? Were we to put everything into Narvik and so gain access to all the ore fields and fulfil our promise to the Norwegians at the same blow? Should we attack Trondheim and Bergen as well? Where were the Germans and how

many of them were there? What forces were available? In addition
to the troops on shore or aboard the transports in Scotland, the
French were now promising six battalions of the Chasseurs Alpins
and some Foreign Legion units: these could not be made available
for some days, but the French—from the grandstand so to speak
—pressed for an attack with enthusiasm; seeing in it more and
more a possible diversion from the Western Front, where they
awaited the long-anticipated German attack in a state of apprehension that was harbinger of the defeat to come. More than this,
nothing could be spared from the divisions in France either by the
French or by ourselves. Nothing could be spared by the R.A.F.,
whose total bomber strength at this time was not much more than
two hundred; and although in the forthcoming days sorties were
to be flown against enemy-occupied landing grounds in Norway
and in Denmark, the attacks were not in sufficient strength and
virtually nothing was achieved by them. Orders were also given
for a mine-laying operation in the Skagerrak—long urged by Mr.
Churchill and long frustrated by argument. In the British Press it
was described as the laying of 'a huge minefield in the Baltic':
it was huge perhaps in terms of square miles of sea but common
sense alone on the part of writer or reader would have shown up
how sparsely the mines were laid. To have laid a 'huge minefield
in the Baltic' would have involved an equally huge number of
aircraft capable of carrying the fifteen-hundred-pound load involved, setting it down from the right height and at the right
speed, unobserved by the enemy. There was not a huge number of
aircraft available nor were there many crews trained in this
delicate and precise operation. Under these circumstances the
minefield was much more successful than might have been
expected and did send at least eighteen and a half thousand tons
of enemy shipping to the bottom, apart from some neutral losses.
This was a good deal less than had been disposed of by Warburton-Lee in his single attack on Narvik, and had we possessed
the resources to provide more than the two hundred mines a
month which could be made available or the aircraft to lay them it
might have had value. It was, like all the other operations, no
more than a pin-prick against the Germans and did not in the
long run interfere with the furious build-up of their forces in
Norway.

Slowly out of the endless wrangles and disputes of the committees as to means and objectives there emerged a naval commander and a military commander for a probable expedition.

'On the afternoon of Wednesday, 10th April, I received a message that the First Sea Lord would like to see me and was informed by him that a combined expedition was to be sent to Narvik and that I was to go in charge of the naval forces, etc.'

So wrote Admiral of the Fleet the Earl of Cork and Orrery in his report after the campaign. His style lacks literary graces—it even lacks the flowing and easy manner which most senior officers acquire in writing reports—and so marks him out as a man of action rather than a man of words. Of action he was to have much less than he desired and of words far too many—especially, one suspects, with General Mackesy. His appointment was a Churchillian one and in the eyes of some a curious one, for this diminutive aristocrat was a very senior officer indeed and carried even more rank than the Commander-in-Chief Home Fleet—an appointment which he himself had held seven years before. He did as well as he was allowed to and his appointment does not, in fact, call for criticism. General Mackesy's appointment was no surprise, for he had been the military officer in charge of that stillborn child, Plan R.4. While Admiral Cork was getting a verbal briefing at the Admiralty in London, Mackesy was on his way to Scapa Flow and the Orders which had been prepared for him for the execution of Plan R.4 were being taken out, dusted and somewhat hastily revised to meet the new circumstances. It would have been better if they had been torn up and started again from scratch, because, as we shall see before very long, they carried the misguided thinking of Plan R.4 on into the operation for the recovery of Narvik and brought their unlucky possessor into head-on collision with the Earl of Cork, who had different ideas and a different interpretation of his own instructions. Tired men, inadequate thinking and shortage of almost everything, including staff, beget tired orders.

So far, therefore, in the face of a very urgent situation the general was on his way even if the army was not. On the afternoon of the 10th crowds around Wellington Barracks saw the army go. There was, it will be remembered, but one battalion of the Guards

Brigade embarked in the Clyde—the 1st Battalion Scots Guards. There had been no 'flap' on when they left London and their going had excited little attention: with a similar lack of publicity the 2nd Battalion South Wales Borderers were on their way from a remote part of the British Commonwealth, Ulster—although the Irish Guards' regimental history, confusing them with the 1st Battalion of their regiment, oddly mentions them as having come from India, which was still remoter. But the Irish Guards set out in the full blaze of publicity that was inevitably theirs in the first wave of public excitement following the news of the invasion of Norway. This magnificent regular battalion, with vast regimental pride and an officers' roll like a page out of *Debrett*, was trained, like any regular Guards battalion, to the last degree and it made its preparations with immense care. All its stores were carefully packed in small boxes and single-man loads. The organization was terrific and for a moment in reading their story one somehow has a vain hope that it would be proof against the confusion of the Norwegian campaign; but this was not to be.

When the Irish Guards paraded for their departure they saw their officers in battledress for the first time. Their families were watching, as were the crowds beyond the railings; and their iron discipline had somehow (you have to understand the Guards to understand this sort of thing) not prevented the row of Green Line buses which was to take them to Euston being chalked with messages reading, 'To Norway', 'See the midnight sun', 'North Pole Express', and so on. The coaches themselves still bore on their destination boards the names of the peaceful weekend beauty spots around London to which they had once plied: like the whole of Britain they were somehow not quite in the war.

To cries of 'Keep your head down, Mick!' and the like they drove away, and the following day found themselves embarked with great satisfaction in the luxury liner *Monarch of Bermuda* in King George V dock in Glasgow. For them at least the campaign seemed to be beginning more auspiciously than for the wretched Territorials in Dunfermline camp; and the same day the Press reported the recapture of Bergen by the British and Trondheim by the Norwegians. This day likewise the South Wales Borderers filed aboard their luxury ship, *Reina del Pacifico*: the two ships presently joined *Batory* carrying the Scots Guards (who never got

their route march) and *Chrobry* which was carrying the Hallamshire Battalion, and set sail for Scapa, escorted by destroyers.
There was a heavy swell off the Mull of Kintyre, but off the
Hebrides the sun came out and the sky was blue: men sunbathed
on the decks and accepted their good fortune with the ease where-
with the professional soldier takes his small mercies. They deserved this much in advance for what they had coming to them.
They now faced a wait of two days in Scapa Flow while their
destination was debated, and this wait was enlivened by a regatta
in ships' boats organized by the Hallamshires, in which General
Mackesy is said to have shown great interest.

The following day the K.O.Y.L.I. and the Lincolnshires were
rescued from the wastes of Dunfermline, entrained for Glasgow
and put aboard *Empress of Australia*. They were still short of
many of the stores and essential items of equipment that had been
lost to them in the panic disembarkation from the cruisers: from
now on they would have to manage the best way they could.

So far, therefore, all that had been accomplished by way of the
immediate aid which had been spontaneously promised to the
Norwegians was the movement of a part of the forces available to
a different concentration place, where in terms of equipment and
preparation they were somewhat worse off than before the invasion started. The discussion in London on both their destination and their rôle went on. From the fog of discussion was
emerging the idea of a quick dash to Narvik and this operation
was presently to receive the code name Rupert—after, it is
thought, the dashing cavalier of King Charles 1st's war. The discussions covered many fields and many possibilities, but they all
shared one common factor—an underestimate of the strength
of the German forces (which was to become more serious the
longer the delay lasted) and a completely unrealistic picture of the
Germans' air power, together with the effect it was likely to have
on operations. This underestimation was the inevitable product
of the wishful thinking from which the War Cabinet in particular
could not shake itself free; for fairly reliable estimates of German
strength had now come via Sweden. The War Cabinet would
suffer for all this because it would lead, together with the Allied
defeats elsewhere, to its undoing, and British prestige and good
repute would equally suffer to an extent which would never be

truly made good. But the biggest sufferers, the victims of all the discussions, changes of mind and indecision over plans and objectives would be both the troops who were enjoying the Indian summer of the Phoney War in the north of Scotland—and the hard-pressed Norwegian people, whose saviours they were supposed to be.

For on the other side of the storm-bound sea, in the wintry land which had for a brief space become the focus of the world's attention, desperate things were being done. In spite of Quisling's attempt to call off the mobilization instructions, the Norwegian Army was managing to get itself together in bits and pieces. None of the five divisions which were responsible for the southern and central part of the country ever succeeded in getting anything like their full strength together: even had they done so and even had so much of their equipment and stores not been lost to the Germans before they were mobilized, they would have been no match for the invaders in terms of equipment, training or air support—though their manpower establishment on paper was roughly equal to that of the Germans. None the less in the extreme south-east, the area of the 1st Division, General Erichson managed to get best part of four thousand men together and equip them: they were to last a week before they were forced over the border into Sweden as the only alternative to extermination or surrender. To the north-west of him General Hvinden Haug also managed to assemble a makeshift nucleus of his 2nd Division and for the moment the safety of the Norwegian King and government was in the hands of these men alone—virtually guerrillas and quite unable to make a stand for long in any one place against the guns and tanks of the Germans and the straffing of their supporting aircraft.

In these very early stages, while the Germans were still building up and readjusting themselves after their first invasion losses, the capture of King Haakon and his legal government was an objective of tremendous urgency. The refusal of the King and his ministers to capitulate had taken them completely by surprise, and while the legal government was known to be in existence the authority of the Quisling administration in Oslo could not possibly be enforced: and so though they were not yet ready to break out in force from their invasion points, they wasted no time over attempting the capture of King Haakon and the cabinet.

When the government evacuated to Hamar, to the north of Oslo, early on 9th April, they did so rather to provide a safe assembly point than with any idea that they would be allowed to stay there: Hamar, however, possessed a radio station; its range, though not large, would enable them to maintain some sort of partial contact with Army and population as long as they could hold on to it.

The Storting, or parliament, assembled there in surprisingly good order and with a remarkable degree of calm for representatives of a people that had not been at war for more than a hundred years. But they had not been there many hours before warning came that an advance party of Germans was only ten miles away, and within ten minutes a train was assembled in the station to move on to Elverum. Here a company of recruits with a bare month's training and a collection of officers who were trying to find their units set up a roadblock. While they were there the German minister, Dr. Brauer, whose demands had been so uncomprisingly rejected early in the morning, demanded a personal interview with the King. He got it, and put to him an even stiffer series of demands than the original ones: in their turn they were once more rejected and once more parliament and ministers confirmed the rejection. The very same evening the German Air Attaché in Oslo determined to substitute action for argument and took a force out along the road to Elverum, leading it himself in one of the legation cars, still bearing its diplomatic licence plates. A hastily assembled collection of armed Norwegians—including some labourers who had never held a rifle before, repulsed the raiders, with losses: as German troops did throughout the whole of the campaign, they recoiled rapidly in the face of opposition. But Elverum was blitzed from the air and the big college building in which the Storting had assembled was reduced to a ruin.

By the time the town was blitzed, however, the government and the King had moved on once more—to Nybergsund near the Swedish border; and once more the German bombers pursued them, devastating the place, which contained no troops and was no more than a few farmhouses scattered around a bridge. The King and many members of the government were driven to the shelter of the snowbound woods as the machine-gunning planes pursued them. For good measure the Germans made a second raid on Elverum in case there was anything of importance left there. Fifty-four people were killed and one hundred and ten wounded: it seemed to the spectators that they made a special target of the hospital and this impression was to persist in other places throughout the coming weeks.

Since it was quite obvious that they were determined to kill or capture the head of the state and obliterate the constitutionally elected government, the parliament adjourned, delegating the conduct of the war to the cabinet—which together with the King and Crown Prince went into hiding in the long and tortuous valleys which cleave their way through Norway to the western coast; and from the first of these anonymous hiding places King Haakon issued his famous proclamation which urged his people to continue their resistance against the 'protectors' and ended with the words, 'God save Norway!'

The defence of the King and government fell upon the shoulders of General Hvinden Haug's 2nd Division, which fought a series of small but bloody actions as it retired. None of these actions amounts to a battle in any sense of the word. To call them skirmishes or fighting patrols would give quite a wrong impression, for they were hard-fought and desperate; but they were encounters between small groups on a small scale—the Norwegians much handicapped in fire power against the Germans and constantly blitzed from the air, but driven by a desperate urge to resist, and fighting on ground familiar to them, in which they were bound to be more at home than the best-trained of foreign troops. There was a very large number of such actions: the pattern of them was so complex that it has taken the Norwegian government's own War Historical Department many years of patient research to build up a complete record. Certainly it would take up a disproportionate amount of space to attempt to describe them in detail; but they cannot be ignored, as they have been in almost every book about the Norwegian campaign published in this country. And while there was never the remotest chance of the Norwegian forces being able to hold the Germans once the latter decided the moment had come to break out in force from their landing points and link them up, they took a heavy toll of

Near Namsos a Norwegian farmer assists an A.A. gun crew to get their Bofors into position.

General Fleischer, Commander of the Norwegian Army in the North.

General Otto Ruge, Commander-in-Chief of the Norwegian Army.

their invaders in killed or wounded. It must not be forgotten that German Army casualties were a good third higher than the casualties of the Norwegians and all the Allied units put together, and that this was not wholly due to the sinkings at sea, the attacks on Narvik and other more spectacular operations.

Moving with his heterogeneous forces in this area was the Norwegian Army's new Commander-in-Chief, General Otto Ruge. On 9th April he had been Colonel Ruge, Inspector-General of Infantry. After the bombardment of Elverum he was promoted to succeed the aged C.-in-C., who was in no state physically to face up to so arduous a campaign. Never to have met Ruge, who died not very long before this book was started, is a matter of very great personal regret to the author, for whenever one meets and talks to people—Norwegian or British—who were involved in the Norwegian campaign, the personality and character of this man shines through the conversation like a flame. His picture—it is nearly always the same picture, though all pictures of him are consistent—is often enough brought out, shown and carefully and lovingly put back again. Under the soft ski-cap of the Norwegian Army, the face is tanned and lined: it is a face of humour, experience and great understanding. The eyes are deep-set beneath bushy brows, the nose is aquiline, the lips are narrow but the mouth is wide. A face of humour, yes, but also a face of great determination and unbounded courage; and by force of determination, courage and sheer personality—by virtue also of the fact that he typified in his person the will of a nation to resist—he made his mass of scattered, half-mobilized units with their scratch equipment and inexperienced commanders into the working semblance of something very near an army. This was how he described it himself:

'Remember what kind of an army this was. From Oslo, for instance, came hundreds of men who could not mobilize because the Germans held Oslo. They gathered around some leader and became a "company", they met other groups of the same kind and became "battalions" under the command of some officer. Casually assembled infantrymen, artillerists, sailors and aviators, with cars and chauffeurs collected from God knows where, became fighting units. A commissary department was improvised, the women on the farms doing the cooking and looking after things. Sanitary service we had none, but it seemed to spring up out of the ground under the hands of energetic and resourceful physicians. I visited one hospital in Gudbrandsdal which was full of wounded and fairly well equipped for its work. The doctor in charge was a civilian who said that he had started at a cross-roads near Eidsvold with one box of aspirins in his pocket. Willing hands had done the rest.

'The railway station at Dombaas was bombed every day, burned and laid waste, the railway and telegraph connections broken—but every night it was repaired sufficiently to use. The unknown men who, in great danger of their lives, did this work night after night, seeming never to sleep, will not be forgotten by us who saw them.

'I remember the military labourers who were given guns at Midtskogen. Some of them had never held a gun in their hands before and were rather surprised to find themselves soldiers, but they stopped the Germans. The tough Opland squadron covered the retreat of the British until they were themselves surrounded by Germans—"a splendid regiment," the British commander said.

'The so-called Sörkedal Ski Company consisted of men who had escaped from Oslo and met in the ski hills in Nordmarka outside the city and turned up as a fighting unit thoroughly welded together. Our fliers with their old Moths and Fokkers darted in and out among the fast German planes, ready to take any risk. The 4th Division—that of the west—fought a suicidal battle at Tonsaasen for four days, holding back a large German force and thereby easing the situation in Gudbrandsdal while the British troops were landing in Romsdal. Hegra, an old abandoned fort, held out for a month, manned by casually assembled people who simply would not give up.

'I bring to mind my "travelling" officers who were sent wherever the need was greatest—always in the firing-line. I remember the students of the Technical Institute in Trondheim who worked as volunteers. I remember the old taxi-driver who by chance had given me a lift the first day and who stayed permanently, was on the road day and night, bombed and machine-gunned, but always smiling and with a firm grip on the wheel. I remember the escaped college boys who served with the ordnance, and all the courageous women who helped us, the nurses, telephone operators, and Lottas. I remember a cup of coffee at night in a bombed Lotta station and a young girl in ski trousers who served the telephone in a burning kiosk.'

Incredibly, when Lieutenant-Colonel King-Salter, the newly appointed British military attaché, succeeded in reaching Ruge's headquarters at Öyer in the Gudbrandsdal six days after the invasion had begun, he found internal security checks in operation, roadblocks created and manned and a headquarters machine in operation. And he was impressed by the strength and calm of the Norwegian commander, who got up from his bed at one-thirty in the morning to greet him.

But at this stage, as he fought his desperate delaying actions from village to village and farmhouse to farmhouse down the valleys, under the unending menace from the air, Ruge's contact with the rest of the Norwegian forces was practically non-existent and his knowledge of them scanty. Inland from Bergen, where the first German onslaught had failed to reach the mobilization depot, General Steffans had succeeded not merely in setting up a headquarters for the 4th Division, but in organizing a complete field brigade which was able to hold the Germans for an appreciable time. There were some small forces beyond Stavanger; but farther south, round Kristiansand, the Norwegian troops had already capitulated in face of a German threat to bomb the town into dust if their resistance continued. Little was known of the 3rd Division, whose area was north of Namsos, though it had, in fact, mobilized nearly three thousand men. Around Trondheim the 5th Division was certainly in existence, though its only co-herent operational force was the 5th Brigade under Colonel Getz with a machine-gun squadron of dismounted dragoons—the brigade at half strength, with an ammunition supply of no more than one hundred rounds per man. And three hundred men were beginning the defence of the antique fortress of Hegra, under Major Holtermann, which has become one of the epics of Norwegian history.

Completely out of touch with its Commander-in-Chief—and for that matter separated from Central Norway by bitter mountains and trackless wastes of snow—was the country's only fully-organized fighting force—the 6th Division, of which we have already heard, under another fighting Norwegian officer, Major-General Carl Fleischer. Writing the record of this division in America in 1944, Colonel Munthe-Kaas gave it the same name as we gave our own XIVth Army in Burma—'The Forgotten Army'. It had no war correspondents, no contact with the outside world and has been correspondingly forgotten by most historians outside Norway: it could certainly not be forgotten by the Germans. Their lucky seizure of the infantry and engineer depot at

Elvergaadsmoen and their occupation, immediately after, of
Bjerkvik at the head of the little fiord, certainly established them
in a commanding position north of Narvik and lost Fleischer one
of the battalions of his 1st Infantry Regiment, together with his
Haalos Engineer Battalion. Colonel Sundlo's treachery cost him
another battalion, a Bofors gun battery and another engineer
company. But two battalions and his signals company were saved
to him, and he was astride the way through Bardu to Tromsö, the
administrative centre of Arctic Norway, with its stores, good
harbour and factories. In Troms province he had under arms an
infantry battalion, a mountain battery and a motorized field
battery with twelve guns in all, a transportation company and
signals, medical and administrative units—in Finmark three
infantry battalions and a garrison company, a field battery with
four guns, some field artillery, signals, transport and staff. To all
these he was able to mobilize and add three more battalions, and
was certainly not out of business.

The same snowstorm which enabled the Germans to forestall
him at Narvik, Elvegaadsmoen and Bjerkvik also put a stop to
the first wave of their own advance. On the day after, they were
able to push on to the important road junction of Gratangen,
where a handful of staff from the 6th Division's officers' school
failed to hold them. From here they pushed out eastwards to
Lapphaugen, and here Fleischer and the mountains together
definitely stopped them—so that from this point their front ran
ten miles or more south in a salient before it turned east again to
finish up secure against the Swedish frontier. On the west they got
little beyond Bjerkvik—were held clear of the whole area where
presently the Allied bases were to be established and later mount
their own part of the attack on Narvik.

Having got the Nazis under control, Fleischer proceeded
to harass them with the clear intention of going over to the
offensive at the earliest possible moment. Had the extent to which
he was pinning down German forces been understood or even
known, even General Mackesy might have thought differently
about the frontal attack on Narvik.

Beyond this front and within the German lines Narvik itself,
occupied but unsubdued, seethed like a cauldron. Insecurely in
possession and with no hope of reinforcement, the Germans had

many problems besides the threat of General Fleischer's forces and the menace of the British Fleet. Much of their supplies had gone to the bottom of the fiord and food stocks in the little town were low, except for vast quantities of fish awaiting export to Germany: there was (oddly enough in this frozen land) a shortage of ice, and for the next two months both occupiers and occupied were to live on imperfectly salted fish—which, the Mayor of Narvik tells us, tasted better than it smelled. The people of the town were stubborn and unyielding in their attitude: the Germans were bewildered by their refusal to accept them as 'protectors'. Sturdily independent of authority in normal times, they now followed implicitly the directions of their own elected Mayor and council and with equal steadfastness refused, overtly or covertly, direction by their invaders. They might be cut off from the rest of the country, but they had better sources of information than many of their people farther south; for reception of the Swedish radio was good and from Tromsö to the north of them, in the only unoccupied provinces of Norway, news of the resistance of the King and government came regularly over the air. News of the fighting on their own front was lacking from the radio reports, but ski-runners brought tidings over the mountains. German censorship found itself unable to deal satisfactorily with their newspaper, which was suspended after one day's publication under the new order, but typewritten bulletins passed secretly from hand to hand. The Royal Navy had come once: it would come again. It was not beyond the 'cowardly British', the Germans admitted, to try another attack.

Tromsö radio had urged evacuation, which the Germans would not permit. But they were unable to prevent a constant stream of people slipping away across the fiord—especially young men burning to join up with General Fleischer and to feel a rifle in their hands.

And on Sunday afternoon, 13th April—the first Sunday of the occupation—the British came again. The harbinger of their coming was a rumble and distant thunder of gunfire from the seaward end of the fiord—heavier gunfire than anything that had yet been heard. A young man came running breathlessly into the town, to report that the fiord was swarming with ships—among them 'a colossus of a warship'. German officials, the command headquarters and most of the troops were seen leaving the town: only a handful remained behind for the defence of the harbour and key points. The gunfire grew louder; from time to time it was punctuated by tremendous blasts that could only be coming from the guns of the 'colossus', and the echoes of these were hurled backwards and forwards across the water—as though the mountains, Theodor Broch, the Mayor, thought, were playing ball with them. He once counted the diminishing echoes seven times before they died. Shells were soon whistling through the anchorage; some of them landed on the town itself. Women and children were hurried into cellars and basements and into a new railway tunnel that was being cut in the cliff; but few of the men-folk could restrain their eagerness to see the battle and the gunfire brought them exhilaration rather than fear. General Mackesy was shortly to refuse to accept the responsibility for a bombardment that would involve heavy civilian casualties in the town. Nothing could have been more misguided; the people of Narvik did not expect to regain their freedom without blood.

The previous evening Admiral Whitworth had received a signal which released him from the storm-tossed monotony of his patrol off the Lofoten Islands and bade him go in and finish off the rest of the shipping in the Narvik fiords. Of the three capital ships now available to him—the battle cruisers *Repulse* and *Renown* and the battleship *Warspite*—the latter was chosen for the job, to the particular chagrin of *Repulse*'s company, who were itching for a chance at least as good as their sister-ship's encounter with *Gneisenau* and *Scharnhorst*. But they had to admit *Warspite*'s claims: she was much more heavily armoured against air attack and her guns were capable of greater elevation. To her, early on this morning, Whitworth transferred his flag—'with consider-able difficulty,' he reported, 'owing to the heavy swell': a sidelight on the movements of admirals not without its humour, even amid the grim business of war.

Even so, there were tremendous risks in taking this great and valuable ship into the land-locked fiords. Apart from the danger of air attack she was vulnerable to submarines and to ship-fired torpedoes, and it was by no means certain that there was no cruiser among the pent-up German forces. There were wrecks—*Rauenfels*, *Hardy* and the sunken German merchant ships and destroyers. The mythical shore defences still existed in rumour, and there were reports of a minefield on the way.

There were things on the other side of which Whitworth did not and could not know. There was no cruiser, there were no minefields, there were no forts: the Germans were short of both oil and ammunition and some of their destroyers were already damaged. In addition, following on Warburton-Lee's onslaught and the death of Commodore Bonte, they had suffered that curious demoralization which invariably seemed to afflict the Germans in general and their naval forces in particular in the face of a setback.

The operation was planned with meticulous care. Aircraft from *Furious* and *Warspite*'s own plane would reconnoitre, and the former would later come in to attack. Of his nine destroyers (some of the large Tribal class) three would sweep ahead, five form an anti-submarine screen, while *Cossack* (of *Altmark* fame) would patrol off Tranöy light and then follow the force in.

The Swordfish aircraft of *Furious* found nothing to report, but *Warspite*'s plane covered itself with glory. In the first place it sighted one of the German destroyers lurking in an inlet to the south of the main fiord, bows to the eastward and torpedo tubes trained to take the British by surprise. Forewarned in turn, the British destroyers advanced with their own guns and tubes trained on the opening. The Germans did indeed get off one salvo, which passed by harmlessly—she was then herself torpedoed aft and forward, within three minutes was on fire and was finally blasted into wreckage by *Warspite*'s fifteen-inch guns. Passing on, the aircraft investigated Herjangsfiord, whence the fresh German destroyers had come down to destroy Warburton-Lee. Off Bjerkvik it spotted a U-boat, which it promptly bombed and sank. Rarely can a crew have been hoisted back aboard so pleased with themselves.

Meanwhile the main force advanced at a steady ten knots up the Ofotfiord towards Narvik town, driving the German destroyers before it: gunsmoke obscured *Warspite*'s view as she followed the destroyers in, but as it cleared from time to time, the shattering blasts were clearly distinguishable to the jubilant Norwegians in the town. Torpedo tracks were sighted, but she 'combed' them successfully and the torpedoes blew up ashore.

'We felt like the princess in the fairy tale,' wrote Broch, 'about whom the princes were fighting. We felt the joy and the pride when the white prince rode in with victory and also the humility of being only a passive prize. The horrifying inactivity of it all!'

Then came a tremendous explosion, still greater than anything yet. One of the disabled German destroyers had been moored at Narvik quay to act as a floating battery. She was raked by *Warspite*'s guns, then torpedoed by *Foxhound*: she was soon on fire and *Foxhound* closed in to board, but was driven away by machine-gun fire from the shore—which was as well, because she had barely drawn clear when the German blew up with such force that the quay itself was badly damaged.

There were now what appeared to be but three enemy destroyers left: on our own side *Punjabi* had been hit in the engine-room and had to retire temporarily to repair damage, while *Cossack* had fallen foul of one of the many wrecks and was struggling to free herself, coping at the same time with a small-calibre gun somewhere ashore. The last of the German ships fled through the narrow entrance to Rombaksfiord and into a trap from which there was no escaping, for here at last the long system of waterways that runs from the Lofoten Islands deep into this narrow strip of Norway comes to a dead end on a cast-iron shore. Steaming through in hot pursuit, *Eskimo* was caught by a torpedo and had her bows blown off: she came out stern first to let *Foxhound* and *Hero* take her place. The other destroyers piled in behind them, but the Germans had fired their last shot. One was aground in the mouth of the fiord, her crew in flight: she was destroyed. The others, as the fiord opened up, were spotted together at the far end, and now there were seen to be three. They did not reply to fire and closer investigation showed them to have been abandoned: one was scuttled and aground, one already sinking and a torpedo soon made sure that the third was doing likewise. The extra one was a casualty from the earlier battle.

The battle was over: there was not a single German ship of war left afloat at Narvik: the crews of those that had been there were either dead, captured or in flight ashore. A captured German officer declared that there were submarines in the fiord—certainly one was detected later trying to sneak away submerged and depth-charged—but Whitworth thought the report purposely exaggerated. After all the shooting was over—at six o'clock—twelve enemy aircraft were sighted and came in but only carried out a half-hearted attack on one destroyer.

With this action the ascendancy of the Royal Navy in the Narvik fiords was completed—and ended. It was the end also of naval ascendancy throughout Norway's coastal waters, and this fact was to be thrown up in harsh relief by *Suffolk*'s attempted bombardment of Stavanger aerodrome in the south a few days later, in which she came out a very second best to the dive-bombers which hounded her home. There were to be other bombardments in Narvik fiord, as we shall see, but none on such a scale as Whitworth's attack; and long before the enemy even got possession of more advanced airfields in his relentless penetration up on the coast, the Navy was hereafter to find its movements and its capabilities increasingly dictated by the constant threat of aerial attack. In other words the Navy was to be denied the freedom of movement which it had always been assumed would follow from its overwhelming superiority at sea—and this in turn would impose a tremendous handicap on what the troops could do on land. Given the possibility of only partial protection against air attack, the Navy could remain on the offensive to a modified extent in these northern waters; but south of Narvik three things would dictate the movements of the Fleet—the necessity for avoiding the dive-bombers as far as possible, the necessity for either putting ashore or re-embarking land forces and the necessity for acting as floating anti-aircraft batteries to the land forces in their brief sojourns on Norwegian soil.

Mr. Churchill, the First Lord, had dreams of a battleship with its main armament exchanged for anti-aircraft guns, making it a sort of floating hedgehog to accompany the Fleet. This might, indeed, have worked, because battleships alone had the heavy horizontal armour which made them more or less immune to the bomber—although how they would be able to replenish the prodigious expenditure of ammunition that would be called for, or how they would cope with the rapid deterioration of gun barrels, firing an unheard-of quantity of rounds in a very short space of time, is more arguable. Certainly such a rôle could not be carried out by the Fleet's four anti-aircraft cruisers, which were no more

than 4,000-ton cruisers converted and very vulnerable indeed—
still less by the sloops which had been designed with similar duties
in view. Valuable indeed these efforts might be for the protection
of convoys on the high seas against the high-level bombing of
long-range raiders or reconnaisance aircraft spotting for the
U-boats; but they were thrown away and wasted in the battle of
Norway. Fighter aircraft were the only answer to bomber aircraft.
Fighter aircraft demanded aircraft carriers or airfields on land:
we had less than a handful of the former and none at all of the
latter until the battle was already lost.

In his report on the action he had so successfully carried out,
Admiral Whitworth laid stress time and time again on the
possibility of a landing directly upon Narvik itself while the
enemy forces were demoralized. He had, indeed, considered immediately putting a party ashore himself from his ships, but
soundly appreciated that not merely could only small numbers be
spared but that the men would all be tired from the recent action
and no match for at least two thousand hardened German troops
when their courage returned—as it undoubtedly would when they
realized the smallness of the forces they had to cope with. He went
on to say:

'The cumulative effect of the roar of *Warspite*'s fifteen-inch guns
reverberating down and around the high mountains of the fiord, the
bursts and splashes of these great shells, the sight of their ships sinking
and burning around them must have been terrifying to the enemy.
But such an effect cannot be of a lasting nature to the soldiers on shore,
and I felt that to be taken full advantage of, it would have required a
trained, organized military force, ready to land directly the Naval
engagement had ceased. If such a force had been present, I believe that
they would have succeeded in establishing themselves so strongly in
Narvik that its eventual capture would only be a matter of time and
reinforcements.'

In his signal to the Commander-in-Chief he said: 'I recommend
that the town be occupied without delay by the main landing
force,' and added that in making this signal he knew that the troop
convoys were already at sea and envisaged them being re-routed
straight for Narvik itself.

All this was not to be. But even Whitworth himself, not being
ashore in the town of Narvik, cannot possibly have realized that

his picture of the situation there was, if anything, an understatement. Theodor Broch has given us an eye-witness account of how the statuesque deportment of the German troops broke down under the thunder of the bombardment and the sight of their ships burning, blowing up and sinking before their eyes—how they smiled and laughed half deliriously, went singing arm-in-arm in the streets and chattered nervously with the Norwegians. When the Norwegians told them that they were finished they smiled half-heartedly and muttered, 'Kamarad!' And long before the bombardment was over they were drifting out through

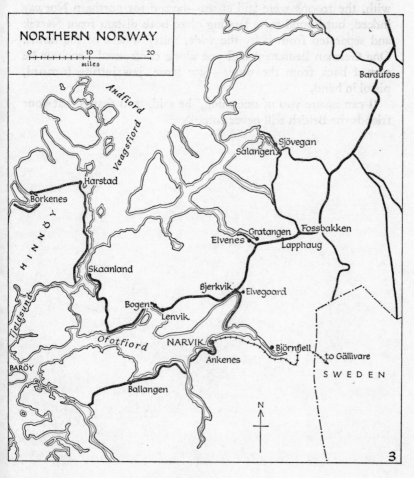

NORTHERN NORWAY

0   10   20
miles

the town and up the mountains in flight, so that Broch and others were able to wander through their abandoned billets and examine curiously the small personal trifles they had left behind. Standing on the shore, Broch tried with all the mental force at his command to project his thoughts and his knowledge across the water to the British ships, with a crazy half-hope that by some miracle of telepathy he could conjure up in their own minds the understanding of the situation as he knew it to be and the will to put the troops ashore.

But there were no troops to put ashore. Delayed and dithered with, the troops were still at sea—bound for northern Norway indeed, but bound for a landing place both distant from Narvik and separated from it by the wide, misty waters of the fiords. One German lieutenant and one alone confronted Broch as he turned back from the water—face tense, jaw jutting forward, pistol in hand.

'I can assure you of one thing,' he said, 'and that is that your friends the British will never come!'

CHAPTER 7

'BOLDNESS IS REQUIRED'

ABOARD the troopship *Monarch of Bermuda* the Commanding Officer of the 1st Battalion Irish Guards was opening a conference. His orders, he explained, had been that with the other units of 24 Brigade he was to occupy Narvik; his intention had been to issue maps to his officers and study them.

'The Germans, gentlemen,' he said, 'are in Narvik and the maps are on another ship. The War Office are trying to find another landing place for us.' He might have added that the maps in any case, printed in 1909, were obsolete, too small in scale and lacking in vital details—they were 'all contours and white spaces'. But the situation as it stood was sufficiently typical of the way in which the forces which were to drive the German oppressors from the soil of the Vikings went to sea. Had Admiral Whitworth, in writing his dispatch and advising the immediate occupation of the town to follow up his own overwhelming and complete elimination of the German naval forces there, been able to see the true state of things, his emotions would (to say the least of it) have been strong.

Best part of two days after the original invasion movements had been reported for certain, the War Cabinet had decided on a policy and appointed the two commanders already referred to—Admiral of the Fleet the Earl of Cork and Orrery for the naval force and Major-General P. J. Mackesy for the Army. Their decision was to seize and hold Narvik. It was a decision arrived at without consultation with the Norwegian government (which, to be fair to them, was virtually impossible at this stage) and apparently without any realistic consideration of the military situation in Norway as a whole. Had it been arrived at in the light of Whitworth's successful attack and had its object been to lay hands on the town before the German troops could return and their morale recover, even as Whitworth had suggested, it would have been entirely praiseworthy. But nothing of the sort was the case. The facts which they had had before them were that the Germans had succeeded in gaining a foothold in various key points in Norway, all of which except Narvik were in the centre and the south. Though these troops could not yet have fully consolidated themselves and though they had suffered severe losses at sea, apart from anything else, the War Cabinet proposed to counter-attack them by sending a force to the extreme north of the country: the equivalent would have been to send a force to the Shetland Islands to counter an invasion of the south coast of England, the Severn estuary and possibly the east coast as far north as Ipswich.

It is quite impossible to do otherwise than feel that, consciously or unconsciously, the War Cabinet's thinking had not been altered in the slightest by the German invasion. They were still obsessed by Narvik and their iron ore strategy; and vital though Swedish iron ore might be to the prosecution of the war, the obsession was a fatal one. Moreover, it took no account whatsoever of the fact that in central and southern Norway the Norwegians (who were now by our own invitation rather than by their request our Allies) were fighting a desperate battle with improvised forces against the Germans, which the dispatch of a force to the extreme north of Norway would do nothing to assist in. For months the Cabinet had hankered after Narvik and the iron ore—for months they had boggled over Norwegian neutrality and the apparently insuperable objections to doing anything while that neutrality remained. Now, suddenly, the objections had disappeared. The door had been opened. We were free to go to Narvik. This complete disregard of the dire straits of the Norwegian Army and people was cynical in the extreme: it was also unrealistic.

It was unrealistic because the War Cabinet had apparently failed to grasp a simple fact. This was that whoever held control of central and southern Norway could ultimately gain control of Narvik, but that the reverse did not apply—in other words, to attempt to capture and hold Narvik as a possible base for operations against the rest of Norway was a completely fallacious strategy. Especially when the power that had occupied central and southern Norway was building up its already strong forces at a frantic rate, had airfields and ample supplies of aircraft to operate from them, troops who could move in the difficult conditions of the Norwegian winter and adequate transport, armoured fighting vehicles and other support weapons for them.

What is more, this force was not to be put down at Narvik or, in fact, anywhere within easy access of Narvik. For its base, Harstad had been selected. Harstad is best part of forty miles from Narvik as the crow flies—and to talk of distances as the crow flies in that snow-bound mountainous country, intersected by long, wide fiords around which the few and scanty roads run tortuously, is to do no more than use a figure of speech. The troops still had no transport—but had they had transport it would have been of no avail for a movement on Narvik, for Harstad is on an island. Admittedly Hinnöy is the largest of the islands of the Lofoten group, but it is an island none the less; and it is separated from Narvik by the Vaagsfiord and the Ofotfiord. It may be supposed that a force to be landed on an island—one of a group of islands, in fact, scattered like confetti on the map—would be equipped with boats; but boats there were none, apart from ships' boats and the vessels of the Royal Navy itself. In the concluding stages of the operation five landing-craft—the first five landing-craft to be employed by our forces on active service—arrived, completely inadequate in numbers and subject to mechanical teething troubles of the most virulent kind. For the foreseeable future the commander of the force would have to improvise as he would in everything else from rations for the troops to anti-aircraft defence. Somehow or other he would have to lay on his own civilian craft of whatever sort could be mustered for the necessary transport of his forces. It was not the way to run a war, let alone win one.

Who were these troops? They were the three battalions of the Guards Brigade together with the half-trained Territorials of 146 Brigade, the 1/4th K.O.Y.L.I. the Hallamshire Battalion of the York and Lancaster Regiment and the 1/4th Lincolnshires. They were embarked in five liners, except for two companies and Mackesy's Headquarters which had been transferred to the cruiser *Southampton*, in which was the General himself. The other incomplete Territorial Brigade—148 Brigade made up of the 1/5th Royal Leicestershire Regiment and the 1/8th Sherwood Foresters —would be following on as a second flight. French troops— Chasseurs Alpins, alleged to be trained and equipped for moving under snow conditions—and others were to follow later, but how much later was largely theory: certainly it could not be for at least ten days. Somewhere in England was 147 Brigade. It was fortunate: it never left the country. The quartermasters had never succeeded in fully making up the stores that had been lost by the units hastily evicted from the cruisers in the Clyde and further muddle and confusion involving more embarkations, disembarkations and re-embarkations had not improved things in the slightest. They were still deficient in signals equipment, mortars, ammunition, rations and cooking equipment, to mention but a few major items. There was neither artillery nor anti-aircraft artillery for them, although there was a Bofors battery without any Bofors guns—certainly there was not so much as a mention of aircraft to cover and support them, nor were there any possible landing grounds for aircraft in the frozen mountains of Hinnöy Island. They still, however, had the base equipment for the garrison duties which were to have been their original lot and to make up for everything they were now issued with Arctic kit on a fantastic and lavish scale—it was apparently the only thing of which the British Army had an over-sufficiency. It consisted of one pair of Arctic boots, one pair of rubber boots, eight pairs of socks, two pairs of footless socks, three pairs of gloves, two sweaters, two leather jerkins, one Arctic cap, one Kapok sleeping bag, and one Arctic Tropal coat lined with sheepskin and weighing about fifty pounds. This gear occupied a minimum of two extra kitbags per man, making three kitbags per man in all or about two thousand kitbags per battalion. The battalion, remember, had no transport for them—not so much as a motor-cycle—or any other means of carrying them except humping them by hand. Of the kitbags the K.O.Y.L.I.'s regimental account declares that until they were abandoned they 'literally hung like millstones around the neck of each officer and man'. General Carton de Wiart declared with some heat that the men could not carry all their kit, while if they put it on they looked like paralysed bears and were unable to move.

The pleasant weather of the voyage around the coast of Scotland had been a brief interlude. The troopships were soon in heavy seas and moving towards the Arctic Circle; their passengers began to get a foretaste of the conditions in which the naval forces had been keeping the sea since the beginning of the emergency.

Presently, as they reached the latitude of the Lofoten Islands, the Irish Guards' war diary was to record the breath of intense cold that came to the ships from the still ice-bound coast. Norway was going to be no picnic, and there were not so many jokes about the midnight sun.

But by the 14th something else had happened. Admiral Whitworth's ships had done their job in Narvik and Admiral Whitworth had made his report on the situation there to the Commander-in-Chief, Home Fleet; and this in turn resulted in such a wave of optimism in official circles at home that it triggered off a whole chain of fresh thinking. Narvik was obviously ours. The only thing we had to do was to take it—although this part of the process was to be curiously overlooked and somehow omitted. In this situation forces could be spared for other purposes, and at last the War Cabinet gave more serious consideration to the fact that it was in southern and central Norway that the war was really being fought. The many discussions which had taken place had already touched on the possibilities of landing forces elsewhere at points not occupied by the Germans: Namsos and Aalesund, north and south of Trondheim respectively, had been mentioned. And certainly to the Norwegian government the recapture of Trondheim was vital. Somehow or other, if their forces were ever to get beyond the point of improvisation and their resistance to the Germans ever become an organized operation, it was obviously imperative for a centre of government to be captured and held: a country could neither be governed indefinitely nor a campaign be run by an anonymous government being hunted through the valleys without any sure means of communication or co-ordination. The recapture of Oslo was not to be dreamed of—it was too strongly held and too easily accessible to reinforcement. But Trondheim could be captured. The German position in Trondheim was still rickety: it had not yet been possible for the troops landed there to break out nor had any movement yet started to join it up with the other occupied centres. There were Norwegian units, no worse equipped than most and better than some, in the area. There was the fortress of Hegra. Above all, Trondheim was a key centre of road, rail and water communications both with the rest of Norway and with Sweden. It was Norway's ancient capital and Norwegian kings had been crowned there. The recapture of Trondheim and the establishment of the Norwegian government there would not merely have been a military achievement of the first importance but would have put tremendous heart into the Norwegian people —infinitely more so than anything happening on the distant Arctic front of Narvik about which virtually no tidings could reach them at all.

At this point more direct information about the situation inside central Norway was beginning to reach London from a new source: for a brief few moments a figure emerges to play perhaps a more significant part in the movement of events than his rank might have allowed under different circumstances. He was Lieutenant-Colonel E. J. King-Salter, a Rifle Brigade officer and an enthusiastic and talented soldier. He was the sort of man the Norwegians would take to—among other things he was one of the best marksmen in the British Army and knew his trade exceedingly well—and take to him they did. At the beginning of March he had been appointed British Military Attaché to Finland —an appointment which soon lost its practical value when the Finnish armistice was signed. On 11th April he became Military Attaché to Norway and was on his way by air from Helsinki in something over two and a half hours after receiving the cypher telegram appointing him. He got quickly as far as Stockholm with the help of the Attaché there, Lieutenant-Colonel R. Sutton-Pratt, where he was able to equip himself with a car, some necessary funds and a small but vital staff of two, of whom one was an Anglo-Norwegian. At the same time he was able to make contact with some members of the former British Legation at Oslo, who had got out of the city and into Sweden on the morning of the invasion but were now rejoining their Minister, Sir Cecil Dormer, who had moved with the Norwegian government on its first evacuation and, travelling with it, stuck to his post till the evacuation. He was now at Nybergsund. This far King-Salter got, again without much difficulty, on the 13th, and found not merely the British Minister but also the French Naval and Military Attachés: together with the two latter he was able, after only a brief delay, to contact the Norwegian Foreign Minister, Dr. Koht. It soon became very clear that reaching the Norwegian Army G.H.Q. was going to be a much more difficult matter; but in the meantime he sent an urgent message to the government at home—transmitting it through Stockholm in a special code which he had arranged with the Military Attaché there—reporting what he had found, urging the importance of landings in central Norway as well as in the north and mentioning Namsos in particular. He represented that Norwegian morale was very low and that some sort of active help in the area where the Norwegians were closely engaged with the Germans was vital. The fact was that the Norwegians were completely bewildered. They had not asked for help—the British Government had offered it. They had assumed quite naturally that the help offered would be forthcoming very quickly; they had expected supplies of arms and ammunition for themselves (both were necessary because British ammunition would not fit their small arms) and the speedy arrival on their soil of adequate and fully equipped forces to help them in their desperate struggle: it was only, indeed, the expectations of much help from day to day that made their own struggle to hold on a thing that could be faced. They could not be expected to know of the Allies' dire straits both for trained men and for arms and equipment of all sorts: they could not be expected to know that the British Air Force was hopelessly inferior in numbers to the Nazis' and that the latter's air superiority was already denying the British Fleet the freedom of the sea around their southern coasts. Least of all could they be expected to know of the state of indecision in the War Cabinet and its committees which made it very difficult to take any rapid action at all. It was fortunate—unexpectedly fortunate—that King-Salter's message should arrive at the moment when thought in the War Cabinet was moving in the direction he urged.

His report was sent in the early hours of 14th April. On the previous day, the 13th, Captain Pegram of the cruiser *Glasgow* had, in fact, received permission to put ashore a small force of 350 seamen and Royal Marines from his ship and from *Sheffield*, which was in company with him, on either side of Namsos. This was the first actual landing by British forces on Norwegian soil. As the form demanded, it was given a name—Operation Henry. It was unchallenged by the Germans, although it is considered certain that it was observed: perhaps this is an indication of the weakness of the Germans in the area at that time or perhaps, on the other hand, the Germans considered the force to be too insignificant to be of any importance. Pegram's men were able to make contact with the Norwegian forces and to report back on conditions there. The reports were frankly not encouraging—they warned of continual air reconnaissance, of the difficulty of movement in the snow-covered terrain and the virtual impossibility of concealing movements on any scale. Be that as it may, they were ashore and could act as advance party to any force sent there. A decision was therefore taken to divert part of the force already on its way to Narvik to the Namsos area as the first instalment of a plan to cut off Trondheim from the north and the south in preparation for a frontal attack on the port itself. For the northern part of the operation—the Namsos part—the name Operation Maurice was chosen, and the forces selected for it were the three Territorial battalions of 146 Brigade.

It is always easy to be wise after the event, and nothing is more dangerous in the writing of a war history than hindsight. None the less, if the recapture of Narvik had now become such an easy operation as the War Cabinet at this stage admittedly imagined it to be, it is very difficult to understand by what sort of reasoning they reserved for that job one of the finest Brigades of trained regular soldiers in the British Army, but designated for the other task—for the first landings in strength in an area known to be occupied by enemy troops under unfavourable conditions already reported upon—three Territorial battalions which could not possibly have the same kind of chance as the Guards. One of the extraordinary consequences of this decision was that in the vital days of the brief campaign in central Norway the regular battalions were kicking their heels around Hinnöy Island and the fiords, seeing very little action except for air raids and slightly mystified as to what they were supposed to be doing—while the untried battalions of the K.O.Y.L.I., the York and Lancaster Regiment and the Lincolnshires were flung into an impossible offensive from which more of them than the War Cabinet had any right to expect were lucky enough to escape with their lives.

On the 14th, therefore, the two transports carrying 146 Brigade, *Chrobry* and *Empress of Australia* were detached from the Narvik expedition and, escorted by the cruisers *Manchester*, *Birmingham* and *Cairo* with three destroyers, turned south and plunged away out of sight. We shall follow their fortunes—or their misfortunes—before very long. One of the many deficiencies with which they started their operations was their commander, Brigadier Phillips: it had been quite overlooked that he was aboard a different ship and that nothing in the world could now prevent him landing up at Narvik while his Brigade was disembarking at Namsos. Improvised tinkering with military and naval operations —especially operations as rickety in their planning as the ones we are discussing—is bound to have the same sort of unforeseen consequences that arise when an architect makes an ill-considered amendment to a working drawing and finds that he has well nigh wrecked the building of an entire house. It was comparatively easy for the Brigadier to be hustled back to his brigade, but it was not so easy for the substantial bits and pieces of the brigade's stores and equipment which reached the wrong destination to be re-routed to the right place under the prevailing circumstances in time to be of any use. It was just another of those things which made a difficult state of affairs even more difficult than it need have been for men who were trying to fight a war.

In the meantime, the remainder of the convoy entered the Vestfiord, to find themselves once more in calmer weather, with the sun coming out on landscape of a sort with which neither of the two battalions of the Guards had ever been faced in their long regimental histories. To a shipload of peacetime tourists the prospect would have been far from displeasing. Under a brilliant blue sky the mountainous coast of Norway unfolded magnificently in vistas of spotless white. The snow came down to the very water's edge: there was not a patch of green or so much as a bare rock to be seen. Dotted very occasionally here and there were isolated trees, and, as the landscape unrolled, small villages appeared and disappeared—wooden houses clustering picturesquely around a church. From time to time great clouds of eider duck rose from the water. It was splendid scenery for a Christmas card, but quite a different prospect for officers and men who would have to soldier in this place without either the equipment for getting about under such conditions or the skill to use it. Officers wondered whether their Bren-carriers for instance would be able to move in this snow. They need not have bothered because most of the carriers would end up in the sea, but this knowledge was, perhaps fortunately, denied them. Certainly it was most unsuitable ground for the regimental runner on the orderly-room green bicycle.

By noon on the 15th the transports were at Harstad. So were the naval and military commanders—General Mackesy and his advance party in *Southampton* had arrived ahead of them and were already ashore, while the Earl of Cork arrived in *Aurora* in time to lead in the convoy. Had the Earl of Cork had his way he would not have been there, and neither would General Mackesy. It will be remembered that Mackesy had already left in *Southampton* with two companies of Scots Guards some little time before Cork sailed from Rosyth in *Aurora*—'at high speed' Churchill tells us, which is somehow appropriate to the red-haired and fiery little Admiral. He was absolutely clear in his own mind as to his instructions. Although he had no instructions in writing he had been briefed personally both by the First Sea Lord and by Mr. Churchill himself—had even made a brief appearance at the Chiefs-of-Staff Committee. In his own words, 'my impression . . . was quite clear that it was desired by H.M. Government to turn the enemy out of Narvik at the earliest possible moment and that I was to act with all promptitude in order to obtain this result.' Being a naval officer, moreover, he was no doubt well aware of Nelson's famous maxim, 'the boldest methods are the safest—nothing great can be achieved without risk'.

When, therefore, at sea, he received news of the second attack on Narvik and of Whitworth's plea for an urgent occupation of the town, he immediately made a radio signal to *Southampton* ordering her, instead of proceeding to Harstad, to meet him at Skjelfiord by eight o'clock that evening. Skjelfiord, it will be remembered, is at the entrance to the approaches to Narvik and was where the temporary naval base had been established. *Southampton* never received this signal direct—did not receive it at all until it was relayed by the Admiralty, too late. Radio transmitting and reception conditions off this northern Norwegian coast are full of strange tricks and there is really nothing extraordinary in the message not having been received, except that it is doubtful whether General Mackesy would have wished to comply with it if it had been. He had instructions quite different from Admiral Cork's—or at least instructions which could be interpreted in quite a different light. Neither he nor the War Office had any knowledge of Admiral Cork's instructions—and neither the Admiralty nor Admiral Cork had any knowledge of his.

General Mackesy's orders have already been described as the original Plan R.4 orders, dusted and somewhat hastily revised. This may seem a harsh judgement but it is difficult to believe that they were otherwise. For one thing they involved contradictions. They started off by telling him that the object of Mauriceforce was to evict the Germans from Narvik but went on to tell him that it was not intended that he should land in the face of opposition. They gave some rather vague and not very accurate particulars about the Norwegian forces and about Harstad, where he was told to establish his headquarters in the first place—including the extraordinary remark 'their attitude is not known but it is believed that they will be ready to co-operate': this is surely a left-over from the pre-invasion situation. It gave him instructions about co-operation both with the Norwegians and the British naval forces and a timetable of reinforcements, some of which changes of plan made obsolete before he had set foot ashore. He was also bound (as were all commanders on land, sea and in the air at that time, with the exception of the submarine forces farther south) by the completely unrealistic standing instructions about bombardment where civilian casualties were possible which, if they had been faithfully adhered to, would have rendered military action impossible on virtually any front.

But he had also been handed before his departure a handwritten message from the Chief of the Imperial General Staff, which, in fact, could have been taken to amend his orders completely. This gave him an estimate that there were three thousand Germans in Narvik, adding that they 'must have been knocked about by naval action'. It included two terse and significant sentences which have often been quoted and will stand quoting again:

'You may have a chance of taking advantage of naval action and you should do so if you can.
'*Boldness is required.*'*

That these were the instructions on which General Mackesy should have acted there can be very little doubt. It is ludicrous to

* The italics are the author's.

suppose that if he had shown the same willingness to move in on the situation as the Earl of Cork (not to speak of Whitworth, Warburton-Lee and all those whose cool acceptance of necessary risks is set down over and over again in these pages) he would have been crimed for it. His resistance to taking the kind of action which the Earl of Cork repeatedly urged him to take can be justified to the hilt by his orders, by his deficiencies, by the fact that the stores and his transports were not tactically stowed and many other things; but the impression remains in the minds of virtually all who have studied or written about the Norwegian campaign that he should have acted very differently. Had he done so the ultimate result of the Narvik operation might not have been very different from what it was; on the other hand it might have been completely different and might, at the most extreme, have had a tremendous effect not merely on the whole campaign in Norway but on the campaign in the West—to which, as events turned out, it was no more than a disastrous curtain-raiser.

Mackesy, therefore, got himself ashore, set up his headquarters at Harstad and put his two companies of Scots Guards ashore at the mainland, where they would be fairly close to the outposts of the Norwegian 6th Division, at Sjövegan. In his own report he says that this had an important effect on the spirit of determination of the Norwegian forces. Certainly the Guards were enthusiastically received by the Norwegian population and made very much at home; but for some reason which is not apparent they seemed to have failed to get on with the Norwegian Army: if the impression one gets of this is true it is virtually the only sector in the whole campaign where the Norwegian and British troops were not wholly at one. The landings, said the German radio, had been made by 'unemployed and hired volunteers'. Did any of the Norwegians believe it? Or was the whole thing a series of misunderstandings?

Before the main troop transports arrived in port the following morning they had had an enormous boost to their morale. On the way in there was a submarine contact. Two of the escorting destroyers, *Brazen* and *Fearless*, churned into the attack and quickly depth-charged the submarine, the U49, to the surface. The destroyers raced past the troopships with their men shouting exultantly 'We got one! We got one!' and the Germans, abandoning ship, behaved very badly in the icy water, screaming for help in what the official report describes as a most dreadful manner. They were nearly all rescued: from the submarine itself were rescued all its official documents which included the complete U-boat plot for the entire Norwegian operation. Too much importance has probably been given to this document. It is often assumed that it provided the key to the position of every U-boat in Norwegian waters, was the cause of many submarines being accounted for, as well as Allied casualties by submarine during the campaign being limited to three very small vessels and one storeship. It is much more probable that the real cause of this was the reluctance of submarines to attack convoys and even more so the perpetual torpedo failures with which the Germans were dogged. It is supposed that the peculiar magnetic conditions in Norway affected the magnetic pistols fitted to them; but the fact is that British torpedoes proved very effective both at Narvik and elsewhere and Admiral Doenitz inveighed bitterly against the uselessness of the weapons with which he had been supplied.

The moment the troopships made port the appalling disadvantages of Harstad became apparent. In common with practically all the landing places which the British forces were condemned to use it was not a port at all in the 'big ship' sense. It had a couple of small quays and very few cargo-handling facilities: its normal rate of discharge would have been roughly two ships in five days. The transports had to anchor off-shore and naval and civilian craft used to ferry stores and men. On the one hand this became yet another commitment for the hard-pressed naval forces— particularly the destroyers. On the other it led to difficulties and uncertainties because the skippers of the Norwegian 'puffers' (some Scotsman must have first applied this name to them because the chuff of their single-cylinder diesel engines evoked nostalgic memories of the steam 'puffers' used in the Western Isles) were independent in their habits and averse to risking their craft in the teeth of German air raids. And before the troopships had been in port for very long the first of the one hundred and forty air raids which Rupertforce was to suffer in barely eight weeks was in full swing.

'That Bren gunner is only annoying the Germans,' observed

the C.O. of the Irish Guards the following morning, after a bomb had landed fifty yards away from his first battalion conference.

'The mess,' he added, 'will be draughty without any windows.'

It was not, indeed, possible to do much more than annoy the Germans. One light ack-ack battery with Bofors guns had come with the expedition: excellent weapon though this gun was against dive-bombers and low-flying aircraft, it was easily evaded by the high-flying aircraft operating over Narvik at this time. In any case, one battery was a drop in the sea, insufficient for protecting the sprawling area over which the naval and military forces were spread and giving no help at all to the civilian population on whose heads (since German orders lacked the niceties of ours in these matters) the bombs fell impartially. Carrier-borne aircraft might give what relief they could, but there was still only *Furious* to help: both she and her squadron were rapidly becoming due for refit and, being herself a highly vulnerable target, she was not able to operate nearer than one hundred and fifty miles off-shore. Likewise, the Skuas from the Orkneys could fly the great distance over the sea from time to time, to spend what short period their endurance permitted over the target area. For the rest, there were only the anti-aircraft guns of a fleet insufficiently provided with them and since these ships as well as the aircraft carrier were direct targets for enemy attack they tended to use up vast quantities of ammunition and wear out their gun barrels doing little more than protect themselves.

Amid these various handicaps the Guards Brigade settled down temporarily to a rather curious life, in which snow, cold and air bombardment were the three most important factors. There was, in the first place, to be an enormous amount of humping and sorting of the stores that had been so carefully arranged on their departure from barracks and which had become such a potpourri during the embarkation, the voyage and the unloading. These units were much better off than the units in the south, but none the less ridiculous deficiencies disclosed themselves. The Scots Guards found themselves with only smoke bombs for their two-inch mortars (a common complaint in this campaign), while the three-inch mortars were too heavy to be transported by a unit whose only wheels for the present were bicycle wheels. More ships arriving to choke the little port brought clerks, signallers, bakers and other base personnel in plenty, but there were still no wireless sets; and since the civilian telephone was not secure and the bicycles of limited use under these conditions and in any case not amphibious, runners on foot and in boats carried the brigade's intelligence as they had done in the Crimean War. Messages, says the Scots Guards' regimental history, were 'likely to be of historical interest only by the time they were received'.

Had the troops been able to ski, of course (assuming skis could have been provided for them), things would have been different: even snowshoes would have been a help. Somewhat mortified, they watched very tiny children who had learned to ski almost as soon as they had learned to walk gliding past on their way to school and envied them heartily. Some of the Guards officers could ski—it was an upper-class accomplishment of those times—and so a beginning was made in teaching the guardsmen. They were required as a matter of elementary instruction to learn to toboggan before they could start on skis, and the vast majority of them never got beyond this stage. In the cold, crisp sunlight, when air raids and other duties allowed it, hefty guardsmen bucketed down the slopes and toiled manfully up them again as though it were Boxing Day on Hampstead Heath. How they longed for 'Jimmy Coates' mob'—the 5th Scots Guards, the battalion of skiers assembled with such enthusiasm for the Finnish war and disbanded with such precipitate haste only a matter of weeks earlier!

It was all great fun but it was not a war.

In central and south Norway there was a war—bloody enough but about to be even bloodier because on the 14th the Germans had decided that their build-up was sufficient to give priority to breaking out and linking up the Oslo area with Trondheim by land. There was a war in the north too, for that matter, in the fiords where the Navy were not merely defending themselves but endeavouring to keep down the morale of the Germans in and around Narvik by snap bombardments at whatever targets they could find: this in addition to submarine hunting, running a general ferry service, looking after their damaged ships at Skjel-fiord and building up their more permanent base at Skaanland opposite Harstad where the depot ship *Mashobra* had landed a Marine fortress unit with heavy guns.

Near this naval base the South Wales Borderers were established, the Irish Guards at Bogen—overlooking the Ofotfiord and almost in sight of Narvik itself but separated from their base by mountains, lakes and sea—and the Scots Guards, half at Sjövegan and half in reserve at Harstad.

On the 15th the Earl of Cork and General Mackesy met for the first time. No verbatim record exists of the discussion: it is possible that it was at times something less than polite but this can only be surmise in the light of the opposite characters of the two men and the apparent opposition between their instructions. Mackesy was absolutely inflexible. He was absolutely convinced of the impossibility of a frontal assault in the snow against the prepared enemy positions which he was certain existed. He was determined to sort his stores, get his force into apple-pie order and plan a considered encircling operation on the town to be put into operation with the coming of the thaw, which was due at any time.

Straight away the latter was an illusion—born perhaps of sunny skies and calm weather. In fact the thaw was exceptionally late this year although the nights were already shortening to a degree that gave only a brief cover of darkness in respite from the Luftwaffe. In succeeding days the weather was to deteriorate into snow and blizzards in which even Lord Cork would reluctantly have to concede the ineffectiveness of bombardment and impossibility of landing forces. Nothing could shake Mackesy in his determination and every moment that was spent in arguing was a moment of opportunity slipping by. When the British did not come (even as the German officer had said they would not) the morale of the Germans began to mount again and they were soon beginning to take it out on the civilian population who had so gleefully watched them go during *Warspite*'s attack. They began to build the machine-gun emplacements which Mackesy's military imagination had already envisaged in being. They began to receive a small trickle of supplies by air and before long supplies were also coming through Sweden.

The Admiral and the General continued to argue. The government at home, nonplussed by the effect of the contradictory orders for which the responsibility was entirely theirs and astonished by the fact that Narvik had not fallen at a blast of trumpets, pressed urgently for the action which was overdue and which would now be many weeks in coming. Before Narvik was to fall 25,000 men of one category or another would be concentrated in an area where German numbers had been in the first place reliably estimated at no more than 3,000. It is an extraordinary contrast to the situation in central Norway—where the 1,000 men of Sickleforce, for instance, were faced with the simultaneous tasks of encircling Trondheim from the south and stopping a whole German army pressing up the Gudbrandsal. It was to have, if not all, at least a working portion of the things which the other forces in Norway were denied in the face of much heavier odds. It was to hold or pin down every ship in the fleet that could be spared, including two aircraft carriers. It was to have heavy ack-ack guns: it was even to have two squadrons of fighter planes. And the only result of it all was to be that Narvik was captured too late to make any difference.

Who was right and who was wrong? All General Mackesy's arguments could be justified and even the redoubtable Admiral Cork, setting out to see things for himself, sank to his waist in snow. But the facts must speak for themselves. The attack on Bjerkvik, prelude to the main Narvik assault, cost only thirty-six casualties; while in the last resort Narvik fell to relatively small forces at the cost of no more than one hundred and fifty killed or wounded—of whom sixty belonged to the Norwegian forces attacking from the north.

While the argument continued and the Guards tobogganed in the snow, the German movement from the south towards Trondheim began and the need for the recapture of Trondheim became more and more urgent. General Ruge managed to get an appeal through direct to the British Prime Minister, urging the immediate necessity for help. Colonel King-Salter had by this time succeeded in making his way to the Norwegian headquarters and commenced from there to send his own series of urgent dispatches. Technical considerations limited the number of these messages but they were urgent enough, detailed enough and very much to the point. He was convinced that the Norwegians were about to crack. He was convinced that if aid both in men and in arms and ammunition were not immediately forthcoming, they would crack. It was quite apparent to him that the Norwegian

forces were already worn out by the impossible odds against them
—were being held together only by the strength of a few resolute
commanders and, above all, by Ruge himself. If Ruge became convinced that the hope of British support was a delusion, he would
throw in his hand. If Ruge threw in his hand, central Norway
would be lost before we landed in any strength; and if central Norway were lost, northern Norway could not in the end be defended.

The Prime Minister replied to General Ruge. His reply said
specifically that we were coming 'in great strength'. Now Mr.
Chamberlain must have known—who could have known better
than he?—what was the total strength of the forces which were on
their way to central Norway—in other words, the three Territorial battalions which had been diverted from the Narvik convoy,
the small naval party waiting to receive them and the other
equally insignificant force whose acquaintance we shall make
before long. The wheel has turned full circle and more than one
attempt has recently been made to convince a later generation
that Mr. Chamberlain was not so black as he was painted. But
what can be said of a man whose wishful-thinking mind magnified
these trifling detachments into an army 'in great strength?' He had
fooled himself that Munich was peace with honour, he is recorded
on two separate occasions as declaring that Hitler had missed the
'bus—heaven alone knows how many times he used that favourite
phrase of his without it being recorded—but here were facts that
could only give him the lie as soon as they became apparent,
discrediting him and discrediting the people whose spokesman he
was. Three battalions of troops cannot be magnified by words
into 'great strength', and herein lie all the folly, all the illusions,
all the impalpable nonsense which wrecked the good name of
Britain and brought her to her knees. Is it to be wondered at that
the Norwegians very soon came to regard us in the same light
as that in which we were to regard the French after their collapse
on the Western Front the following month? This is really the
background to the distrust and lack of understanding between
Fleischer's forces and our own in the north and to many things
large and small which subsequently happened. Later the Norwegians would know and understand; for the moment their
emotions would change from hope to bewilderment, from bewilderment to contempt.

It is true that a much more ambitious operation was now under consideration—no less than a direct naval and military onslaught on Trondheim itself, which was given the portentous name of Operation Hammer. As an operational plan its history was not unlike that of the embarkations and disembarkations of the original troops: it started with deliberations and arguments, worked up to an extraordinary pitch of unanimous enthusiasm that lasted perhaps twenty-four hours and then suddenly collapsed. It envisaged the employment of two more British brigades, together with Canadian and French troops: it involved attacks in strength by R.A.F. on German-held air bases and naval aircraft and the bombardment from the sea of Stavanger aerodrome. Most of all it involved a descent in force upon Trondheim fiord by all the available units of the Home Fleet—a project which the Commander-in-Chief, Admiral Forbes, not unnaturally viewed with considerable misgivings. We shall presently have to look more closely at the curious story of the birth and death of Operation Hammer: its importance is that the force which was already on its way (minus its brigadier) to Namsos and the force which was about to be dispatched to Aandalsnes—the latter consisting of the two battalions of the original Plan R.4 force which had not yet left England—became subsidiary parts of the bigger operation. The task of these would be to encircle Trondheim from the north and south, pin down the Germans and prevent their reinforcement. As earnest of this the southern half of it was christened Operation Sickle.

When the main operation met with a premature death—or to be more accurate when it died before it was born—the subsidiary operations to the north and south remained, and these, in fact, were the sum total of our land operations in central Norway.

In preparation for the landing of Sickleforce to the south of Trondheim, a naval detachment set out from England, to play a rôle similar to that of the forces landed by Captain Pegram at Namsos: they were to act as advance party to Sickleforce the same way as Pegram's men had landed in advance of Mauriceforce, now on its way down the coast after its diversion from Narvik. But this was truly a comic-opera operation—except that there was nothing comic about it to the men engaged in it. These unfortunate troops were some seven hundred seamen and marines belonging to ships refitting. They were scraped together hastily with no more than the usual shortages and omissions—there was, among other things, a searchlight unit minus its searchlights—and squeezed together with their stores and equipment in a state of shocking overcrowding in four sloops, *Bittern, Flamingo, Auckland* and *Black Swan.* The weather turned bad on them and, apart from causing the most intense misery to the men packed like sardines in the little ships, very nearly led to the whole force foundering—a disaster which was avoided only by its commander deciding to put in at Invergordon. Out of all the curious names given to operations in this campaign—some ambitious, some allegorical and some merely whimsical—none was more inappropriately named than this, Operation Primrose. It survived this unlikely beginning, however—largely owing to the Royal Navy's infinite capacity for improvisation. Its men bolstered up some of the shortages of 148 Brigade, and its two-pounder guns on scratch mountings provided the only ack-ack defence their base ever owned. It even provided the Royal Engineers with explosives for demolitions in the retreat.

Let us leave the wretched men of Operation Primrose about to set forth again from Invergordon; Mauriceforce—or rather the solitary brigadier-less brigade of which Mauriceforce still consists—is at last nearing Namsos. Things are looking up for Mauriceforce: additional troops have been found for it, a demi-brigade (three battalions) of French Chasseurs Alpins, originally intended for Narvik. These, too, are about to leave England in transports and everyone regards them as a great asset in a snow-bound land. They are referred to as 'splendid mountain troops'. Their establishment, however, is only seventy ski-troops to a battalion and by no means all of these have learned to ski: in any case they have no skis, so that they will not be able to ski at all—but nobody at Namsos knows this yet. It is one of the pleasant discoveries awaiting the new commander of Mauriceforce, who has just been appointed.

At this point we find ourselves confronted with one of those fabulous characters who sometimes emerge, larger than life, from the humdrum pages of official documents and reports. A fiction-writer might get away with a character like Major-General Sir Adrian Carton de Wiart, V.C., as long as he put him in the first

Wrecked supply jetties at Namsos after German bombing.

Major-General Carton de Wiart at his Headquarters near Namsos.

Elizabethan age, where he properly belonged. Captain Roskill, the Navy's official historian, describes him as 'an officer with a remarkable fighting record in the First World War', which is a typically naval understatement. This polyglot old buccaneer of nearly sixty had lived his life at a tempo that would wear ordinary men out in early middle age. He was one of those rare people who know no fear, who experience a genuine exhilaration in the face of extreme danger. His body was full of odd bits of unwanted metal that had been shot into it at various times: he was virtually indestructible. He had decamped from Oxford to enlist as a trooper in the South African War. In subsequent years he had crushed his ribs and suffered other minor accidents in India. In the First World War he had lost an eye in the Middle East, a hand in France, followed by miscellaneous wounds in ankle, hip, ear (twice), leg and head—in the latter case a bullet went in and out without doing any apparent damage on the way, and the General swore its only after-effect was that every time he had a haircut, it tickled; later he was to recover from a broken back at an advanced age. Apart from his V.C., he had risen from captain to brigadier-general in less than a year; and he was to describe the Norwegian campaign as the dullest he had ever fought in. He strode on to the stage with an artificial hand and a black patch on his eye, and the blacked-out, colour-starved British public took to him greedily. He symbolized the adventurous waging of war for which, almost without realizing it, the public craved.

But Carton de Wiart, the happy warrior, was no superannuated blimp. He was a man of intelligence and great sensitivity, and had knowledge of which both the Chiefs of Staff and the War Cabinet might have availed themselves. Finding himself in financial straits between the wars, owing to the failure of his father's business, he had discovered it was possible to live a satisfactory life in Poland and had made his home there. When Hitler's war came he was dug out, being on the spot, and made Military Attaché. He had seen the German *blitzkrieg* on Poland at first hand, had noted the threefold lessons of its mobility, its devastating use of air power and the new device of the fifth column. It made a profound impression on him, both as a professional soldier and in human terms. 'I saw the very face of war change,' he wrote afterwards, 'bereft of romance, the glory shorn, no longer the soldier setting

forth into battle, but the women and children buried beneath it.'
He was the only senior officer in the British Army to have witnessed with his own eyes a *blitzkrieg* in action. He could have
told the War Cabinet what to expect in Norway, and it is a
thousand pities that he was not sent for and asked for his views in
advance instead of having to make his points in a series of urgent
signals from the battle area—where his whole reactions to the
situation were quite rightly and understandably conditioned by
his personal knowledge of the workings of the German war
machine.

'It dawned on me it might be Norway,' he noted when ordered
to report to the War Office, 'especially as I had never been there
and knew nothing about it.'

'Here comes Carton de Wiart,' he heard someone say, 'to
collect another gong.'

Carton de Wiart wasted no time: he was a man of action who
would have been a much better stable-mate for Admiral Cork
than General Mackesy. In particular, he detested staffs and paper-
work and disregarded his orders to collect a staff before setting
out, deeming it essential to meet his troops on their arrival.
He left Scotland in a Sunderland flying-boat on the 14th, taking
with him one solitary and ill-fated Staff Officer, Captain Elliot,
who was air-sick all the way across. The Sunderland had no
sooner touched down at Namsos when German aircraft, which
had been busy attacking the destroyer *Somali* in the harbour,
descended joyfully upon it and peppered it with their machine-
guns. Elliott was wounded and so ended his campaign in Norway.
Carton de Wiart, as we know, was indestructible and presently
managed to get himself aboard *Somali*. From there in turn he made
contact with the naval advance party and proceeded to inspect his
base.

He found it to be another of the microscopic ports which figure
in this campaign. Its quay space and unloading facilities were
utterly inadequate and both the harbour and the long fiord leading
in to it were very cramped indeed—unsuitable generally for large
ships and especially for *Empress of Australia*, which, for technical
reasons, was very clumsy to manœuvre. Searoom, moreover, is
essential to ships under air attack, and accordingly the two big
transports and their escort had already been re-routed to lie off

Lillesjona, a hundred miles to the north: from here the destroyers would ferry the troops to Namsos. In other words there was to be another trans-shipment; and another trans-shipment meant more trouble—especially as this time it was going to be carried out under the malevolent eye of the Luftwaffe. It had been hoped that the convoy would escape detection at Lillesjona: the hope was false.

CHAPTER 8

TOO LITTLE—TOO LATE

It was on this day, 14th April, that 'landings at several points in Norway' were somewhat prematurely announced to the world by the British Government. The Norwegian government (in a pardonable effort to boost morale) announced that 'assistance was assuming great proportions'. The information was most helpful to the Germans but most unhelpful in the concealment of the troopships: it was also slightly puzzling to the troops aboard them.

The men of the K.O.Y.L.I., the Lincolns and the Hallamshire Battalion were not impressed by the scenery. A bitter wind was blowing as the transports anchored: it was 'laden with fine snow which swept the fiord and the desolate shores'. The water was dotted with lumps of ice, while inland the white hills rose cheerless, immense and daunting, thickly mantled with snow. Even to these Yorkshire troops, used to the winter aspect of their own bleak moors, the brooding landscape of this grim land in all its grandeur and immensity brought a foreboding of harsh days to come. In training, experience, equipment and everything else (except that ridiculous and unmanageable Arctic kit) they were totally unprepared and unfitted for it.

It was not long before the Heinkels found them out, and to their first sight of Norway was added their first experience of air attack—particularly unnerving for men helplessly cooped up in crowded ships. The aircraft fought shy of the barrage put up by the cruisers and destroyers and flew high, but there were some near misses. The K.O.Y.L.I. made the best they could of it—Hibbert's rigorous training had made all the difference in the world to them. Lining the rails of *Empress of Australia*, they bet on the bombs. They were never to lose a life from air attack, nor were casualties in any unit to be more than fractional. It was morale that was wounded by unremitting and unopposed air bombardment—the helplessness of it, the restriction; the feeling of being naked and pinned down.

Half the Lincolns had already been transferred to *Nubian* and *Sikh* when the attacks came in: half were still aboard *Empress*. The destroyers seemed especially singled out for attack and promptly made off for Namsos at top speed—a further hammering for the unfortunate troops. While they churned on towards their final destination the troops remaining in the transports settled down to desultory bombing for the rest of the day. It was some sort of small acclimatization for what was to be the normal background to their lives for the next fortnight.

Carton de Wiart (who had sailed to collect his troops on one of the destroyers) realized, in the light of his Polish experience, that it was vital to get the men and their stores ashore and dispersed as quickly as possible before they became a convenient, concentrated target for the unopposed bombers. Although winter weather still held central Norway hard in its grip, the nights were shortening and no more than four hours of complete darkness could be relied upon for cover. There would be congestion at the tiny quays: in the absence of any unit transport he would have to rely on civilian lorries and the single branch railway line which ran inland to the big junction at Steinkjer, where it joined the main line coming out from Trondheim—on these and the hands and backs of the men themselves. They, too, were confined to the roads, the surfaces of which alone were free of the hampering soft snow. One saving grace was that the country in this part of Norway is thickly wooded, offering help in concealment.

It was obvious to him that the men were raw and untried and that their officers had little experience in handling them. But they were willing and quick—probably the more so because of the sense of personal helplessness which the strange conditions bred in them. In the brief four hours of darkness he was able to get the men and their kit and stores ashore, away from the quayside and dispersed, while the destroyers thankfully stood out of the narrow fiord where they were sitting targets for air attack and where the high cliffs and mountains blanketed the approach of raiders until the last moment. Such a disembarkation would have been impossible for a brigade properly equipped with transport, artillery and other heavy stores: it was, perhaps, the only occasion for thankfulness at their ill-found state. And little though they had, the haste and the blackout inevitably added to the losses caused by the previous embarkations and disembarkations.

All this was thrown up much more sharply when the rest of the brigade came in the following night. Rather than leave the troops at Lillesjona sitting around under the air raids for another day while the destroyers got back, it had been decided to transfer the men and everything that could be moved in destroyers to the more manœuvrable *Chrobry* and bring them to Namsos in her. And so, while the half-battalion of Lincolns was hurrying ashore at Namsos, the other half and the K.O.Y.L.I. were suffering yet another panic disembarkation—with blackout as one more aid to chaos. The destroyer came alongside: chutes were rigged and down these were hurled stores, kit and whatever else could be manhandled. Some of it landed on the destroyer's decks—in one piece or otherwise—some of it fell into the sea, some of it could not be moved at all. It was at this moment that the three-inch mortars and other gear that the K.O.Y.L.I.'s quartermaster had begged and prayed for were discovered in *Empress of Australia*'s holds: there was not a chance in eternity of getting them out. The transfer completed, the transports weighed anchor and put to sea —*Chrobry* and the destroyers to stand off out of the way of the bombers till the evening, *Empress of Australia* to make her way home. She took with her in all 170 tons of stores it had been impossible to transfer, ammunition and rations included. Instead of two weeks' supplies with which it had been issued, 146 Brigade now had two days'—apart from the appalling deficiencies in their already meagre scale of equipment. This was the 'great strength' in which we were coming to the aid of Norway.

As evening approached on this day—the 17th—*Chrobry* entered the fiord and made towards Namsos, still miraculously undiscovered. Her way led through some of the loveliest scenery in Norway: peaceful for the moment (though it was not to remain peaceful much longer) the winding fiord threaded its way, narrow as a river, through thirty miles of fir-clad slopes and rocky islets. The snow showers had ceased and the landscape shone spotless and dazzlingly white in the sun. It was dark when the ship berthed at the little wooden quay, and the now familiar

scene began to repeat itself. Zero hour for finishing the disembarkation was three a.m.: in the blackout every thing the units
possessed—including the kitbags with the Arctic kit—had to be
manhandled off the ship, got to the station a mile away and loaded
on to the train to start for Steinkjer before full daylight. Much of
it, once more, was literally hurled on to the quay, to land on top of
whatever else might already be lying there in the confined space.
Kit and equipment belonging to one unit were mixed up in shocking confusion with kit and equipment belonging to another. The
surprising thing was not that there were further losses and
deficiences but that the units managed to emerge with as much of
their own belongings as they did.

Once more the men obeyed orders with alacrity and worked
with a will: so far they were standing up to these testing conditions far, far better than anyone had a right to expect. When dawn
came the quay was as clean as a whistle; *Chrobry* was on her way
out to sea again—she still had 130 tons of stores aboard, but was
able to return with them the following night—and the troops
were rattling on their way to Steinkjer. Overburdened, yet ill-
equipped, their regimental historian aptly calls them. Most of
them still had their three kitbags: but they had no transport,
mortars, ack-ack guns or supporting artillery, no signals equipment, not so much as a bicycle and no other means of communication. At the end of their eighty-mile journey they were billeted
in a school which the Norwegians had cleared for them; and here
the cooks set about their business as best they could with borrowed utensils which included buckets and tin baths, to cook
food obtained by ingenuity rather than indent. Solely owing to
the devotion and resource of their quartermaster, Lieutenant W.
Wride, they never went short of a meal. They were now also re-
united with their much-travelled brigadier and, as another chore
to be added to its many duties, the Navy was somewhere ferrying
down to them such of their stores as had been discovered at
Narvik. At the same time the naval force which had acted as their
advance party was re-embarked: in this sector it played no further
part in the campaign on shore.

So far, largely due to the General's stringent precautions, they
had escaped the all-seeing eye of the Luftwaffe—they had yet to
make the acquaintance of George and Henry the Hun. But in a

real sense these would-be saviours of Norway were already a force on the defensive.

De Wiart had, however, further reasons for moving these troops out from his inadequate base area so quickly: the demibrigade of Chasseurs Alpins (having left behind their skis, their mules and much else) were on their way in four large liners with their own general and his staff and would need to be disembarked rapidly and got clear in their turn. Invaluable though they would have been as ski-troops, they were now as snowbound as the British troops and could only be similarly employed. And in the light of what he had seen with his own eyes in Poland (albeit no one at home had seen such things or had any inkling of them) de Wiart had little doubt of the sort of offensive operation which was going to be launched upon them at any moment. Already, at this early stage, his signals home were stressing the necessity and urgency of air support and warning that his base could not be tenable for long once the *blitzkrieg* on it started. He was convinced in his own mind that unless there were a radical change in the shape of things, the campaign would be of short duration—he did not, in fact, think it worth while putting up the insignia of Acting Lieutenant-General, to which rank, by virtue of his command, he was promoted.

None the less, his troops had an operational job to do and he lost no time in deploying them to carry it out. His orders spoke formally of providing encouragement for the Norwegian government, providing a rallying point for the Norwegian forces, securing a base for subsequent operations in Scandanavia and so on: for his part he was abundantly clear that his job was essentially to hang on until the Navy and assault forces appeared and then move in on Trondheim—in other words to act in support of Operation Hammer. There were two things he did not know. One was that Operation Hammer was out of favour and about to be cancelled. The other was that the German movement northwards from Oslo in strength, ordered on the 14th, was now well under way and that the already exhausted Norwegians opposing it were on the verge of cracking, as crack they were bound to. In any case, therefore, Operation Hammer would have been forestalled, even if it had not been cancelled. The doom of Mauriceforce was already upon it. The same was true of Sickleforce—

under which name 148 Brigade, even thinner on the ground and even worse equipped than Carton de Wiart's force—was now landing at Aandalsnes, to the south.

With the final transportation of 148 Brigade to its destination the last of the original R.4 troops were at last got on the move, and their movement was, in terms of the refinements of chaos, the most outstanding of them all. It will be remembered that 148 Brigade—Sickleforce—had started off by being a battalion short. It was now, on its first landing overseas, to be made a further half battalion short, so that it would be at exactly half its paper strength in terms of infantry—without, of course, any supporting troops at all. Its equipment was already in confusion: it was to be still further confounded. When the rest of the force set off for Narvik the brigade was earmarked for Namsos, and Brigadier Morgan accordingly began to scrape together what information about Namsos he could. On 13th April the Leicesters were embarked in the troopship *Orion* with half the battalion of Sherwood Foresters: the rest of the latter were put aboard the cruisers *Galatea* and *Arethusa*. *Orion* lay well down the Firth of Forth and the embarkation of both men and stores was carried out by means of lighters in the blackout. This naturally led to stores being stowed anyhow in the holds as it arrived: fortunately the holds were roomy with plenty of space to work, and in the ensuing couple of days the troops laboured hard under the quartermaster and R.S.M., getting everything sorted, straightened out and tactically disposed. They had no sooner got everything straight when they were ordered to disembark and everything was immediately in confusion again. Eventually the Sherwood Foresters and half the Leicesters left early on the 17th in two cruisers and the small anti-aircraft cruisers *Carlisle* and *Curacoa*. The transfer had been another blackout operation with a stiff breeze added for good measure, and further stores that were left behind included all the brigade headquarters equipment (wireless transmitter and all) and all the Foresters' mortar ammunition. At the last moment a battery of Bofors guns had been added—it left without its predictors. B and C companies of the Leicesters, shut out of the party for want of space, were trundled off to Aberdeen to be shipped as a second flight. They sailed several days later in two tiny ships, *St. Magnus* and *St. Sunniver*. With them (this is anticipating things a little but the picture may as well be completed) went the brigade's transport in the vessel *Cedarbank*: it would not in any case have got there in time to be of any use, but the fates that somehow seemed to brood over this operation made certain that it never got there at all: *Cedarbank* was torpedoed before the very eyes of the two companies—the only storeship or transport to be sunk by a U-boat in the whole Norwegian campaign.

Their destination, while all this was going on, had been changed from Namsos to Aandalsnes,* and so any brief preparations Brigadier Morgan might have been able to make were undone. It is significant that later, when King-Salter, the Military Attaché, met the exhausted units retreating on Tretten, he found himself the only person in possession of a map.

This time the troops were shadowed across the North Sea by German aircraft but they were not attacked and once more, in the same almost miraculous fashion as in the case of the other landings, the Navy got the battalion and a half safely ashore, where the naval detachment had prepared the way for them. As elsewhere the country was under heavy snow and the nights were bitterly cold for the unacclimatized troops. In these strange and difficult surroundings it appeared at first that they would make contact with the Germans almost immediately; for a paratroop force, in advance of the main German movement from the Oslo area now proceeding, had been dropped near Dombaas, where the branch line from Aandalsnes joined the main line from Trondheim in the same way as that from Namsos joined it at Steinkjer. Fortunately this force was mopped up by the Norwegians, helped by a British naval gun, which had been landed and sent forward: the troops were hurried off by train to Dombaas out of the disembarkation area in the same way as Mauriceforce had been.

Here, therefore, were the troops of Mauriceforce on the north and Sickleforce on the south—got ashore safely against all expectations for what they could do in the Norwegian winter with the equipment still left to them and ready for their encircling movement on Trondheim in preparation for the main assault of operation Hammer, which was never to happen. Far away to the north the well-trained regular troops of the Guards Brigade were

* Pronounced 'Undulsness'.

still dodging air raids and making trifling movements round the Narvik fiords while Admiral Cork and General Mackesy pursued their separate policies, the Norwegians in Narvik waited for the British to come, the Germans struggled to consolidate their defensive positions as best they could and General Fleischer prepared for the one and only counter-attack that for the moment held out any promise at all.

At Aandalsnes the naval advance party was absorbed into the military force instead of being re-embarked—they had no ships to re-embark in and the depleted brigade was very short indeed in manpower for the tasks that faced it. There had been linked to their landing another operation which was carried out at the same time as 148 Brigade was coming ashore—the bombardment of Stavanger aerodrome by *Suffolk*. Although some accounts give the impression that this bombardment was a part of Operation Hammer which somehow got into execution, it was, in fact, an operation of its own and for once it was given a name entirely appropriate to what happened—it was christened Operation Duck. It was a misguided operation because it came known afterwards that the Luftwaffe units from whose attentions it was intended to relieve the British troops at Aandalsnes were not operating from Stavanger at all but from airfields in Denmark; and its results were not merely revealing and foreboding, but also underlined the objections which, as we shall see, Admiral Forbes was at that time putting forward against Operation Hammer.

Suffolk sailed from Scapa Flow on the 16th—it was to be her last sailing for a long time. That night she made rendezvous with the submarine *Seal*, whose job it was to pin-point her position for her, and made ready to start the bombardment at first light. In preparation for it she catapulted off first one then the other of her Walrus amphibians and waited for sight of a flare which a Hudson aircraft of Coastal Command, R.A.F., was due to drop over the airfield to mark the target. Both these air operations went wrong: radio contact with both the Walruses was blacked out, as so often happened in these parts, so that they were useless as spotters, while the Hudson attracted to itself an extraordinary quantity of flak which made the flare quite indistinguishable from the general firework display. None the less, *Suffolk* stuck to her schedule and opened fire at the appointed time. In three runs she fired two hundred and two rounds from her eight-inch guns at a range of twenty thousand yards. She did, indeed, cause both casualties to German troops and damage to the airfield, including the setting ablaze of two petrol dumps; but the damage was nothing like as heavy as had been intended and certainly not heavy enough to put the airfield out of action. The only real purpose it served, like the Bren-gunner at Narvik, was to annoy the Germans—who by this time were already in the air and after her blood.

A few minutes after six o'clock in the morning she completed her last run and made off to sea at thirty knots. Having put some distance between herself and the enemy-held coast, she reduced speed somewhat and turned due north to carry out a sweep she had been ordered to make on the way home. At this point she expected to make contact with an R.A.F. long-range fighter escort, but, like all the other aerial parts of this adventure, the rendezvous did not come off, because the fighters had expected to find her closer inshore. At eight-twenty-five the first of the German bombers did find her, and from then until after three o'clock in the afternoon she was more or less continuously under bombardment without a single friendly aircraft to help her and dependent entirely on her own guns for defence. She was in action without respite and fired off most of her ack-ack ammunition. Appeal after appeal were made for fighter support (there was obviously no point in her attempting to keep radio silence), but no support was forthcoming. Her report precisely lists thirty-three bombing attacks and a total of eighty-eight bomb splashes observed at varying distances from the ship. Twenty-one of the attacks were by high-level bombers, the remaining twelve—much more deadly—by Stuka dive-bombers; had the Stukas not been less practised than they afterwards became she would have been at the bottom of the sea. As it was they scored only one direct hit, which went more or less right through the ship aft, damaging very severely indeed both her hull, her machinery and her weapons, causing ammunition explosions and leaving a trail of dead and wounded. Other near misses caused damage of varying degrees: by the time the action was over she had taken aboard two thousand five hundred tons of water and her steering gear was badly affected. She steamed the last one hundred and sixty-four miles steering by her screws alone and just managed to make Scapa Flow with the seas breaking over her almost submerged quarter-deck. Operation Duck had ended, lives were lost, and a valuable ship was to be out of action to bring no relief whatsoever to the two slender brigades strung out to the north and south of Trondheim like two pieces of elastic ready to snap—waiting for Operation Hammer.

Now Hammer, be it remembered, was conceived in the moment of optimism following on the second bombardment of Narvik and in response to the appeals of both General Ruge and Colonel King-Salter for help in recapturing Trondheim. Churchill tells us that the violent surge of opinion in favour of such a direct attack went far beyond official circles—that it was urged by the public, the clubs and the newspapers. By his own side he had, egging him vehemently on, his old friend and colleague, Admiral of the Fleet Sir Roger Keyes—'champion of forcing the Dardanelles, hero and victor of Zeebrugge'. It was, of course, the whole appalling episode of Gallipoli and our failure to force the Dardanelles which had led to Churchill's disastrous fall from power at the Admiralty in the First World War, and in the obvious parallel between the two situations he had found himself in a state of indecision quite uncharacteristic of him. On the one hand he felt that the mistake of Gallipoli, with its disastrous national and personal consequences, must not be repeated—on the other that the unlaid ghost of Gallipoli might be urging him on to back an operation which would in turn lead to disaster. Further, the French, still hoping that operations in Norway might be a distraction from the Western Front, backed the Hammer proposal and the Supreme Allied War Council agreed to troops being withdrawn from France for it—ten battalions in all, half of them British, half French. Indeed, although all the plans and discussions about the operation eventually came to nought, one good thing resulted from it—the British 15 Brigade, made up of three absolutely first-class battalions of regular troops, trained to the last degree and full of confidence, was almost immediately ordered home from the Maginot Line and so was available later to be flung in to central Norway in support of the battered 148 Brigade. This alone made the withdrawal of the remains of the brigade possible.

The proposals were now put to the Commander-in-Chief Home Fleet, Admiral Forbes, who was asked for his opinion both on getting the troops into Trondheim fiord and conducting a successful bombardment with all his available ships. This involved a thirty-mile approach through narrow waters by both troopships and naval vessels under air attack and with the shore defences in German hands. He rejected the operation as he was bound to, in view of the fact that German control of the air had already forced the Fleet out of southern Norwegian waters and was steadily forcing it out of central Norwegian waters as well. But under pressure and with promise of air support, bombardment of airfields and thorough preparation which would take a full week, he reconsidered his decision and—reluctantly one feels —agreed to make his disposition: units of the Home Fleet were withdrawn to Scapa to oil, prepare and take aboard the special bombardment shell which would be needed. On the same day that *Suffolk* was being harried home from Stavanger—the 17th— the military commander was appointed and briefed, Major-General Hotblack. This time the peculiar fates that somehow ruled the Norwegian campaign produced a great portent: General Hotblack had a stroke and was found after midnight lying at the foot of the Duke of York's steps in no condition to command an invasion force. His second-in-command, Brigadier Berney-Ficklin, took over and left for the north: on his way by air to Scapa Flow his plane crashed at Kirkwall and he broke his jaw and suffered other injuries. These personal disasters obviously cannot have had anything directly to do with the abandonment of Operation Hammer but one cannot help feeling that they contributed psychologically to the change of attitude about it.

For during the 18th what Churchill calls a 'vehement and decisive change' came over the opinions of all who had pressed for Operation Hammer. Changes of opinion are familiar enough in the history of these months, but there is, perhaps, no other instance of one being so unanimous as this. For some reason or other realization seems to have dawned simultaneously on all concerned of exactly what Admiral Forbes's ships would have to face, pent in the narrow fiord, of what the troops would have against them on the enemy-held and Luftwaffe-dominated shore. No doubt the gruelling experience of *Suffolk* brought it home in Admiralty circles: events on land had not yet reached the point when they would bring it home to the War Office also. Churchill was at first dumbfounded by the change—more particularly as Admiral Keyes was still by his side begging to be allowed to lead a force, even of older ships of war, to storm the German defences. After having steeled himself to kill the ghost of Gallipoli he found it particularly difficult to undo his resolution; but he had no choice but to accept the situation and to report the facts to the Prime Minister. Operation Hammer was dead.

In its place it was decided to reinforce the two arms of the pincer movement against Trondheim from the north and the south so that Trondheim could be encircled from the land and so reduced without the perils of a frontal attack. In preparation for this, Lieutenant-General Massy was appointed to command the whole operation and for a brief period held the appointment of Commander, North Western Expeditionary Force. The rapid movement of events that followed gave neither time nor opportunity for him to set up his headquarters in Norway and for the short time that his appointment lasted he exercised his command from England—perhaps the only occasion in history in which a British general has commanded a force overseas without setting foot out of the country: he can therefore be fairly forgiven for some inaccuracies in fact and for some misjudgements of conditions which appeared in his official report.

There was nothing wrong at all with the decision to substitute the pincer movement on Trondheim for the frontal assault, which would almost certainly have resulted in a massacre. What was wrong was not the decision but the way in which the decision was implemented: in the first place the reinforcement of Mauriceforce and Sickleforce was not proceeded with at the speed that was now obviously called for; and for some reason which positively defies all divination, the commanders of these forces were not told that they were no longer merely in support of a major operation but were now the major operation itself. So Carton de Wiart would string his small force out, weak, vulnerable and lacking both in mobility and communications equipment, in preparation for the hammer blow on Trondheim that would never happen: and Brigadier Morgan with his still smaller and worse-equipped force farther south would have to put himself in a still more difficult position. General Ismay in London was working on a paper for the Chief of Staffs Committee in which he dwelt at some length on the hazards of the operations in central Norway (in the same paper he declared that the possession of the Gällivare ore fields was 'the main objective of the operations in Scandinavia' which shows that there was still considerable emphasis in the wrong direction in the minds of influential people) but his paper was not produced until 21st April—by which time the rot in central Norway had already set in. Beyond all doubt the urgent necessity for bolstering up the Norwegian government and its scratch though valiant army was not convincingly realized—nor was there yet any realization that defeat in central Norway ultimately meant defeat at beloved Narvik.

When we left Carton de Wiart, he had got his solitary brigade ashore, obliterated the traces of its disembarkation and hurried his troops away out of the disembarkation area. He had made contact with the Norwegian 5th Brigade under an energetic and resourceful officer, Colonel Getz. Getz had only his two battalions —got together in the scratch way characteristic of all the Norwegian battalions except those in the north—and the dismounted dragoons with Vickers guns. All these had just about enough ammunition for one day's serious fighting, but since they could move in the difficult country they would be very useful as supporting patrols. Moreover, Colonel Getz was able to rake together a sufficiency (though not an abundance) of civilian lorries to move the British troops. These therefore—moving rapidly on the roads, which were clear of snow—fanned out around the inner edges of the fiords in which Trondheim stands, till at one point they were barely sixty miles by road from the town itself. The rapidity of this advance became an additional factor in turning thinking in London towards the possible success of this encircling movement—in utter disregard of the weakness and vulnerability of these troops. Churchill alone, looking at their dispositions, pointed out (it was the kind of situation which his military training of long before qualified him to appreciate) that they were exposed and in danger; that if the ice broke up in Trondheim fiord, as it was due to any moment, the Germans would be able to land and cut them off by sea. But then Churchill knew that Hammer had been abandoned.

The night after 146 Brigade had been hustled out of Namsos the French demi-brigade came in. They, too, were hurried ashore from their troopships: the need for haste had been underlined by air attacks in the long, narrow fiords through which their way had lain—without casualities to the troops, although the French cruiser *Émile Bertin* was sufficiently damaged to have to return to England. Whatever may have been the virtues of these French troops, they were certainly overstrong in one thing—confidence. They were therefore less amenable to strange orders than the raw British troops and characteristically, perhaps, they lacked the habit of tidiness—which is somewhat less of a fetish with the French Army than it is with the British. One must not be unjust to them—there were more of them than there were of the British —four thousand of them—and the landing space was very restricted indeed. Be this as it may, they did not obliterate their traces and the all-seeing German reconnaisance aircraft which came as regularly as clockwork with the daylight soon spotted the signs of a disembarkation. It was, in any case, too much to hope that the concealment could have been kept up for ever. The first German bombers appeared over the neat little town at ten o'clock that morning and from then until late in the afternoon it was bombed repeatedly. There were few dead: the Chasseurs were bivouacked in the woods and the civilian population fled at the first attack—it was easy to escape from so small a place— but the town was destroyed, the timber houses burned, the railhead and everything on it was obliterated. Electricity and water supplies were cut off, even the wharves were wrecked. The destroyer *Nubian*, which came back that night with part of the demi-brigade's stores, found the wooden buildings still aflame from end to end of the town, lighting up the snowy slopes beyond with the livid glare of destruction. Namsos had ceased to exist— so had the base of Mauriceforce. The *blitzkrieg* which Carton de Wiart had seen in Poland had come to the shores of the western seas, even as he had feared and known it would; and the rest of what he had feared would follow just as certainly. In the morning he signalled the War Office, making it clear that he saw no possibility of carrying out any operations at all unless air cover could be provided.

But air cover could not be provided. No R.A.F. fighter—not

even the long-range Blenheim fighters, which were neither faster nor more manœuvrable than the Heinkel bombers—could operate over Namsos. *Furious* was still with the Fleet but had no fighters: *Glorious* and *Ark Royal* were on the way from the Mediterranean to join her. These ships, sitting targets themselves, would have to operate well out to sea, thus reducing the endurance of their fighters over the target: none the less the one day's respite Mauriceforce was to have was when a carrier was close at hand. The R.A.F. were attacking German-held aerodromes, at extreme range and therefore ineffectively. For the rest there were the guns of the anti-aircraft cruisers and sloops in the fiord: all these could do was defend themselves, and an exhausting time they had of it—under steam all day to manœuvre as best they could in confined waters under the continuous onslaughts of the bombers that came without warning over the hills and cliffs of the fiord, firing away their ammunition, wearing out their gun barrels. The only real relief they brought was that while they were there they drew the enemy attacks upon themselves—and this was of little service to the troops who had already pushed out many miles away.

Look at the map of central Norway. Its most easily distinguished feature is the Trondheimsfiord, curving between the mountains till it all but cuts the narrow land in two: almost at its extreme end, far beyond Trondheim itself, it breaks through a narrow neck and spreads out again into the Beitstadfiord. This is roughly parallel with the end of the main fiord and separated from it by the Inderöy peninsula, itself joined to the mainland only by two narrow strips with a lake between. This waterway system lies right athwart communications between Namsos and the south. Road and railway skirt it together: inland from these there is nothing but mountain tracks, with rare bridges over the few precipitous and narrow valleys. It would have been difficult country for movement at the best of times: just now it was covered, like the rest of Norway, in deep snow and therefore impossible for troops without the equipment to move in snow. The three British battalions were thus restricted to the road and railway round the fiords, and it was on this road and railway that they moved and operated. But the German mountain troops could move in the hills, and there was peril in the fiord also;

because though the winter was still hard on the mountains, it was near its end—and the first sign of its end coming would be the breaking-up of the ice on the waters, which were under German control and gave direct access to German-held Trondheim. Were the ice to break, the British would be trapped between the fiord and the hills.

But there was no choice for them. Their orders were to encircle Trondheim, and they must, perforce, encircle it by the only route on which they could move. The Lincolns had spent the day after their disembarkation at the little railway junction of Grong (where they had their only pay-out in kroner) while the other two battalions had gone direct to the bigger junction of Steinkjer. The Lincolns joined the others the following day—a bitter journey through desolate landscape in the freezing cold. Remember that these men had already been through the demoralizing experience of the embarkations and disembarkations, the transit camp, the muddle of orders given only to be altered, the sea journey, the trans-shipment under enemy bombing, the chaotic landing. Now men and junior officers had no idea where they were, where they were going or why; they were turned out early into the bitter morning and told to get on the move before Jerry spotted them—discouraging in itself to men with no weapons to deal with Jerry. Their small arms they had, and grenades: miraculously, they had one three-inch mortar left them. They had no anti-aircraft or anti-tank weapons, no machine-guns. The other two battalions had had a few hours more to take stock of Steinkjer, albeit there was little to take stock of—a typical Norwegian town of timber houses, its population no more than four thousand, its most prominent feature the railway junction and the combined road and rail bridge over the river that ran into the fiord. Below this bridge, the Hallamshires' diary, at least, notes that the ice was breaking fast. The other thing of importance noted this day was the first appearance of a Henschel float-plane which flew low and in a leisurely fashion, inspecting them. It is a sign of spirit that they christened it Henry the Hun.

To the Hallamshires fell the most northerly positions around Steinkjer and the northern side of the Beitstadfiord. Of the Lincolns, two companies remained in the town itself, where the brigade's advance headquarters had been set up: A company went a few miles north, D company five miles down the railway to Vist. Their orders were no more encouraging than their journey— they were to keep cover during the day and not give away their whereabouts by firing their small arms at aircraft. They alone of the three battalions gave their personal recce aircraft no name.

It was the K.O.Y.L.I.—Hibbert's rejuvenated battalion—that moved the farthest from its base. It moved by train, the companies dropping off one by one into the night—at Sparbu, at Strommen, at Röra and far round the fiord at Stiklestad, in support of a Norwegian machine-gun detachment holding a road bridge beyond them. At this point they were the nearest of all the troops in Norway to German-held positions—outposts of a thinly-strung-out, solitary brigade manning a front fifty-five miles long with no communications between platoons, companies, battalions and headquarters except on foot. Their advance headquarters was not much more than thirty miles from their base at Namsos on the map, but nearly eighty miles by rail. And Namsos would next day cease to exist.

Hibbert did what he could. He rounded up eighty ancient civilian lorries and two decrepit 'buses. He protested that his troops, tied to the road and hemmed in by the mountains, were virtually trapped. He pointed out that he had no artillery and that his only hope of warding off an attack would be if the Germans landed right among his positions. This was unlikely, because his battalion had, like the others, acquired its own particular Henschel recce plane, which flew low in leisurely and constant attendance. His men named it George.

Here, then, 146 Brigade rested uneasily for the night of the 19th and the day of the 20th, while Namsos burned behind them, the ice in the fiord disintegrated and moved on the tide and the Germans investigated and weighed up their dispositions. Already the attackers were on the defensive; and, so far from encircling and cutting off the Germans in Trondheim, were themselves at any moment liable to be encircled and cut off from their bases.

But this was a picnic compared with the situation of fearsomely named Sickleforce to the south—148 Brigade, still only one and a half battalions strong. We left them disembarking at Molde and Aandalsnes, shadowed by enemy aircraft but not yet attacked, and being in their turn hurried forward far from their base to their own junction with the main railway line at Dombaas. From here the Gudbrandsdal, one of Norway's main natural communication arteries, led directly through the mountains all the way to Oslo. On this route, for a short, desperate time, King Haakon and his ministers were resting and hiding as well as they might at Otta—still the legal King and government of Norway, still bearing with them Norway's gold reserve, their passport to independence and their first stake, if need be, to their right to buy fresh arms and re-equip themselves as equal allies in the battle for a free world. Beyond these, again, was Ruge's headquarters at Öyer; beyond Ruge his desperate, improvised army—already at war for well over a week and near exhaustion, but still grimly hanging on to positions south of Lillehammer, around Lake Mjösa. The German break-out in strength from Oslo had now been gathering momentum for several days. The Norwegians were feeling the relentless pressure of Army Group Pellengahr—seven full divisions, including mountain troops, with tanks, artillery, air support and all the accoutrements of total war. The breaking-point was very near: what could one and a half battalions of unsupported infantry at Dombaas do to avert it?

Now Ruge did not know—how could he?—that the 'great strength' of the forces sent to help him was one and a half battalions, that they had no arms and ammunition but what they could carry, or perhaps even less than that. King-Salter and the French Attaché had now been living for some days at his headquarters and messing with his officers: he saw them constantly and they, for their part, quickly made themselves familiar with the country, the situation and the needs—King-Salter continuing to send as many messages home as conditions allowed him to. Everything they saw and heard pointed to the one conclusion on which Ruge continually dwelt—that to make their grip on Norway a reality the Germans must link up their forces in the south with their holding force in Trondheim—that the only way through was up the Gudbrandsdal, and the Österdal which runs parallel to the east. These could be defended by comparatively few troops, if they were properly equipped: even the Norwegians, badly off as they were, were at least delaying the advance through them, but now the pressure upon the tired troops was becoming intolerable and there were no reserves to relieve them. All the features of the *blitzkrieg* in Poland were being repeated, as they were to be repeated again in the Low Countries and in France. Carl Hambro talks of the bombing of towns where there were no military establishments at all, of hospitals, of people coming out of church, of a funeral procession: he speaks of Norwegian men and women tied to the fenders of cars or forced to stand on the running boards to shield the Germans inside. He speaks of German parachutists taking shelter in farmhouses and small homesteads and covering up behind women and children when attacked. Getting on towards a generation later these atrocity stories sound synthetic and hackneyed, as the stories of the Belgian atrocities in the First World War had sounded in the 1930s; but there was no point in inventing them—no one, until the German *blitzkrieg*, would have thought of inventing such things, which had passed from the civilized world—and the evidence of them is overwhelming.

But Ruge was becoming increasingly bitter about the delays— and bitter too about his complete lack of any information on Allied plans to bring him the substantial aid he had been promised. The landings at Narvik heartened him for a little—but why Narvik, or at least Narvik alone? Why not landings by the British and French with the great reserves of troops they were reputed to have, the arms and equipment with which they must be well endowed, right in the heart of Norway, where the battle could and must be won but where there was only a little time left for its winning? From his headquarters on the hillside above Öyer he, his officers and the Allied representatives, could sometimes look down and see German aircraft flying up the valley below them at zero altitude, completely unchallenged by any antiaircraft weapons at all. It was infuriating and frustrating. How much longer could it go on?

At last, on the 17th, came a message telling them to watch Aandalsnes. On the 18th it was followed by the tidings that the troops were actually landing. This could only be the help that was so urgently needed: could there be any doubt that it was to go where the need was greatest and that the Norwegians had a call upon it?

Now Brigadier Morgan's orders, as we know, were to encircle Trondheim from the south—more specifically, to secure the

Dombaas junction, 'then operate northwards and take offensive action against Germans in the Trondheim area'. This might well be thought sufficient task for a mere thousand troops and it was perhaps understandable that no further tasks were specified for him; but telegrams from England to Ruge's headquarters gave the impression that these troops were his expected reinforcements and King-Salter in particular had no doubt in his mind that Ruge could call upon them. Accordingly he contacted Morgan and asked him to bring his troops south. He followed it up on the morning of the 19th by a journey up to Dombaas to meet Morgan personally—the German parachutists between having fortunately just been cleaned up. Arriving in the town with the full urgency of his mission upon him he was overjoyed to see British troops for the first time in Norway.

What followed has more than once been both misreported and misinterpreted. General Massy's official report asserts that King-Salter 'stated to Brigadier Morgan that the War Office had sanctioned the 148th Infantry Brigade coming under the command of the Commander-in-Chief Norwegian Army'. The British Attaché, in fact, did nothing of the sort. He contended that in the view both of General Ruge and himself the telegrams they had received from the War Office gave them a call on the Brigade; and he represented to Morgan that the Norwegians to the south were in such dire straits that he, as the commander on the spot, must make a decision on his own initiative and go where the rapidly deteriorating situation undoubtedly called for him. In any case, other considerations were quite obvious to Morgan. His troops at Dombaas were already more than sixty miles from their seaward base at Aandalsnes on a line of communication which was for all practical purposes completely unguarded: the only reinforcements he could expect, as far as he knew, were the two missing companies of the Leicesters, due in on the 20th. If he were now to turn north with his handful of troops while the Norwegians south of him were retiring by large bounds before the German onslaught, he would not merely be open to attack from the rear but would also be easily cut off from the coast—in other words his only way of securing his communications was to endeavour to secure his force against the German advance; and this amounted to as near what the Norwegians were asking as made no difference. He therefore agreed to the Norwegians' demands: before himself returning by special train down the valley with King-Salter to meet Ruge personally he signalled the War Office asking for confirmation of his action. As a matter of history the reply (which was not received until the following day when the troops were already in action) agreed with him, sanctioned his co-operation with the Norwegian C.-in-C. while making use of Dombaas, 'if you can spare troops'. If he could spare troops, forsooth! Had someone at home forgotten how many troops he had?

The interview with Ruge began badly. The Norwegian was not the most easily ruffled of men but some orders Morgan had given to Norwegian railway staff earlier in the day had struck a discordant note. When cordiality was restored Ruge made two things absolutely clear: the first was that he and he alone was responsible for keeping the Norwegian forces in being and that Norway's continuance in the struggle depended upon himself—the second was that the British troops must not merely go south but go south under his command.

Morgan, on the spot and fully grasping the situation, saw that he had no choice. He was not happy about surrendering control of his troops to Norwegian commanders but it is to his credit that he did not hesitate—at other times and in other theatres of war precious time was lost over arguments as to who should be in command. It is doubtful if he would have changed his mind even had he received by then a telegram from the War Office stating specifically that he must retain command of his troops; albeit the official responsibility for him not receiving this message in time rests with King-Salter, who has admitted delaying its delivery. Although it may be argued that a strict interpretation of his duties would probably find him guilty of exceeding them, there is no doubt that both he and Morgan were doing their best to stave off the imminent collapse of the Norwegian resistance, of which only they on the spot could be fully aware. They did, in fact, stave it off, and had the British troops been more numerous, better acclimatized, better trained and better equipped—had they had air support and artillery and the means to operate in the snow-bound country—the Germans might well have recoiled as effectively as they did later when they came up against 15 Brigade.

Accordingly, on the 20th, the troops were moved from Dombaas. Both battalions had now been almost continuously on the move since their first departure from their quarters in England a fortnight before, except for their brief spell at the miserable transit camp at Dunfermline. They were cold and bewildered, but still game. The Leicesters' regimental history, speaking of the next twenty-four hours, says that it would be 'hard to imagine a worse position for any battalion to find itself in in its first experience of modern war'. Yet they still were to have spirit to scrawl on their buses and lorries slogans that read 'Tours to beautiful Norway', 'See the midnight sun' and so on. This much, at least, they had in common with the Guards departing from Wellington Barracks! They hurried south down the single railway which follows the Gudbrandsdal, leapfrogging with the road and river—a tenuous thread putting a further one hundred and forty miles between themselves and their perilously insecure base. At the southern end of Gudbrandsdal is a long lake, Lake Mjösa. Near its southern end are Elverum and Hamar, where the Norwegian King and government had first sought refuge on their flight from Oslo—at its northern end is Lillehammer. The Germans were now firmly in possession of the approach from Oslo to the southern part of the lake and were pressing up in force through the mountainous country on both sides of it. On the west side of it there were two main organized Norwegian groups—one under Colonel Dahl, the other what was left of their 4th Brigade. On the east side there was a Norwegian battalion of about five hundred men and a dismounted dragoon regiment of about one thousand. These were under the Norwegian General Hvinden Haug. All were in action and all very hard pressed indeed by the Germans who were battering at them with infantry, motorized machine-gun units, artillery and air support. They were worn out and their need for relief, rest and reorganization was urgent. So there was no pause for the British battalion and a half (the two missing companies of the Leicesters were only on this day about to disembark at Aandalsnes) when they arrived at Lillehammer. They had a brief glimpse of Ruge, their own brigadier and of Colonel Beichmann who had scraped together civilian transport to take them into the line and who was to continue for the rest of their brief campaign to scrape together such transport as could be vouchsafed to them. They had time to take in the vista of spruce forests marching up the lower slopes around them, the snow-capped ridges above. They had time even to retain a brief impression of Lillehammer—'a colony of quaint wooden houses, clear, compact, picturesque. . . .' They saw the river Laagen widening into the lake, still frozen over from edge to edge. Then into this pitiless landscape they were deployed; A and D companies of the Foresters to the west of the lake, B and C to the east. Hard on their heels came the Leicesters, already suffering before the battle had even begun from an acute shortage of ammunition, on top of all the equipment they had lost. The westward companies of the Foresters arrived at their destination at two o'clock in the morning and for a brief period found warmth at least in the parish church of Nykirke, which was heated for them; but in a matter of hours they were pulled out again to bolster up the Norwegians nearer the lake, who were already breaking, and that night half of them at least slept out in the snow. The eastern section, likewise, had a brief few hours' respite in a village, but the following day found themselves pushed forward and directly under German pressure. Their mortar section opened fire but was quickly silenced.

Coming up behind them the following morning, the Leicesters were soon under air attack as they advanced to relieve the Norwegians on an icy slope more than a thousand feet above sea level and already being bombarded by German guns less than two miles away. They, too, endeavoured to open fire with mortars: all they had for them was smoke bombs. Colonel German, their C.O., protested that he was being asked to take over a whole divisional front and himself selected another position for them to stand farther north. His selection was difficult because the only map he had was on far too small a scale to be of much use and the position had to be astride the main road, which was the only place where his troops could put one foot before another. During the afternoon the exhausted Norwegian troops began to pass through them and soon they found themselves covering a general withdrawal of the whole of the Norwegian forces east of the lake. These passed on until they were more than twenty miles in the rear, endeavouring to reorganize. Either by chance they had arrived at the precise moment when the Germans were stepping up pressure, or the Germans stepped up pressure because of their arrival.

It was not long before the Norwegian commander decided to withdraw the whole force north of the lake. The civilian transport laid on for the Leicesters did not materialize and they were faced with the alternatives of either marching or being captured. Thigh deep in snow and in a bitter wind they struggled fourteen miles to Aasmarka, where the transport picked them up and took them to Lillehammer—but almost immediately they had to withdraw again because the Germans were right on their heels, and a party of six officers and fifty men was cut off. Some of the transport over-ran and so their strength was temporarily still further reduced. With them withdrew the Foresters: an attempt was to be made to make a stand at the Balbergkamp where a bridge crossed the head of the lake to Faaberg. The units to the west, under less heavy pressure, would have to withdraw in step with them or be cut off themselves—so would the Norwegian forces on their side of the lake, now in grave jeopardy. There were no effective reserves north of them: the Norwegians were no longer in any condition to fight until they had been rested somehow and pulled together again.

The history of the party of Leicesters who were cut off is typical of more than one similar little Odyssey that was to happen in the coming days. They were not captured, as the official history says they were. They picked up some stragglers from the main body and then were lucky enough to lay hands on a single lorry, which got as many men as it would carry back to the battalion. The remainder marched through the night—raw Territorials though they were, with no ammunition except a few pistol rounds and no other means of defending themselves; unfed, unrested and freezing, but determined to rejoin their units—and about midnight came to a fork in the road. With no map to guide them they picked the left fork: ten minutes later the Germans, rapidly overhauling them, picked the right fork and, unknown to them, overtook them. They traipsed wearily into Lillehammer about eight o'clock in the morning and sought breakfast and a wash at a small hotel. The proprietor regretfully refused them—he had, he said guardedly, just been asked for somewhat wider facilities by the German Headquarters. Tired though they were, the Leicesters needed no second hint—they fled from the town and took to the mountains; and for ten days they floundered north over this impossible and inhospitable country, finding food and rest where they could, but little of either, still determined to outflank the Germans and rejoin their battalion. Then they heard in a farmhouse news of the British evacuation on the radio and, turning east, escaped into neutral Sweden.

News that the British troops had been forced back so quickly on the heels of the retreating Norwegians caused consternation at the headquarters at Öyer, only seven miles north of the bridge at Faaberg where they had temporarily halted—already with Bavarian ski-troops on their flanks and mortar bombs lobbing down from the hills. The German advance was acquiring impetus—if it could not be stopped or slowed up there would be no stopping it at all; and if it could not be stopped the Germans would soon dominate the whole Gudbrandsdal, the link with Trondheim almost in their grasp. King-Salter hurried south with Morgan's Brigade Major to see what he could do, but they had gone barely half a mile when they began to meet British troops withdrawing, crammed into civilian lorries. They had held their position until after three in the afternoon, had even repulsed attacks by the enemy pressing in on their unprotected flanks, albeit with casualties; but the Germans had worked around them everywhere and before they finally withdrew they were under *blitzkrieg* fire from heavy machine-guns at short range on their front. This time the withdrawal was even more hasty: kit, rations and ammunition had to be left behind: they were being rapidly reduced to the state of retreating with little more than what they stood up in. Somehow or other it was vital for these men to stand. Where could they stand, and with what?

At home in England the public was seeing a very different picture—another wishful-thinking picture, just like all the pictures of this campaign. The previous day, a Sunday, the day when the Leicesters and Sherwood Foresters first came up against the massive German attack, there had been released to the Press a Norwegian communiqué announcing that units of the British Expeditionary Force were fighting in Eastern Norway against the Germans advancing from Oslo: the Norwegian Legation in Stockholm said that 'what was presumably a mobile column' had already reached Lake Mjösa, forty-seven miles north-east of Oslo. British units had therefore already travelled nearly two hundred miles across Norway from their place of disembarkation. The news-starved Press speculated and the news-starved public speculated even more—both Press and public were convinced that the British were within striking distance of Oslo, and it was stated positively that Hamar had been recaptured. It was mentioned that 'two stations on the railway they might have used, Dombaas and Lillehammer' had been bombed by the Germans—'presumably in an attempt to hold them up'. Somehow or other these stories give the impression of troops entraining in parade-ground style at some sort of Clapham Junction with a few German puffballs being ineffectively dropped from the air. Very different indeed from the agony that was now descending on Dombaas, on Lillehammer, on every village up the Gudbrandsdal where the harried British might rest for a moment, on Molde, on Aandalsnes itself—until Norwegians became, with reason, almost panic-stricken at the sight of a battledress, lest it should bring retribution from the air down on their heads.

But it was not only Sickleforce—the intended southern half of the pincer movement on Trondheim—that was in trouble. Mauriceforce, the northern half, was in trouble too; and its trouble had begun on the very same day that Sickleforce had been transformed from an avenging host that was going to purify the soil of the Vikings, to an army in retreat.

We left Mauriceforce strung out perilously along the farthest shores of Trondheimsfiord and Beitstadfiord, road-bound, on the defensive, watched at leisure by George and Henry the Hun, while the ice on the fiords broke up.

On the morning of the 21st, at first light, a German cruiser and a smaller vessel were reported in the Beitstadfiord. Before long there were two hundred Germans ashore to the south of the British positions and before much longer another four hundred of them ashore to the north, dividing in two and advancing on the Lincolns who—since the Germans had not been obliging enough to land in the middle of their positions—could do nothing but watch. The Germans were equipped with skis and snowshoes and drew their mortars and machine-guns behind them on sledges. They would most certainly not be road-bound. Part of the Lincolns moved down the road in civilian lorries to meet the threat from the south but in a couple of miles they were within range of the Germans, whose fire made the road untenable. Floundering off it they took up position in some farm buildings and managed to hold on there until the evening. Then German incendiary bullets set fire to the hayloft and in minutes the whole farm was ablaze. Most of the Lincolns got away into the woods, but two sections were cut off and, having fired away every round they possessed, surrendered. Still floundering in the deep snow the others got as far as the little town of Vist, but enemy shells were already falling upon it and in a very short time Vist also was ablaze from end to end. In the flames went up not merely the wooden homesteads but all the Lincolns' spare clothing, rations and ammunition.

Now though these troops had been shown up naked and vulnerable at the first German attack, their line of retreat was still open to them. The Hallamshire Battalion was still intact and in the hills on their landward flank the Norwegians were still able to give them some little security against encirclement—although they themselves would not counter-attack because if they did so and failed they were positive they would find the way back closed behind them. Moreover they were all hopelessly short of ammunition and still waited with growing impatience for the British supplies they had expected. For the K.O.Y.L.I.—the most advanced battalion of all—the position was very much worse because they were threatened on three sides, and if they failed to keep contact with the rapidly retiring troops to the north of them they would most certainly be cut off. During the day Colonel Hibbert struggled to do two things at once—to hold the Germans on his front and to keep contact with the rest of the brigade in his rear. In both these tasks he failed, as he was bound to—not because of the strength of the Germans (who were barely equal in numbers to his own troops) but because under the conditions both movement and control were as near impossible as makes no difference. The troops could not deploy because they were tied to the road: they could not move with any coherence or speed on the road because there was not sufficient transport to move them in one piece; and in any case the only means of getting orders to the scattered companies and platoons was by runners struggling along on foot. In the midst of it all 'George' buzzed around in his leisurely fashion, carefully observing every movement, which was thus more or less checkmated before it could begin to be carried out. By nightfall the K.O.Y.L.I. and the Norwegians on their front were still intact, but the Germans had a firm grip on the road both to the north and the south of them and counter-attack along the road was impossible because it was sealed off by superior enemy fire they had no artillery to answer. As it was getting dark orders came through to them from Brigade to hold on to their positions that night and withdraw in the morning: but this was a very ill-considered order, because under the watchful eye of the German aircraft no movement by day could possibly escape detection and a fighting withdrawal in conditions where the troops could barely stand up and only walk with difficulty was unthinkable.

Carton de Wiart had hurried south at the first news of the German attack and at once saw that the only course open to the Brigade was to withdraw as rapidly as possible—if indeed it was not already too late for them to withdraw at all. It was no good—as he had known all along it would be no good. If the attack on Trondheim was not coming (he did not yet know Hammer was cancelled) these light forces could not stand on their own. If there was to be no air support they were defenceless. And he was not going to leave them there like sitting rabbits. He had no troops to put into the line to safeguard their retreat except for the Chasseurs Alpins—whose skis had now arrived, but in a condition that made them quite unusable, so that their mobility was just as restricted as that of the British troops. Where the force could retire to was a secondary problem, but one that would have to be faced before many hours were up: it was a long road back to their base. If they could be got there the base offered them no security, for it was already constantly being blitzed from the air and it was impossible for ships to berth except in the few short hours of the decreasing night. As if to emphasize the danger and hasten his decision the Germans started bombing the town of Steinkjer behind the threatened battalion; and this, with its road and rail bridges, offered the only major crossing place in the little neck of land between the fiords on one side and the lakes on the other.

Here, then, darkness at last came down on the night of Sunday

21st—while at home in Britain and all over the world people were hopefully speculating on the extent of the British advance in Norway. To the south the K.O.Y.L.I., still in one piece, with few casualties as yet but ready for 'chopping' as soon as daylight made movement possible again. North of them the Lincolns, mauled and already depleted. North of these again the Hallamshire Battalion not yet in action but expecting action any moment— the more so because local rumour had it very definitely that the two forward battalions had been completely annihilated. The Hallamshires watched through the night and in its strange, macabre way the night was not without its humours. A report of enemy light machine-gun fire turned out to be a Norwegian chopping firewood, and noises that were positively identified as Germans digging a mortar position turned out on investigation to be caused by some civilians pulling a cow out of a snow-drift: Norwegian cows, it seemed, were no more snow-proof than British troops.

The Germans made no further move after dark. Over the whole of this campaign the Germans fought and moved by day and rested by night. They may have been determined to keep their men fresh—they may have been doubtful about committing to night action in difficult country troops of whose quality they were uncertain. The same for that matter is largely true of their air force—which only in the final stages of the battle followed up its daytime bombing attacks on the bases by blitz at night. By night, therefore, there was a little respite, but not much chance of recovery. Dawn would bring first George and Henry the Hun doing their morning rounds almost to a timetable, and following George and Henry would come the bombers, the shelling, mortaring and machine-gunning and the German infantry.

So it happened. With first light the undamaged Hallamshire Battalion was withdrawn well to the north to hold a line on which the other two battalions could withdraw, if they could make it. All morning the Lincolns attempted to stand, to safeguard the retreating K.O.Y.L.I. in front of them—vain hope, because the Germans had already driven a wedge between them. The enemy were in the woods all around them. Pressure built up from hour to hour, with mortar and heavy machine-gun fire and light artillery. Not long after noon they were ordered to withdraw:

as a matter of fact the order had been given several hours before, but it took all this time for it to reach the battalion. In the midst of all the techniques of modern war orders were being transmitted by the methods of the Dark Ages—except that in the Dark Ages a runner might at least have had a horse.

Withdrawing was more easily said than done. Time and again aircraft came sweeping low and machine-gunning. They caused few casualties, but the demoralizing effect they produced can only be truly understood by those who have experienced it, and every time they came the troops would scatter and lie in the deep snow till they had gone. Steinkjer—their only means of crossing the river to the line the Hallamshires were now holding—was now burning, as Namsos had burned: its people had fled, the railway was out of action, the railway bridge was breached. But the road bridge was still in one piece. Part of the Lincolns got there and, hurrying across, struggled on for three miles farther before they felt it safe to rest. Rest could not be long—they could see the Austrian mountain troops advancing into the burning town, drawing their mortars, machine-guns and mountain-guns comfortably on sledges. At this point they managed to find enough lorries to take them on through the darkness another fourteen miles.

But some two hundred of them did not get the withdrawal order until even later in the afternoon—brought by a company runner crawling on his hands and knees in the snow. They abandoned their Bren tripods, their boxes of ammunition—they even discarded their steel helmets to avoid recognition from the air. And, of course, they abandoned their fantastic Arctic kit. Then they joined hands and so stumbled away in file as darkness came down upon them. The crawling runner had brought with him a fairly accurate map. With this and a compass to guide them, as well as the beacon of burning Steinkjer ahead for a guide, they plodded up the mountainside, too weary even to curse their lot. By three o'clock in the morning they had made good a mere one and a half miles and were worn out. They found a barn and rested there.

The K.O.Y.L.I. were now well and truly out on a limb. All Colonel Hibbert knew of the position to the north of him was that the brigade was withdrawing and now might already be leagues away. All his companies were under attack. They were dispersed and out of touch. Somehow or other he must disengage and concentrate them—and what then? The road to Steinkjer was barred to him—in any case the Germans would be in Steinkjer by now. Certainly the Germans were to the west and the south of him. To the north of him was the Ogna river with no bridge marked on his ancient map east of Steinkjer. To the east of him there was a roadless country of mountain, forest and snow: some sixty miles in that direction was the Swedish border—it might have been the moon. He might stay and fight it out—with what result was obvious to the blindest eye, since even if he could keep the battalion intact, food and ammunition would soon both be exhausted. He might, on the other hand, get his men out to fight again in a less one-sided battle. Somehow or other he must take to the country and get across the Ogna river.

He did manage to disengage and he did manage to concentrate his troops: had they been in the condition in which he had originally found them not many months before, both would have been impossible for a start. With him at this point there were two companies, A and D—both intact save for one platoon of A Company which, cut off from the main body, had attempted to make contact with the Lincolns but was mopped up. Having concentrated them, he withdrew off the road to his eastern flank—an operation which, his regimental historian points out, is not mentioned in any textbook. The enemy missed them and, like a posse of Keystone Cops in a silent film comedy, pressed on up the road towards Steinkjer. With any luck, he might yet gather the whole battalion together.

This, then, was the sorry pass to which British forces in central Norway had been reduced by the night of 22nd April. Although they had been ready to move the day before the invasion of Norway broke, it had taken a good ten days to get them there. After no more than four days in the country they were in full retreat on both their fronts—both the jaws of the pincers that had been intended to nip the Germans in Trondheim off from both retreat and reinforcement had been broken. 146 Brigade was in retreat from what was really no more than a desperate German sortie from Trondheim, in numbers no greater than their own but irresistible in face of their own lack of artillery, air support and even the means of movement. But their comrades of Sickleforce were in much direr straits—split in two by the lake and the river Laagen with the whole of the main German attack from the south bearing up rapidly upon and all around them. Facing them was not merely retreat, not merely hardship, but a real threat of positive annihilation; and while around Namsos the Norwegian forces were still intact and had hardly been in action, on the Gudbrandsdal front the failure of the exhausted British to stand for just a brief space while the two big Norwegian groups still to the west of them got across the river would mean surrender or annihilation for the Norwegians too. Still not very far north of them the hunted Norwegian King and Cabinet, with the precious burden of Norwegian gold, was in desperate danger too. Should these be captured, the last visible symbol of Norwegian resistance would be erased and the German *blitzkrieg* on Norway would be complete.

Yet while all this was going on the best trained troops—the only likely troops we had so far sent to Norway, were still doing virtually nothing. All the arguments between the Earl of Cork and General Mackesy had come to nothing. The weather deteriorated: Mackesy persisted in his long, ponderous plan for a slow advance through the difficult country and around the complex system of fiords, to encircle Narvik by land; and even the urgent pleas for action from London would not move him from it. In the beleaguered town the Germans had recovered their morale long since and were making it very clear to the stubborn citizens that though they might have come in the guise of protectors there was nothing benevolent about their protection. Rations were short: life was grim and already much of the modern workings and installations that had brought prosperity to the town after many years of hardship had been destroyed. Why, they asked themselves, would the British not come?

Relations with General Fleischer had deteriorated rapidly when it became clear to him that the British were not moving in. Two incidents illustrate—as small things often illustrate—the suspicion and distrust that arose between the British and Norwegian forces at this time and in this part of the country. The two companies of Scots Guards on the mainland were the nearest to the German units whom Fleischer was holding desperately at bay while he strove to organize his counter-attack. These, from time to time, had minor contact with German patrols and, suffering from the universal difficulty of the British over moving in the country, obtained the local co-operation of some small local detachments of Norwegian troops. When the Norwegian Command heard about this (according to the Guards' history) they were withdrawn—the Guards were told that the Norwegians were there to defend their own homes and not the Allied troops. Yet when these same Guards were later placed in support of the first Norwegian attack the Norwegian accounts point out bitterly and pointedly that they were assigned for defensive purposes only.

In an effort to get some action into the situation at Narvik the War Cabinet decided on the 20th that the Earl of Cork should assume supreme command of all the forces in that area: no doubt it was remembered that it was he who had vainly ordered the immediate occupation of Narvik on the first arrival of the British forces, hoping and indeed assuming that Mackesy would fall in with his views. But it was too late to put the clock back. Only a few days had passed but many things had happened—most of all perhaps the deterioration in the weather which now offered to the Germans all the help and to the Guards Brigade all the perils that Mackesy had argued in support of his own delaying tactics; in any case, in supreme command or not, Cork saw the enormous difficulties of forcing the military commander into action which was against all his wishes and inclinations and which he would obviously not pursue with any enthusiasm. The time for putting Cork in supreme command would have been in those brief hours of opportunity following on *Warspite*'s attack, when Rupertforce had first arrived. To use that phrase so beloved of Mr. Chamberlain, the War Cabinet had missed the 'bus.

So only the Navy continued on the offensive in the Arctic waters. There would never be a repetition of Warburton-Lee's tempestuous daring nor of the splendid hours when Whitworth's destroyers, guns ablaze and torpedo tubes in action, had stormed their way to the utmost limits of the mountain-girt waters, with *Warspite* booming away in their midst as though she were Churchill himself. But there was what the naval reports call 'continuous harassing in a smaller way' by detached squadrons of cruisers and destroyers as they were available. There were no more targets afloat for them, but there were targets ashore, as the Germans strove to set up gun sites and defensive positions against the attack which they had told the Norwegians would never come but which, to them, in their weakened and besieged state, seemed an inevitability from an enemy in full possession of his senses. These harassing attacks were only one of a formidable

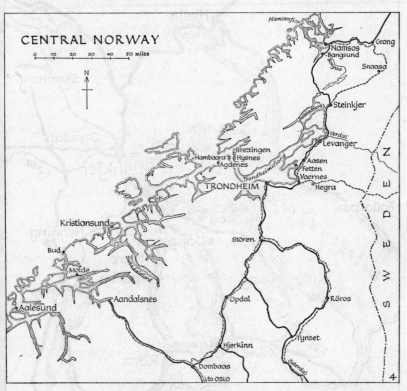

catalogue of chores that fell to the Navy's lot—fetching and carrying troops and supplies, bringing in supply ships, establishing their own permanent base at Skaanland and guarding their damaged ships at Skjelfiord. Above all there was the job of providing as well as they could for the anti-aircraft defence both of themselves and of the troops ashore; for there were still no shore-based fighters and still only a mere handful of light anti-aircraft

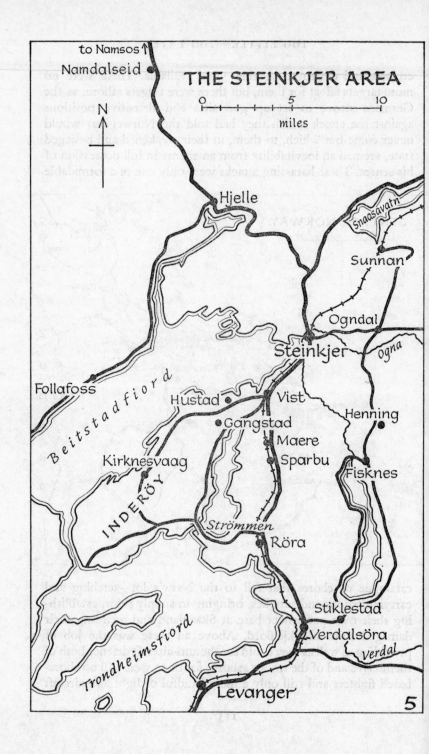

THE STEINKJER AREA

to Namsos ↑
Namdalseid

N

0   5   10
miles

Hjelle

Snaasavatn

Sunnan

Ogndal

Steinkjer

Ogna

Follafoss

Beitstadfiord

Hustad

Vist

Henning

Gangstad

Maere

Kirknesvaag

Sparbu

Fisknes

INDERÖY

Strömmen

Röra

Stiklestad

Verdalsöra

Verdal

Trondheimsfiord

Levanger

5

guns, and the raids were continuous. Movement in and around the whole area was always under air bombardment—every movement and every suggested operation, however small, had to take into account the constant bombing raids which had become part and parcel of day-to-day life. The deadly dive-bombers had not yet come, nor would come until bases nearer to the Arctic Circle fell into German hands—but while the high-level bombers were much less effective and in particular caused few casualties on land, they were a constant affliction and a constant threat to morale, for defencelessness against any form of air attack is not a condition to which people become either accustomed or reconciled. But the air attacks—even high-level air attacks—were much more dangerous to ships on the water than they were to troops on shore: troops could scatter and take cover, but ships were compact and convenient targets which could not go to ground. As elsewhere, one of the unforeseen ways in which they provided air defence for the Army was by attracting the enemy's attention to themselves. *Ark Royal* and *Glorious* were hurrying north from the Mediterranean—they reached Scapa Flow on the 23rd—and they would have fighters to put in the air, although the usefulness of these would be limited by the fact that the carriers themselves were sitting targets and had to operate well out to sea. There were still the naval aircraft from the Orkneys, which could make brief appearances between the long flight out and the long flight home. Naval personnel were also endeavouring to find what possible landing grounds there might be under the snow, ice and slush for land-based aircraft when they could get there: the Navy would have to ferry those across as well. The Navy could, with some justification, feel that every bit of dirty work that was going fell to its lot—largely because it was the only service which had the means of doing anything at all. The immense amount of steaming, shooting, fetching, carrying and everything else shows up vividly in the naval reports of the time. Most hard-worked of all were the Navy's maids-of-all-work, the destroyers: *Electra* reported on 8th May that she was at more than half an hour's notice for the first time since 8th April, while in the later stages of the campaign *Fame* claimed to have had steam on her main engines continuously for nearly four weeks.

But there was a shortage of destroyers. Indeed, there was a

0   5   10 miles

Dovre

Molde

Rosti gorge

Heidal

Rudi

Otta

Aandalsnes

Kjörem

Veblungsnes

Kvam

Setnesmoen

Vinstra

Verma

Ringebu

Romsdal

Rauma

Gudbrandsdal

Laagen

Lesjaskog

Gausdal

Tretten

L.Lesjaskog

Tolstad

Öyer

Faaberg

Bridge

Balbergkamp

Lillehammer

Dombaas

Nykirke

Biri

Mjösa

Dovre

Braastad

6

shortage of naval craft of all sizes from battleships and aircraft carriers downwards. It was a shortage which was soon to become greater, for in not much more than a matter of days, signs of the coming of Hitler's offensive on the Western Front—which we now know had been planned to follow the Norwegian adventure at the interval of one month—were becoming as plain as the prelude to a thunderstorm, so that every ship that could be spared as well as many that could not would have to be withdrawn for duty elsewhere.

It was but one portent of the fact that time in Norway was running out. It was running out not only for the virtually immobilized forces at Narvik: it was running out for the sketchy units reeling from the main German attack up the Gudbrandsdal and retreating from the sortie out of Trondheim. It was running out for the Norwegian forces who had held out too long and too desperately in the south for the reinforcements, supplies and ammunition that alone could save them and their country—for the Norwegians round Trondheim conserving their few battalions and their meagre store of shot and shell to support an Allied attack that was long overdue. It was running out even for General Fleischer's division north of Narvik who were holding the Germans at bay until they should be strong enough and well-armed enough to drive them into the fiords or over the Swedish border. Indeed, time was running out.

CHAPTER 9

MEN WITHOUT WINGS

BUT even as time ran out the old wishful thinking and the old committee-fathered changes of objective and plan were still in evidence. Wishful thinking arrived at King Haakon's hiding place on the disastrous 21st April in the person of Admiral Sir Edward Evans—who had won great distinction as Evans of the Broke, a survivor of Scott's last expedition to the South Pole and well known to the Norwegians: he was worthy of a better mission. He had originally been appointed to command the naval forces in the ill-conceived British plan for an assault on Norway to forestall the Germans. When that petered out, with the disgruntled troops marooned on the quayside and the cruisers careering off to sea, he had been appointed to the military mission to Sweden and had now been sent on a personal errand to Norway as part of the process of 'putting heart into the Norwegians'. He, too, appears to have been ignorant of the abandonment of Operation Hammer, because he positively assured both King Haakon and General Ruge that the direct assault on Trondheim by the Navy would start that day: he is said also—according to the official historian—to have talked of a first instalment of 40,000 Allied troops.

There was never any likelihood of 40,000 troops; but at this time there was yet another change of thinking at home and a fleeting attempt to revive something that looked very like the ghost of the deceased Operation Hammer. This never came anywhere near to being really put into effect. It had a twilight life of perhaps four days. Once more it included a direct bombardment of Trondheim, the landing of regular troops, to be withdrawn from France, the bombing of airfields to keep the German bombers on the ground, and the establishment of land-based fighters in Norway. It also involved the appointment of yet another general to command the whole of the forces south of

Trondheim, Major-General Paget. He had originally been sent north in a hurry when Berney-Ficklin was put out of the running by his air crash, to take charge of the troops in Operation Hammer: when Hammer was cancelled, so was his appointment—now he was appointed all over again and his brief, in fact, was to revive the dying embers of the fire that was to have encircled Trondheim, link up Mauriceforce and Sickleforce and stop the German advance.

Paget was a most able officer. A completely different sort of officer from Carton de Wiart—an ex-commandant of the Staff College, an outstanding administrator, a good tactician and an irrepressible personality. General Ruge and his staff would take to him, and his indisputable personal honesty in the handling of relations with the Norwegians would ameliorate some at least of the bitterness that inevitably arose when failure had to be admitted and the withdrawal came. Carton de Wiart in the north and Paget in the south, both given adequate forces and the minimum tools of their trade, could have accomplished all that was needed: as it was, the only achievement the fates granted to Paget was a skilful withdrawal in very difficult circumstances which saved many men to fight again—and one fresh regular brigade, which made it possible for him to accomplish this.

The withdrawal of 15 Brigade from France has already been mentioned. It consisted of the 1st Battalion, the York and Lancaster Regiment, the 1st Battalion, the King's Own Yorkshire Light Infantry and the 1st Battalion, the Green Howards, commanded by Lieutenant-Colonel Robinson. All three were units of regulars with a very high standard of training, but the Green Howards, by good fortune, were a battalion of quite exceptional quality, with a tremendous tradition and colossal confidence. This is how their regimental historian proudly describes them:

'Men from the Dales, from the rich central plain of York: men from the mines of Cleveland and from the industrial town of Middlesbrough, from the market towns of Thirsk and Northallerton and from the seaside towns of Scarborough, Redcar, Whitby and Bridlington. . . .'

This was the 'Green Howard Family'. They were troops who

had seen action, for they had only returned from Palestine in the spring of 1939, and their commanding officer had served in the First World War. For some of the winter of the Phoney War they had been in the Maginot Line: in turn with the other two battalions in the Brigade they had spent some weeks out of these sheltered fortifications in the Saar Valley, living hard in the snow of that severe winter. To some extent, therefore, they were a little conditioned for what they were to find in Norway; but Major-General Robinson (as he now is) is convinced that even more important was their experience in the almost guerrilla warfare of Palestine. Palestine, as he puts it, was 'a section commander's war': indeed, their brief campaign in Norway, with its lack of communications as well as everything else, called for this kind of experience to the utmost.

On 17th April, 15 Brigade was withdrawn from France in both secrecy and mystery. As part of the usual preparation for the Norwegian débâcle they were ordered to leave all their carefully tended transport behind—and a very great wrench it was. They were whisked rapidly across the Channel and at Dover hustled off virtually under guard into a special train—if the rest of the preparations had been as good as the security arrangements all would have been very well indeed. The train took them via Didcot northwards and at Rotherham in the midst of their own country there was a halt. There was a certain opening of lavatory windows and a certain mysterious melting away of men; but with equal mystery they all melted back again before the train went, and there were no absentees. They bedded down for the night and morning found them first at Edinburgh and then at Dunfermline, where a little Scottish staff officer, complete with kilt and sporran, made an enormous fuss over their detraining and caused immense and ribald joy to the troops. In the transit camp (where the unfortunate Territorials had spent their days in limbo not so long before) they met the Canadian troops and were regaled with gruesome rumours about a death-or-glory assault on Trondheim. They were issued with Arctic hats, then, to confound the rumour-mongers, with topees. Then sealed orders arrived. Upon the staff officers of the Brigade the horrible truth burst: it was Operation Hammer, and they did not feel called upon to be enthusiastic about it.

At least there was no nonsense this time about an unopposed landing. 15 Brigade arranged its stores and equipment as the Guards of 24 Brigade had done—everything in one-man loads, everything ready to be moved by hand. Tanks and artillery there were none—neither was there transport. There would be virtually no signals equipment beyond Brigade H.Q., nor any medical services forward of base. There was certainly no air cover, though the force commander was now being told optimistically of a squadron of Gladiator fighters to be based on a frozen lake. There would be anti-aircraft ships and two carriers off-shore. In theory, one light and one heavy anti-aircraft battery was to accompany the Brigade: little was seen of the former and the disembarkation of the latter proved quite impossible.

The abandonment of Operation Hammer caused very little change in these preparations. It caused a delay of a couple of days, during which the Canadians faded from the picture and that mysterious entity, 147 Brigade, was once more prevented from entering it. It did, as a matter of course, result in the usual confusion over ships, the loading of them and the apportionment of men and stores in them: it was not until the 22nd that the first units of the Brigade were on their way in three destroyers (which only sixty-six men each) and the cruiser *Birmingham*— a proposal that they should march to Rosyth having been firmly resisted and eventually abandoned in favour of S.M.T. 'buses. Paget and the second flight (which included the Green Howards) would not be on the way for another two days—by which time Paget's orders would be even more out of date than they were when they were first written and the only rôle left for these first-class regulars to play would be the stopping of the victorious German army groups for long enough to allow of the withdrawal of the shattered Territorials and themselves. For on the 22nd, in fact, the fate of the campaign south of Trondheim was being decided.

We left 148 Brigade—or rather the split-up and scattered portions of the one and a half battalions with which 148 Brigade had started the battle—being relentlessly pushed up the Gudbrandsdal Valley; those on the east relentlessly harried by the Germans, those on the west, together with the two Norwegian groups, falling back to keep pace. This western portion still needed to recross the river: the last point at which it could do so would be at Tretten, now not very far to the north. If it failed to recross, it would be cut off from the base completely.

Inevitably, in reading the official accounts, these small points along the valley at which attempts were made to stand—Biri, Aasmarke, the Balbergkamp and so on—read like a series of small individual actions. In fact they were part of a continuous process —a process of withdrawal and disintegration which had started with the troops being lightly equipped and ended with them in possession of nothing but the clothes on their backs and the rifles in their hands.

The attempt to hold the river crossing between Faaberg and the Balbergkamp had collapsed almost before the half-battalion of Leicesters and the half-battalion of Foresters had got into position: it was in the course of their withdrawal from it that King-Salter and General Hvinden Haug had met the cold, exhausted and hungry troops fleeing northwards in their lorries. Öyer—from which General Ruge had withdrawn his headquarters the previous night—was but half a mile behind them—and here there was a position with a good field of fire, where they might once more endeavour to make a stand. Hopeless now, but still obeying orders with weary acquiescence, the men were got into position there by the Leicesters' C.O., Lieutenant-Colonel German. They were heavily bombed as they climbed from their vehicles: two sticks of bombs fell right among them, and though they caused little damage and few casualties, the effect on these exhausted and demoralized Territorials was very serious. They might have broken altogether at this point, had not the remaining half-battalion of Leicesters arrived, hurried straight from their disembarkation at Aandalsnes along a line of communication which was now being constantly straffed from the air. It was difficult to see what difference they could make, but their coming raised morale a little. Three light anti-aircraft guns—the only three to appear at all in this sector of the campaign—followed them as far as Otta, but were brought no farther: by the time they got there, there was no more point in trying.

King-Salter busied himself helping to recover transport from which the Norwegian civilian drivers had fled. Then he went in search of Hvinden Haug once more, to see what more could be done, and found him waiting for the German aircraft to go home for the night before moving his headquarters back. He repeated that the British troops, whatever state they were in, must stand that night and the following day, so that their companies to the west of the river and the Norwegians beyond them could get across the bridge at Tretten. Here is his own account of the hours that followed—a rare, eye-witness description of 148 Brigade's last, lonely action in Tretten Gorge, with which this book opened. A forgotten action in a forgotten campaign, fought by troops whose plight and whose condition was an indictment of the nation that had sent them there, wishfully magnifying them into a fully equipped and conquering army:

'I passed these orders on, and a little after dark was on my way back to General Ruge when I passed Lieutenant-Colonel Ford, commanding the Sherwood Foresters, moving to the new position at the head of some of his battalion. He spoke to me and asked me urgently to represent at Headquarters that our troops were not capable of holding the position on the next day. It should be pointed out here that most of our troops had had several nights without sleep and many of them had apparently not received their rations. They had come across from England in a rough sea, had travelled straight down by night a distance of some two hundred miles and some of them had to go straight into action, being harassed by the German Air Force on the way. Many also had had a terrible night's march through the mountains. They were simply rifle companies with no artillery, tanks or aircraft to support them. Consequently I agreed to take his message. I found General Ruge at his new H.Q. near Ringebue about midnight and told him that our troops could not hold the position next day. He replied at once that they must hold it, because otherwise the whole of the Norwegian force on the west of the lake would be cut off. Their only way back was across a bridge at Tretten two miles behind the position that he had ordered must be held. He then made me an urgent appeal (though obviously I was absolutely ready to do what he asked) to go forward again at once and ensure that the troops did hold the position. I said that I would, and he shook hands with me. I stopped a short time at his Headquarters to get some food; and then Brigadier Morgan appeared —possibly about one a.m. on the 23rd. It will be remembered that he was not in operational command of his troops but he had been visiting them and he came back with exactly the same comment as I had brought, that they were too exhausted to hold the position the next day. General Ruge held a conference and Brigadier Morgan agreed, as I had, that our troops must try to hold it. Brigadier Morgan wanted to go forward to Lieutenant-Colonel German himself but General Ruge wished me to do this as I knew the position which it was required to hold, having taken the orders from the Norwegian staff officer the previous evening. Brigadier Morgan was to go and see General Hvinden-Haug and urge him to collect Norwegian troops to help. General Ruge was also very anxious that Brigadier Morgan should meet the fresh British troops reported to be landing on the 23rd at Aandalsnes, under Brigadier Morgan's command until General Paget arrived, and bring them south.

'I accordingly went forward again almost immediately after the conclusion of the conference. I found a number of the British troops at Tretten and gave orders for all fit to fight—including personnel of Brigade H.Q.—to move south again into the forest; and I was told that Lieutenant-Colonel German was with the outposts on the south edge of the forest. It was now perhaps 0500 hours. I then went on to see him and found him in the front line of the outposts. He had had some fighting in the night. It was decided he should remain where he was as long as he could while I went back and reconnoitred the position in the forest in front of the mountain saddle and helped our troops to occupy it. I alone had a map.

'Lieutenant-Colonel German gave orders for a company he had in reserve to move to the position; and I went back and began to reconnoitre it. Its strength lay in a high spur jutting out from the main ridge and precipitous on the side facing the enemy's advance. Apart from the main road at the foot of the spur and in its immediate vicinity, there were only two passes over the spur. Its weakness was that it was closely wooded, except on the actual precipitous slopes, and except for a very narrow open stretch up the re-entrant at its foot, giving a field of fire sometimes of less than one hundred yards—too little in the absence of trenches and wire. The Norwegians had made an emplacement by the road and had done some clearance of field of fire.

'Seeing that some of the troops had now arrived, I went down again so as to start as soon as possible getting some into position, in accordance with what I had agreed with Lieutenant-Colonel German. There was a little delay, however, as units and sub-units were mixed and had to be re-organized. As each sub-unit was ready it was sent up the re-entrant to me and I allotted it its area. I addressed the men of some of these sub-units and told them how important it was for them to hold this position. I had not yet reconnoitred farther up the re-entrant, where there appeared to be no open ground at all. The company commander who was to be on the left (i.e. east flank, high up the re-entrant) now came with me to reconnoitre. We had to go farther and farther trying to find a suitable position to cover the left flank; the ground had now flattened and we were on a wooded plateau. There had been no time to get a covering party and I momentarily expected to meet German ski patrols. At last the forest came to an end and we got a fairly good field of fire over the plateau covering the left flank. Returning down the mountain we met his company on its way up. Going on down, I met Major Roberts, 2 i/c of the Sherwood Foresters. He had been commanding the half-battalion Sherwood Foresters, operating on the west side of the lake. During the night his two companies had been brought back to Tretten (two or three miles north of our present position). He told me he had left one company holding the bridge-head at Tretten facing west and the other company was spare. I said that I would send it up.

'I was thankful that we had got the troops on the ground in time; but I was worried because there was no wire and they had no tools— even if it had been possible to dig in this frozen, rocky ground. With the short field of fire, in places there being no open ground at all, the danger of infiltration was great. The steeply rising ground in rear made movement of reserves within the position extremely difficult. It was a case of having "everything in the shop window". The position however seemed absolutely tank-proof, the road being the only possible route for tanks. In the absence of tools or mines there seemed to be no possibility in the time available of making an anti-tank block on the road unless we had sacrificed one of the few coaches for carrying personnel, which perhaps we should have done. The Norwegians had promised a company to help in this position but it had not arrived. A Norwegian motor machine-gun unit was sent up, however, and occupied the two passes high up on the precipitous spur. I do not know at what time they got into position.

'I went back to Tretten—at perhaps about 1000 hours—intending to send forward the other company to Major Roberts, to inform General Ruge that the position was occupied, and to try and arrange for protection of the left, or east, flank from the Tretten side of the high spur; because I was still not satisfied that that flank was adequately protected and an approach through the deep snow over the plateau was more direct than the line of the road which went round two sides of a triangle. I sent forward Major Roberts' spare company, telling them, as Major Roberts had asked me to do, to drop one platoon to give depth to the defences on the road itself. While looking for a telephone I met a Norwegian staff officer (Colonel Beichmann) who promised to pass my message to General Ruge; and then I motored up a mountain road above Tretten to reconnoitre; but found that owing to the forest it was very difficult to do anything to protect that flank adequately. Eventually I decided to post a small party of troops on the eastern outskirts of Tretten where they could oppose, across some open snow-covered fields, any attempt to attack Tretten from over the mountains. While this party was being organized from some of the H.Q. company troops still in Tretten, I had some dinner which they offered me.

'Shortly afterwards I again happened to meet the Norwegian staff officer and with him the O.C. norwegian motor machine-gun unit. They were both extremely anxious lest the enemy should be working up the west bank of the valley, on the other side of the river or lake, and asked me if I could send some troops southwards on that side. I was surprised, as I had assumed the forces on the west bank were responsible on that side. The river was in many places so wide as to resemble a lake. When receiving this request from the Norwegians, I was uncertain whether to take action, not knowing if Lieutenant-Colonel German was back yet or if Brigadier Morgan had resumed control now that his units were together again; I felt that I had accomplished the special task which I had been given. But the Norwegians were very insistent and I agreed to act. They sent a Norwegian officer with me to find a local guide and I motored to the west side of the Tretten bridge where I found Major Kirkland, at perhaps about 1400 hours, holding a bridge-head with his company (one of the two which had been under Major Roberts on the west of the lake). I explained to him what was required and he agreed to take his company one or two miles south down the west side of the valley. Dinners were to be served soon and I told him to wait until the men were fed; a difficult decision because it seemed of great urgency for him to move without any delay.

'I then decided to revisit the defensive position. I had heard no firing whatsoever and as it was by now about three o'clock I was feeling very hopeful; and the shock was very great when about half a mile south of Tretten at the entrance to the forest I met some stragglers, utterly exhausted, who told me that German tanks had just broken through their position. An R.E. officer, Major M. R. Jefferies, was with me, who had earlier been carrying out demolitions on his own. I sent him back in my car to warn the troops at Tretten of what had happened.

'More men appeared, all with the same story. There were some felled trees at that point and some of the men helped me to make an improvised tank obstacle. All this time—about fifteen minutes—I felt that I ought perhaps to go forward to see what the situation was and to help if I could. I always remembered that it was vitally important to hold the position all day if the forces on the west bank were to be saved. Then an officer, I think an I.O. called Barratt, arrived with a message for the commander of the forward troops to hold their position until 2000 hours. I felt that he must go on with his message and decided to go with him. An officer called Bradley who came up at that moment volunteered to come with us. We three then walked up the road, each carrying a rifle. We had gone about three-quarters of a mile through the forest when, on approaching a bend, we heard shots just round it, some of which passed over us. As we had been prepared to meet tanks at any moment we immediately ran into the forest and lay down in a slight depression about twenty yards from the road, but in full view of it. The snow had melted here and we were not conspicuous. A few seconds later we could hear tanks; and we then lay motionless, momentarily expecting to be discovered, as we watched the German tanks and infantry go by.

'From now until the 27th I was behind the German lines, but before describing what happened to me during that time, I will give a short account, as I know it, of the general events that followed that afternoon of 23rd April. When I sent Major Jefferies back to Tretten, I told him to try and get hold of Major Kirkland's company if it had not already started off. I have subsequently met Major Kirkland who tells me that he did receive fresh orders and that these orders were to take one and a half platoons to the east bank and go forward and "deal with a German tank which had broken through and broken down!" He came up the road with his one and a half platoons shortly after us and encountered the German advance just inside the forest. The Germans were halted and Major Kirkland saw them first and deployed an anti-tank rifle and a Bren gun, to engage the leading German tank and the infantry section immediately behind it. He opened surprise fire but the German tank came on notwithstanding and Major Kirkland's troops were overrun. He himself was wounded and captured, and lost a leg. The Germans then proceeded to bombard Tretten heavily both with 6-inch infantry guns and from the air, and with machine-guns which had worked forward on the other side of the water. Eventually they advanced on Tretten and captured it. The garrison of Tretten can only have consisted of those men who had been too exhausted to be put into the defensive position earlier in the day, and of the remainder of Major Kirkland's company, and of various H.Q. details. After capturing Tretten the Germans pushed on some miles, before being checked by Norwegian troops at Faavang.

'As a result of the failure to hold the forest position the whole of the Norwegian force on the west bank was cut off. I have heard from a member of that force, subsequently, that their Commander, Colonel Dahl, tried to get his troops back into the main valley, over the snow-covered mountains. He was, however, unable to succeed unless he abandoned his transport, which he did not wish to do. He accordingly returned towards the main valley but was kept away from it by German troops, including tanks. Colonel Dahl's force remained bottled up in the mountains in this area until it received orders from General Ruge to surrender about the 3rd or 4th May, i.e. after our troops had left Aandalsnes.

'I am not clear as to exactly how the breakthrough in the forest position occurred. It would appear that the German tanks were not stopped by our anti-tank rifles and that they succeeded in forcing an entry into the position down the road. Infantry followed and the troops higher up the re-entrant had their position turned and were cut off. Many of them got away into the mountains. Most of these were eventually captured but some reached Sweden. At the end of that day there was virtually nothing left of the two battalions of the 148th Infantry Brigade as a fighting force. They had tried to carry out a vital task which we had thought was beyond their powers, exhausted as they were, and completely lacking in artillery, tanks or aircraft; and the enemy in fact proved too strong for them.'

The British troops on the west of the river had actually succeeded in reaching the bridge in time to cross after the long night detour in open lorries over ice-covered roads. They had not been seriously engaged from start to finish although, like all the rest of the troops, they were completely exhausted. Even with them, when the remnants were assembled at the Heidal after that last night flight from Tretten, there were but nine officers left all told—five of the Leicesters and four of the Sherwood Foresters—and three hundred men. These were split up into parties of fifty or so to make their way back to Aandalsnes the best way they could: the railway north of Dombaas was now wrecked beyond repairing and there was little or no road transport still available—most of the journey would be on foot. At Aandalsnes that very day the first instalment of the regulars had landed to reinforce 148 Brigade, which as a fighting unit had ceased to exist.

King-Salter saw nothing of this, for with all the advance troops who had been cut off he was behind the German lines. His appointment as Military Attaché was at an end: he had done a good job and, like the troops, might have done a better one had he had the means of doing it. His story of the three and a half days that followed is not inappropriate because it is typical of so many stories that can be told—some of them ending in escape. After several narrow escapes, which included being fired at from point-blank range, he and those with him got up the mountain, collected some more men, found a car, nearly ran into the Germans again, abandoned the car and took to the woods—coming under almost point-blank fire again for the second time that day. During the following three and a half days they tried to march round the flank of the Germans to get back to the brigade: the party steadily grew, until by the evening of the 24th they were about ten officers and eighty other ranks. Everyone was now completely exhausted from lack of food and sleep and many of the troops had lost their arms—although he notes that two stout-hearted men still carried their Bren guns. On the second day they found an impassable peak in their path and had to make a wide detour over the mountains away from the valley; but that night they managed to lie up in an empty mountain hotel together with some Norwegian soldiers. During all this time they could still hear firing in the distance, receding: they were still sufficiently conscious of what they were supposed to be about to wonder whether perhaps they could not stage a raid on the German lines of communication—but there was little that exhausted men with few arms and practically no ammunition could hope to do, and they thought better of it.

The mountain hotel was at the very edge of King-Salter's map— the only one—but a young Norwegian on skis who had appeared during the night offered to guide them. The country in front of them was becoming increasingly mountainous—their choice lay between going over open mountains, which the men had not the strength to tackle and where they would show up for miles against the snow to any German aircraft that might pass overhead—and following the upper tracks in the valley, which at some points, forced in by the mountains, descended close to the valley where the Germans were bound to be. It would have to be the track. At a fork in the road King-Salter, with a small advance party, got separated from the Leicesters' commanding officer, Lieutenant-Colonel German, and the main body with him, so that the larger and the smaller parties took different ways. And to cut a long

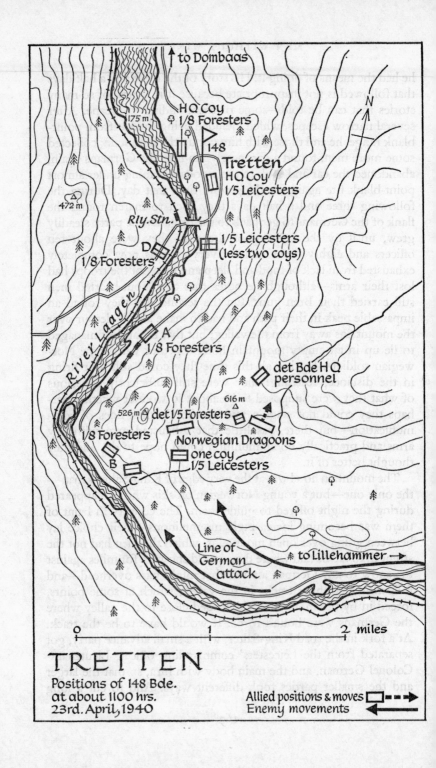

to Dombaas

HQ Coy
1/8 Foresters

175 m

148

Tretten
HQ Coy
1/5 Leicesters

472 m

Rly. Stn.

1/5 Leicesters
(less two coys)

D
1/8 Foresters

River Laagen

A
1/8 Foresters

det Bde HQ
personnel

616 m

526 m   det 1/5 Foresters

1/8 Foresters

Norwegian Dragoons

B   one coy
C   1/5 Leicesters

Line of
German
attack

to Lillehammer →

0   2 miles

TRETTEN

Positions of 148 Bde.
at about 1100 hrs.
23rd. April, 1940

Allied positions & moves ☐ ▪▪▪▶
Enemy movements ◀━━━

story short, both routes took the respective parties by an all-night march straight into the hands of the Germans. Attempting to escape, King-Salter had his right foot almost completely shot off, so that this was the end of his active soldiering as well as the end of his campaign.

But not all the detached bodies of wandering troops ended up in captivity. In spite of their exhaustion, in spite of their inexperience and of everything else, these raw Territorials showed remarkable determination and a will to fight again. In twos and threes some of them got over the Swedish border after a nightmare trek of a good hundred miles over the snow-covered mountains in low temperatures. Others got to the coast and found their way to Scotland in fishing-boats—as some of the Norwegians did. When one considers that these men had no maps, no knowledge of the country, no training, no food except what they could find—or indeed anything of any significance except the will to remain free—their resourcefulness is as outstanding as their grit. What could these men not have done had they only been properly equipped, properly supported and used in a consistent and well-thought-out plan of action—instead of being misused in the way they were! As elsewhere in Norway, such a little more would have made so much difference, and the legend of German invincibility would never have been born.

So much for Sickleforce, the troops who were to have invested Trondheim from the south. What of Mauriceforce on the north? We left these, too, in full flight—in this case from the German sortie from Trondheim by land and sea. The Hallamshires, the rearmost battalion, had got away pretty well intact. The Lincolns had been less lucky—C Company and their battalion H.Q., some two hundred men in all, had been cut off through getting the withdrawal order too late. The K.O.Y.L.I. had lost no more than a platoon, but their only way back was over impassable snows in mountain country and their escape even by this route was barred by a river which according to the map was unbridged east of Steinkjer, where the Germans already were.

To help them on this improbable operation the battalion had but two assets: one was a Norwegian, Mathieson by name, who had escaped from Trondheim on skis and attached himself to them —the other was the redoubtable Colonel Hibbert himself. And

Hibbert, by one of those extraordinary coincidences that only happen in real life, had been there before—thirty years before. For his father, a naval man, had been in command of a warship visiting Trondheim and had taken him along for a holiday jaunt. Memory was very dim, but the boy had gone fishing in the mountains and insistently at the back of his mind—was it actual recollection or was it hallucination born of desire?—there was a wooden bridge. The river could only be the Ogna river, running east from Steinkjer and north-east of this present position. Could the bridge be there too? It was a faint thing to go by, but anything was better than nothing: he sent Mathieson off on his skis to reconnoitre a way through the mountains and himself started off with his two companies on the by-road round the east of the lake, which would take them the first part of the journey—leaving behind at last, for whoever could possess it and for whatever use it was, the famous Arctic kit. The road (for want of a better name) was barely wide enough for one vehicle and bounded by snow-filled ditches into which the few ancient lorries continually skidded and upset. 'George' came over at tree-top height—miraculously banked at the moment they should have been in full view, and the observer missed them. So they reached Fisknes, a little village at the head of the lake, undetected: here they could wait a few hours, rest and hope for news of the other two companies. They got better than news—they got B Company itself, weary and on foot but intact: their few ramshackle and over-loaded lorries had all cracked up. And a runner brought news of C Company, the southernmost, ten miles away, very tired but still marching—a nightmare march on a frozen road with a cutting north-east wind bringing snow flurries, that must have made Hibbert's toughening-up exercises seem like a choirboys' picnic. As dawn was breaking, these reached a farmhouse and lay up for a few hours before struggling on to Fisknes. B Company were still waiting for them, while the main party had moved on four miles to Henning. By nine o'clock that evening—the 22nd—the whole battalion, short only of the one captured platoon of A Company, was together. And Mathieson had returned from his journey of exploration.

There was a bridge, he said—maybe Hibbert's bridge or maybe another, but certainly a bridge: it might or might not be intact.

By the river it was but six miles east of Steinkjer but to reach it the K.O.Y.L.I. would have to march several times that distance over a mountain trail, difficult for fresh men, unencumbered and used to the country—well nigh impossible for them. But there was no stopping and no turning back. There and then Hibbert got his exhausted men on their feet, ordered them to destroy all their equipment bar rifles and Brens, got the wounded, swathed in blankets, on to the few sledges they had, and made a start.

It was getting dark. The wind was still bitter and brought a thin snow with it. As dusk deepened into night the sky to the north-west of them was red with the flames of burning Steinkjer, which seemed to reach out and redden the snow at their feet. Mathieson led the way, and man by stumbling man the whole battalion followed after in single file—three yards' distance between each of them, because under their feet the snow packed firm but became slippery, so that one man falling, if too close, might bowl the whole column down like ninepins. Two miles they were from end to end—saviours of Norway in a long, thin thread of exhaustion, winding its way round the track. They were able to make good no more than one and a half miles an hour. Yet here is the most remarkable thing about this battalion that but a few months back had been a dead loss in terms of fitness and a write-off as a fighting unit—not a man fell out and the only man to throw away his rifle was an epileptic.

The night was endless and terrible. There was no resting in the freezing cold. Man trudged after man, beyond weariness—long minute succeeded long minute, hour succeeded hour. And each step brought them nearer the bridge that might be no longer there, might be in the hands of the enemy. If there were no bridge, the only hope would be Sweden; and Sweden was a world away over those impossible mountains.

Dawn came. The sky lightened and the flames of Steinkjer faded. The grim landscape of mountain, snow and forest was visible again. Quite suddenly there was a deep gorge across their path with a rushing river in its depths. And across the gorge was a wooden bridge—intact. The farther side was blanketed with black forest, an ideal ambush, thick enough to hide a division of troops. Not even Hibbert could believe the wood was clear. From his exhausted men he detailed a fighting patrol, and while the rest watched in unbearable suspense, the patrol crept across the bridge and into the forest.

The forest was clear: there was not a German to be seen.

Across the river the K.O.Y.L.I. presently reached a farm held by Norwegians, who at first refused to believe they were not Germans. Here they got four hours' sleep before the Norwegians roused them with news that the Germans were moving up out of Steinkjer. They made good a few more miles and rested again. By seven that evening they were within eighteen miles of the rest of the brigade at Namdalseid, on the main road to Namsos, and the C.O. was able to make contact by telephone. C Company, who had marched the farthest, were unable to go any farther and were left to rest: a few lorries, got together by the rest of the brigade, met the remainder seven miles out and brought them in—so tired that they slept the cold night through on bare boards without blankets. And they awoke to pass the day of the 25th doctoring their inflamed feet amid a mist of exploding meat and vegetables caused by careless heating and hasty handling of tins. It was more than they had dared to hope for.

It was not a victory, but it was a magnificent feat. Once more—again and again this lesson cries out for learning—what could these men not have done if only their government of cabals and committees had got them there in time and given them the weapons for their task? There is one other such march to come in this story, but it is a march by regular soldiers: Hibbert's Territorials had trudged to safety across country that had been unanimously regarded as impassable before they were forced to take to it. In this country the farthermost of them—15 Platoon—had marched eighty-two miles in thirty-seven hours actually on the move, sixty-six hours all told. And now they understood what all Hibbert's 'blood, toil, tears and sweat' had been about!

Last of all came the missing two hundred men of the Lincolns. From their barn on the mountainside they had struggled on to Henning, hoping to meet the K.O.Y.L.I., but missed them by many hours. They thought of making for Grong, the railway junction forty-five miles away, but were lucky enough to meet a Norwegian patrol who told them where the brigade had gone. So they rested the night, and morning brought a Norwegian missionary, who led them along the track the K.O.Y.L.I. had taken the night before. They, too, got across the river, and the end of their particular journey was one of those things about the Norwegian campaign that might have been funny if it had not been so deadly serious. At Mejer they found the telephone working. They also found a horse and trap. In this the company commander set off at a good gallop down the road until, falling in with one of the Hallamshires' outposts, he was able to change the trap for a bicycle. Presently he was able to change the bicycle for a car, and in the car he arrived at Namdalseid, where, once more, sufficient lorries were got together to bring his men in. They had not covered quite as much ground as the K.O.Y.L.I., but in the same impossible conditions they had come forty-five miles in forty-nine hours: they, too, came in, each man with his rifle, and they too left not a single straggler by the wayside. And the same lesson that cries out from the K.O.Y.L.I.'s experience cries out also from theirs.

Mercifully, during those few days, there had been a lull in enemy air activity. The weather had been bitter, tempestuous and overcast, as the K.O.Y.L.I. and the Lincolns knew all too well. The long northern winter, near its very end now, was going out in a spell as severe as anything the unlucky British troops had so far experienced. We shall presently see how this same last burst of Arctic weather frustrated one more attempt by Admiral Cork to get some action into the situation on the Narvik front. The lull was also partly due to the fact that *Glorious* and *Ark Royal* were off the coast, so that there were at least a few fighters available to deal with the Germans in the air—and the opportunity was taken of making some attacks on the landing ground outside Trondheim, which also helped a little.

But the lull would not last. There was about to break on the central Norwegian front a blitz from the air that showed the enemy was moving in for the kill and was determined to stamp out every spark of resistance, Allied or Norwegian. It was necessary for him to do so because the situation at Narvik brooked no further delay. Probably the Germans could not understand what miracle had saved their forces there from liquidation, but it was quite clear to them that the miracle would not be vouchsafed to them for ever—that they must lose no time linking up communications with their besieged garrison in Trondheim.

The battle in central Norway, in other words, was now as good as lost: its doom had moved upon it surely and inexorably from the moment the German forces, immeasurably stronger in almost every way, had started their movement from the south towards Trondheim and began to drive first the Norwegians, then the British before them. Their complete liberty to do as they wished in the air had been an important element to their success. Had it been possible, in the earlier stages of the battle, to get Allied fighter planes into the air against them and ground attack planes to harry their troops and communications as they had harried ours—both in sufficient strength—things might have been different. But only now, when the battle was for all practical purposes decided, was one single and inglorious attempt made to get British land-based fighters into operation. It is a sorry story; but it has to be told and the facts are not in dispute.

There was no level ground clear of snow in our possession from which fighters could possibly operate. The only possibility at all was to use the surface of a frozen lake, if one could be found. The Germans themselves had tried a similar experiment in the Narvik area, but had quickly abandoned it after losing a number of aircraft. Hasty reconnaissance in the few days previously had offered two possibilities, Lake Vangsmjösa and Lake Lesjaskog at the head of the Romsdal; the latter—'Gladiator Lake' as it came to be known to the Navy—was chosen, and 263 Squadron R.A.F., equipped with Gladiator biplane fighters, was selected for the job.

The choice of Gladiators makes more sense than some ill-informed critics have supposed. Any biplane now appears to be a 'string-bag', but the Gladiator was fast, efficient, much more manœuvrable and needing less room for take-off and landing than any monoplane—factors of importance since they would have to be flown in from a carrier and operated on an improvised landing ground. The choice of 263 Squadron is a more arguable point: it was based on Bristol, had seen little or no action and very little operational work in severe winter conditions. Both of these requirements could have been found in squadrons which had spent the previous winter on the east and north-east coasts. The competence and courage of its flying personnel were well up to standard, nor was there anything wrong with the performance, later on, of its ground staff at Bardufoss in the north. But for some unfathomable reason the ground staff were not sent with the aircraft and flying personnel. The staff who were sent instead were strange to the squadron and unfamiliar with the Gladiators. They were short in some essential branches—one trained armourer, for instance, to service the seventy-two guns of the eighteen machines. And their stores were dispatched in a manner which frankly beggars comment: they were neither labelled nor listed, so that they had to be unpacked and sorted piecemeal in snow and freezing cold with enemy air attack imminent—and as they were the most appalling deficiencies were disclosed. Outstandingly, there were only two refuelling troughs, while the single starter trolley's batteries were uncharged and there was no acid for them. In other words, the squadron left England in *Glorious* carrying a built-in disaster with it.

The ground staff, arriving on the 23rd in conditions they had never dreamed of, much less seen before, found a single runway, perhaps half a mile long, cleared of snow by Norwegian labour, and a track, likewise cleared, from the main road to lake shore: from thence to the runway was through snow a foot deep, over which stores needed to be dragged by horse-drawn sledges. Toiling under these very difficult circumstances, they managed to get fuel and ammunition dumps laid out along the runway: needless to say, enemy aircraft watched their activities with interest and attention.

The following day *Glorious*, which dared not venture nearer than one hundred and eighty miles from the coast, flew off the eighteen Gladiators into a blinding snowstorm: escorted by two naval Skuas, all the pilots very creditably landed their machines in one piece on the frozen lake.

They were not bothered by the enemy that night: the enemy did not fly by night and the weather, indeed, could do much of his work for him. In temperature below freezing-point carburetters, controls and everything else froze solid by morning—when the weary and shivering ground staff were faced with the appalling task of attempting to start the engines by hand. It was two solid hours before the first machine was got away—by which time the Heinkels were overhead and some bombs had already been dropped on the vulnerable sheet of ice which covered the lake. One Heinkel was shot down, but there were plenty more to come.

The next two Gladiators up were got away on their mission of bringing some relief to the hard-pressed troops farther down the valley and the exhausted airmen were still struggling with the remainder when the Germans descended upon them in force, bombing and machine-gunning unmercifully—quite undeterred by the two naval Oerlikons and a handful of Lewis guns which were the only ground defences. Five Gladiators were soon wrecked: others managed to get airborne and in the course of that nightmare day no less than forty fighter sorties were somehow or other made and six enemy planes destroyed.

Under the nightmare, the untrained and unacclimatized ground staff, already strained to the limit, cracked. They fled from the shambles of the lake, with its wrecked and burning aircraft—the surface was already beginning to disintegrate—and took cover in the woods around. The pilots and the few who had not panicked were left to refuel, re-arm and re-start their machines themselves; and before long supplies of belted ammunition were running out.

By nightfall there were only five Gladiators left. In desperation the remains of the squadron was moved under cover of darkness to the parade ground of a former Norwegian Army camp near the coast—from whence an attempt was made next day to keep up some show of help to the ground forces. One crashed through an engine failure, three others suffered damage which could not be coped with: the one remaining was never flown again.

The man who says he has never been frightened is either a liar or a superman like Carton de Wiart: there are plenty of the former but few of the latter and it is no shame that the ground crews of Gladiator Lake were not cast in this heroic mould. Of course they should not have run, and of course it is reprehensible that they did. The surprising thing, however, is not that they ran but that more of the ill-prepared troops in the whole of the dismal campaign did not run likewise. The truth is that they were even less prepared for what they had to face than the rawest and least stout-hearted man in any of the Territorial battalions. They were not truly even soldiers at all: they were tradesmen, theirs was the problem the R.A.F. has had to face as the only one of the

three services in which only a small *élite* go into battle. The answer
to this problem is squadron spirit—which these men could not
possibly be expected to have, since they were strangers to the
squadron. The only other possible answers are training and
acclimatization: in the months and years to come—in the battle
of Britain, in the desert and in a host of other places—both these
were to be vouchsafed to R.A.F. ground staffs, some of the fugi-
tives of Lake Lesjaskog doubtless among them. And they would
acquit themselves, in the by and large, at least as well as the
noncombatant personnel of other arms. The failure was not
theirs—it lay at the door of the men who sent them there and
the men and the nation responsible for the whole sorry state of
things.

On the 27th, Squadron Leader 'Bing' Cross of 46 Hurricane
Squadron touched down at Aandalsnes in a flying-boat to explore
possible landing grounds for his own unit. He found himself in
the middle of an air raid: houses ashore were on fire in all directions.

'Where's 263 Squadron?' he asked the Naval S.T.O.

'They didn't get up this morning,' he was told.

He determined then and there that when his turn came he
would not be caught out in this way. But his turn was not to come
in central Norway: by the time he got back to England next day
the evacuation had been decided upon.

While the Gladiators were on their way to Lesja, reinforcements of a different kind were on their way to Carton de Wiart.
They included the advance party of his staff, representatives of the
sub-area units for the base which had already been obliterated, a
Marine howitzer battery, a field ambulance and a dock labour
company, a Bofors gun battery, some of the Lincolns' transport and
vast quantities of stores. In the same ship that brought them were
the rifles and ammunition for want of which Colonel Getz's
Norwegian troops had been more or less obliged to keep themselves at a distance from any serious or prolonged fighting. It
proved impossible to get most of the stuff ashore: some of the
howitzers were landed without any ammunition, the Bofors guns
without their predictors—also landed (to their sorrow) were the
headquarters party and part of the dock labour company. All the
rest sailed home again, including Getz's rifles and ammunition,

and with them went all possibility of his being able to fight on after the British had departed.

In these days, indeed, a strange and illusory peace descended upon Mauriceforce. The Germans did not follow up their sortie from Trondheim: they were not strong enough to follow it up in force and, in any case, they had no need to. They had averted what Allied threat there ever was to Trondheim: the main attack group from the south, which had advanced so rapidly and successfully up the Gudbrandsdal, liquidated 148 Brigade and cut off all the Norwegian forces between Tretten and the coast, would soon join up with them, and until that moment all they needed to do was to sit tight. Carton de Wiart, for his part, had already made up his mind that in default of the promised frontal attack in force on Trondheim and in default of air protection, tanks and artillery for his troops, his position was impossible and his chances of doing anything negligible. He had already told the War Office that evacuation might be necessary, but had been ordered in reply by General Massy to hold on in defensive positions. He says in his autobiography that he sent a staff officer over to find out if he could what was going on. The officer came back with a picture of utter indecision in which the merits of evacuation, holding on, reinforcement and counter-attack were being debated from one moment to the next—he got the impression that Carton de Wiart could do pretty well as he liked. And so the decision on how to act was once more left by default to the commander on the spot. The General therefore refused a second demi-brigade of Chasseurs Alpins: there was nothing he could do with them—especially if they were as well trained and equipped as the first lot—and they would only mean so many more mouths to feed, so many more bodies to defend and in the end so many more men to be extricated. The Chasseurs were sent to Narvik instead, and General Béthouart with his staff departed to meet them—the Navy, as usual, finding a destroyer from somewhere to carry him. General Audet remained, to toy for a little while with a scheme for counter-attack by the demi-brigade already there together with Getz's Norwegians—neither of whom had yet been in action—but it came to nothing.

Meanwhile to the south, where General Paget and the regulars of 15 Brigade were just ashore, the last and belated attempt to enlarge Sickleforce into a sort of revitalized ghost of Operation Hammer was rapidly turning into a desperate action to extricate the remains of 148 Brigade and save the King and legal government of Norway from capture by the Germans. There was no lull on this front and the story of the last fierce battles there, fought with determination but too late, makes another story of grit and initiative which, like all the rest, could have been employed to better purpose had it been employed in the right way.

CHAPTER 10

A TALE OF TWO TUNNELS

WITH barely a week to go before the petering out of all
operations in central Norway except for the brief and
isolated resistance of some of the Norwegian units, time on the
Narvik front was running out even faster than ever. But there
was still no hint of urgency in General Mackesy's lengthy
preparations for the encircling operation which was ultimately
going to end with the recapture of the town and the iron ore railway to Sweden still, in spite of everything, the most important
thing in the minds of the majority of the War Cabinet at home.
Cork was preparing detailed plans for the establishment of his
permanent naval base and defences and was demanding light
and heavy anti-aircraft guns in quantity, heavy guns and equipment for fixed harbour defences—only a fraction of which he
would ever receive, for the air defence of the United Kingdom
itself had nowhere near the number of guns its wartime establishment on paper demanded.

None the less, he did at least strive to keep up the offensive.
While the two brigades in central Norway were living out their
few bitter days of action he was making one last attempt to capture Narvik by direct assault. Mackesy agreed to make the Irish
Guards' Battalion available for it on the understanding that
the troops would go in only if Cork's bombardment battered the
Germans into showing the white flag ashore. The Admiral still
had *Warspite*, the cruisers *Effingham, Enterprise* and *Aurora,
Vindictive*, his destroyers and the carrier *Furious* off the coast—
although the latter was now short of aircraft and in poor shape
mechanically after many near misses by German bombs. He timed
the attack for the 24th, the twenty-fifth anniversary of the landings
in Gallipoli — but there was no significance in this sinister date, for
no landing was accomplished.

It was not an attack on the same scale as Whitworth's glorious

onslaught of only eleven days before—eleven days in which so
many things had happened and the situation had changed so much
that in this narrative they seem more like eleven months. The
weather was against him—the same weather which had added the
final misery to the retreating troops in central Norway but here
intensified by the Arctic latitudes. Snow was falling thickly when
the three-hour bombardment started. It obscured targets, it quickly
blanketed any damage done by the shells and it prevented any
adequate observation of the fall of shot: it was like bombarding in
a world of cotton wool. We know now that some damage was
done and that there were enemy casualties. We know too that it
once more raised the hopes of the Norwegians in the town a little
and once more frayed the nerves of the German garrison. But
there was nothing like the utter collapse of morale that there had
been during the attack of the 13th—perhaps their previous experience had hardened the Germans a little, so that there was very
little likelihood of such a collapse again. Certainly there was
never any likelihood of the white flag and after the three hours
the Earl of Cork had regretfully to call off the action and put
ashore once more at Bogen the Irish Guards who had embarked
in *Vintictive*.

But General Fleischer's Norwegians were at last on the
offensive on this terrible day and they did not allow the snow
to deter them. Perhaps they should have done: three feet of snow
fell in twenty-four hours and although Norwegians live in a cold
country, they are none the less made of flesh and blood. It is
true that the weather conditions kept German aircraft on the
ground, but the cold and fury of the Arctic blizzard more than
counter-balanced this advantage. Nothing, therefore, gives a
more abiding impression of the Norwegians' passionate urge to
strike at the Germans at the very earliest moment they were able
to.

They had reorganized and even been reinforced: troops who
had been on the neutrality watch before the invasion had been
gathered together and brought down from farther north by sea—
another little convoy job for the Navy. In spite of the losses they
had suffered when the Germans captured their depot at Elvegaardsmoen, they were not badly equipped and not badly off
for ammunition. There had been continuous skirmishing on a

small scale ever since they had stopped the German advance towards the north, and they were eager for action.

The German line, where it had been held north of Narvik, was not unlike an elephant's head—the trunk pointing down the Herjangsfiord opposite Narvik town and the neck following the indentation of this little sideshoot of the Ofotfiord, with Bjerkvik at the top, just about where the elephant's mouth would be. The top of the head curved round through Gratangen and Lapphaug, where the Norwegians had stopped their march, and from there the line turned south again for some miles down the valley, with high snow-clad mountains on its eastern side: then it made a sharp right-angle over the mountains to the Swedish border, forming a salient which was less vulnerable than it looks on the map because of the nature of the country.

The attack was to take place on the top of the elephant's head: its only co-ordination with Allied Operations was in the coincidence of the date and the fact that two companies of Scots Guards had been allotted for defensive purposes only. They had been given snowshoes and camouflage cloaks from the Norwegians' stocks, and there is really something shockingly paradoxical about the fact that the ill-supplied Norwegians were compelled to help in this way. The fact that they were so compelled helped to increase the bitterness and contempt that was growing among the Norwegians on this front and the defensive rôle of the Guards is acidly commented on in their own records. Perhaps this is hardly just: there was very little the Guards could do by way of offensive action when they could hardly stand on their feet, and the Norwegians' snowshoes, to which they were not accustomed, cannot have helped them very much.

At this particular point, the left flank of the attack, the Norwegians had about two miles to go. With a climb of about three hundred feet in the terrible weather, it took them all day to cover this distance; and at the end of it they found the Germans well dug in and fighting back both fiercely and effectively: the automatic weapons with which they were well supplied had tremendous stopping power. Frozen and exhausted, the Norwegians were forced to retreat. On the right flank the going had been better—they were able to make progress and get down into the valley to shelter for the night. But the Germans, after driving off the other arm of the attack, came down upon them in force with withering machine-gun fire, so that they in turn had to fall back leaving behind them two hundred and fifty killed, wounded or taken prisoner.

It was only a temporary setback: they were fighting not in a strange and alien land without very much idea of what they were about, but almost within sight of their own homes. The very next day they were reformed and reinforced, and their second attack pressed on in spite of the power of the German fire and took the mountain position. Once ousted from their prepared defence posts the Germans did not attempt to counter-attack and began the very first movement of a slow retreat which, in the days and weeks which followed, was to contract their forces in a ring of decreasing size around Narvik itself. It was this movement, in fact, that, when the Norwegians were at last reinforced with Allied troops, was to lead to the capture of the town.

All this, however, was not much consolation to the War Cabinet who were still trying to urge action on Lord Cork and General Mackesy. They were now casting about for a new commander for the land forces and a certain Lieutenant-General Auchinleck (whose name was then quite unfamiliar to the British public or the world at large) was being informally tipped off that the appointment was to be his. There was also going on a thorough re-examination of manpower: the Chasseurs Alpins, who had been rejected as reinforcements by Carton de Wiart, were switched to the northern front and units both of French Foreign Legion and the Polish Brigade were on their way—the former having embarked from France with ceremonial parades, military bands and presentations of bouquets of flowers. There was even talk of withdrawing another British division from France.

But it was all very leisurely: the tempo of things failed completely to match up to the War Cabinet's feeling of urgency, so that it would yet be several days before Auchinleck was officially appointed, let alone on his way. And the sands were still running out.

How fast they were running out would not become truly apparent to those not on the spot until the brief remaining scene in the tragedy of central Norway was acted out: to play his part in this, Major-General Paget was only now landing at Aandalsnes, with 15 Brigade as the first instalment of the forces that were to restore the situation there and an advance party of his army corps headquarters, led by Brigadier Hogg. His orders and his briefing painted a picture of Carton de Wiart's men to the north of his operational area strung out in partial encirclement of Trondheim, 148 Brigade deployed far along the Gudbrandsdal in support of the Norwegians, the Gladiators about to arrive on Lake Lesjaskog. He was to organize his base and his anti-aircraft defences at Aandalsnes and Molde, secure his line of communication to the south and hold the Germans. And he was to have at least a full division—with everything. His first hint of the rapid and disastrous change in the situation came as the guard was about to whistle off his train from King's Cross, on the way to Edinburgh and the cruiser which was to take him to Norway. An agitated staff officer came rushing through the barrier with a message and the train was held long enough for him to hand it to Paget. Paget read it and gave no hint of the disastrous tidings it contained.

'Hurray, good news!' he cried. 'Good-bye!' And the train went. He remained buoyant and indomitable throughout. So, in fact, did 15 Brigade. The confidence of these regulars was so colossal that they were absolutely certain that once they landed everything would be all right, and even four days of bitter fighting failed completely to convince them that the situation was more than they could handle with the means at their disposal. The Green Howards in particular desperately wanted to do well.

The first part of his force—the 1st Battalions of the K.O.Y.L.I. and the York and Lancaster Regiment—landing on the 23rd, had found Aandalsnes and its even tinier sister port of Molde, across the fiord, still picturesque and miraculously untouched— a few small isolated attacks had done little damage. It was overdue for attention by the Luftwaffe—attention which was made the more certain by the fact that King Haakon and his ministers had now arrived at Molde at the end of their long and reluctant flight along the Gudbrandsdal. The very next day the fate of Namsos was visited on Aandalsnes and on Molde too: the now familiar scene of burning wooden houses, shattered store dumps, wrecked power stations and railways was painted here again, the familiar dying flames lit up the short night after the bombers had departed.

The bombs came down, too, upon Dombaas, the railway junction, the narrow single railway line and the road and every village and hamlet that was likely to harbour or give any aid either to the Norwegians' own troops or their would-be helpers. The two anti-aircraft cruisers in the fiord could do nothing to hold off the attacks—becoming, as they had already become elsewhere, themselves targets for the fiercest of them. It was the beginning of the stepping up of the German air offensive, which was soon to be mounted by night as well as day. Neither here nor at Namsos was there to be any respite at all. The one Bofors battery, which got as far as Otta, was to lose nearly all its guns on its first day in action: the naval vessels and their crews were to be martyred in the restricted waters, firing away their ammunition, wearing out their guns and exhausting their endurance. Against this lurid drop-scene the York and Lancaster battalion (the 23rd, St. George's Day, was their regimental day) and the K.O.Y.L.I. were whisked away, first to Dombaas and then away down that sinister valley which has played so large a part in this story, to plug the gap that had been left by the rout of the Territorials at Tretten.

This was the shape of things when Paget and the rest of the brigade steamed in on the evening of the 25th, to face another of those frantic disembarkations in the ever-shortening night. They had been thirty-six hours on passage and had suffered grievously from heavy weather: they had been bombed by Heinkels, but not yet intensively, and there had been no hits. It was calm in the fiords. The snow-capped mountains towered above them in the half-light and in Aandalsnes, rising up the hill, some houses still burned fitfully. In spite of their confidence, the troops were very silent. Everything had to be manhandled off the ships: there was a mere handful of lorries to help get them, with their stores and kit, to the station. The train they found waiting for them was a Red Cross train and precious time was wasted tying tarpaulins over the crosses—not so much, perhaps, for the observance of international convention as to reduce its attractiveness to German aircraft. Some stores, as usual, were inevitably left behind, though their losses were not so disastrous as those of the brigade which had preceded them: none the less, by seven-thirty next morning they were in Dombaas Junction—a chaos of shattered station buildings, wrecked tracks and smashed and burning wagons.

Paget had been met at the quay by Colonel Beichmann, Ruge's Chief of Staff, who was afterwards to command the Norwegian troops in exile: it was he who had got together the few lorries for the disembarking troops and who was to continue to find them the only transport they had for the rest of their short stay in his country. The General's first call was on the British Minister, Sir Cecil Dormer—still sticking gamely to the Norwegian government but, like it, forced to the edge of the sea at last. It was past midnight: the Minister, garbed in a white dressing-gown and cap, briefly sketched in the grim picture of the situation, explained that Ruge was still holding the Norwegian Resistance together—but only just. Turning over in his mind the shape of things which confronted him—so very different from the picture painted for him in London, Paget set off with Brigadier Morgan of 148 Brigade, for Ruge's headquarters.

It was not merely the situation in the Gudbrandsdal he had to face up to, though this was bad enough to have stampeded his one fresh brigade straight into action from their ships. Parallel with the Gudbrandsdal there runs another valley, the Österdal. It is a less important artery of communication, but, like the Gudbrandsdal, it gives access to the south. Paget, in fact, had originally intended that 15 Brigade should operate down it towards Oslo while 148 Brigade, with whatever reinforcements he received for them, continued to hold the German Army Group Pellengahr in their more easterly valley. Its defence had been the job of the Norwegian 2nd Division—which now found itself faced with a second German group pressing rapidly up from Oslo. Group Fischer was not as large as Group Pellengahr, but its three battalions, backed by tanks, artillery and aircraft, were more than a match for the lightly-armed Norwegians; and they were already within twenty miles of Dombaas. In other words, a threat was developing which might cut off from their base port the fresh battalions already fifty miles down the Gudbrands Valley. And the tunnels at Dombaas now contained pretty well everything 15 Brigade and Paget's headquarters possessed—including the only radio which would reach England. Paget sent off Cameron Nicholson, his Chief of Staff, to the Norwegian 2nd

Division (a pleasant journey he had of it, for the Norwegian driver fell asleep and the car was wrecked) while he went on to Ruge's headquarters.

Now while it must already have been becoming rapidly clear to Paget that he was about to conduct a fighting withdrawal instead of organizing a new campaign, nothing of the sort can have been apparent to Ruge. He was still waiting for the massive reinforcements which he had been promised and becoming increasingly bewildered at their non-appearance. He was becoming increasingly concerned at the difficulty of recapturing Trondheim before the Germans joined up with its defenders. He could have no inkling that the British had already virtually abandoned thoughts of recapturing Trondheim and were already beginning to debate a possible evacuation—not merely in London but in Norway itself; for away back in Aandalsnes, Brigadier Hogg, on his own initiative, was about to signal the War Office that if air cover could not be provided, evacuation would be necessary. Paget corrected this later to his own view that if only air cover could be provided, the situation could be held; the only difference is that Paget, by temperament, preferred the positive to the negative— and since, in any case, there was no longer any likelihood of air support being obtainable, both views would amount to the same thing. At the time of the first meeting with General Ruge, however, all the evidence shows that Paget hoped his fighting withdrawal up the valley might end at Dombaas and that he might hold on here while reinforcements and other weapons reached him. While the withdrawal was taking place the remains of 148 Brigade would be posted (for what, in their battered state, they were worth) as a guard against the possible flank attack on Dombaas from the Germans pushing up through the Österdal. In fact, the brigade was never able to get into position but the course of events were such that its failure to do so did not materially affect things.

Paget and Ruge took to each other. Both were strong personalities, both were buoyant characters and born leaders. The character of Ruge is already known to us: the writer of this book has not heard a man who was under his command speak other than warmly of Paget. It was natural, therefore, that they should get on, and the brief but hectic few days of their campaigning together

produced a most happy relationship. The first fruit of this relationship was that Ruge handed back to Paget the command of the
Allied forces in the Gudbrandsdal which Brigadier Morgan had
surrendered to him. It could, in any case, be no longer contended
that the Norwegians were in command of the operations there—
for most of the exhausted units who had been engaged on the
eastern side of the valley had already withdrawn through the
British lines, while those on the west had been cut off since the
disaster at Tretten and were probably out of the running for good.
Ruge did allot to 15 Brigade some ski-troops to work on their
flanks, and these were the only Norwegian troops most of the
British soldiers engaged there saw. Still more than ski-troops,
however, Ruge gave them transport—what transport he had
available, that is. This was absolutely vital to the British troops,
who could certainly not otherwise have conducted any sort of
campaign or any fighting withdrawal against the mobile German
forces. Things were bad enough as it was: the single main road
was barely the width of a large vehicle—it was not even possible
for lorries to turn except in the villages and things were made even
worse by the fact that the thaw was now just beginning, although
it froze again by night. As to the railway, this too was a single
track; much of its rolling stock and all but a few of its locomotives
had been either wrecked in the bombing of Dombaas and Aandalsnes or immobilized in their sheds by craters. Road and railway,
sharing the same valley—sometimes on the same side of the river,
sometimes one either side—were an easy target for the enemy's
ground-attack planes, which were now stepping up their pressure
in the same way as pressure on the harbours and bases had been
stepped up. They worked to a timetable, they came and went with
such regularity and so predictably that watches could virtually
be set by them; and their coming and going, their bombing and
straffing, thundered between the hills. One of the abiding memories of those who lived through these violent days is the tremendous noise that always seemed to be about them—the noise of
aero engines, the noise of bombs, the noise of mortars and artillery,
the roar of avalanches started by bombs on the hills, the echoing
and re-echoing that magnified it all. The strain on the nerves of
the troops was constant and unremitting. The only respite granted
was that the enemy still did not fly by night (at any rate in the

battle area) any more than the German ground troops operated at night. But the nights were short and becoming ever shorter. 'It took such a hell of a time to get dark', is one of the things survivors say over and over again.

It was under these conditions that Paget's first troops had already been rushed down from Dombaas into the battle area the morning before he set foot in Norway. They had leapfrogged through the few hundred survivors of the Territorial Brigade, still in the Heidal, and taken up their position in Kvam twelve miles farther on. As one looks at the battle plan of this little action in the official history, it is almost a replica, save for the details, of the battle plans of the little actions that had taken place all the way along the valley. The river Laagen rounds another bend with hills on either side, a few islands between its shores, the road and railway run together, little black squares and oblongs show company positions and upwards along the road at the bottom of the map points the great black arrow that appears on all these maps, identified as 'enemy advance'. Here, first into the line, came the 1st Battalion of the King's Own Yorkshire Light Infantry, supported by B Company of the Green Howards on their flank. Their lorries had been bombed and machine-gunned all the way down: this, in spite of the fact that these hours saw the one and only intervention in central Norway by land-based British fighters—the unlucky Gladiators. From their disintegrating base on the lake at Lesja they flew their forty sorties on that tragic day, fought at least thirty-six battles and brought down for certain six enemy planes. By the end of the day they could do no more, and it is only human to hope that by their impossible and unequal battle—in so many ways even more unequal than that of the troops on the ground—they took some mite of pressure off the infantry, made things infinitesimally better than they might otherwise have been. It was not enough—it made no material difference. 15 Brigade would after all have to establish and hold its positions without the aid of the air support which the Government at home had already been told was absolutely essential to them.

The Green Howards had reached their position by crossing the river on the ice and climbing the precipitous hillside. They found it impossible to dig themselves in, as the Territorials had found it before them—but they were fresher, better trained and more resourceful and picked perseveringly at the rocks until they managed to erect little individual emplacements for themselves which stood them in good stead both here and farther up the valley. The view was restricted everywhere by hills and woods: there was not a single position to be had with a really good field of fire. The only difference in weapons or equipment from the Territorials was that at least this brigade had with them their anti-tank company with five Hotchkiss guns.

And it was an anti-tank gun that scored the first hit and momentarily stopped the enemy when their first vehicles came in single file round the bend of the narrow road, as they had done so many times before. Stopped, they deployed on either side of the road in classic German fashion and brought their artillery into action, but only the foremost company of the K.O.Y.L.I. was driven in and the Germans were held there all through the thundering, roaring day until they packed up fighting for the night. The company of the Green Howards had been no more than spectators with a grandstand view of the battle, powerless to intervene effectively because of their lack of anything but small-bore weapons. Captain Fanshawe made his first appearance with his rum jar: the rum jar was to be seen again and is another one of of the abiding memories of the battle.

A part of the York and Lancaster Battalion had come up towards evening, and this enabled the positions to be strengthened during the night; but two of the five anti-tank guns had had to be abandoned and replaced by the only two in reserve. The rest of the York and Lancasters formed a rearguard through which the remainder could withdraw—and withdraw they would eventually have to.

Very early next morning the Germans renewed their attack in a fashion that made it clear they could not be held much longer. From their vantage point the Green Howards saw the tanks and armoured cars moving up the road again, saw them pushing the K.O.Y.L.I. back, saw British prisoners being marched back. Before very long the ground-attack planes came in and more artillery moved up to plaster the K.O.Y.L.I.'s positions. Soon they found that there were Germans on their own flank too. As a matter of fact there were Germans on both flanks, though the

Norwegian ski-troops gave a good account of themselves and prevented them from getting their own way too quickly. There were German troops working down from the rear, so that the York and Lancaster company found themselves in a trap and had to withdraw. The battle was rapidly breaking up very dangerously into a series of isolated individual struggles. In an effort both to keep contact and find out what was going on, a Green Howards platoon set off to try and make contact with the York and Lancasters: they were in time only to take part in their withdrawal under extreme enemy pressure with heavy casualties so that out of the last two sections only one man escaped.

In the middle of the afternoon the K.O.Y.L.I. were ordered to withdraw after dark, but could not hold on that long. The Germans were now using incendiary mortar-bombs, and the very woods took fire. As dark came on there was confused fighting, with bits of all units mixed up together. Many groups were cut off: the majority of them managed to make their way back to their units at Otta the following day; but once more the will to survive and escape produced a few more of the little Odysseys born so plentifully from the fighting in this difficult land. Sixteen men of the York and Lancaster Regiment, headed by Lieutenant-Colonel Tennent, walked a hundred miles over the mountains into Sweden and were repatriated. Another party, with Captain Wilson, found their way to the coast, got themselves a fishing-boat and sailed home to England—perhaps in not very much more discomfort than they had sailed out.

The company of the Green Howards on the flank held on till nearly midnight. There was no question of their recrossing the ice, for the village was in enemy hands. They would have to recross the river farther up at Sjoa—where, according to the latest information they had, the bridge was to be blown at one a.m. They set off in single file and first scrambled down to the level ground by the river; but the thunder of the day's battle had been succeeded by the stillness of the Norwegian night, and the very scraping of their boots against the rocks drew fire from German outposts across the water. So back into the woods they went, split into small groups, stumbling and slipping, often on all fours. Many failed to find the bridge at first, but owing to yet another change of plan it was not blown. By five o'clock in the morning

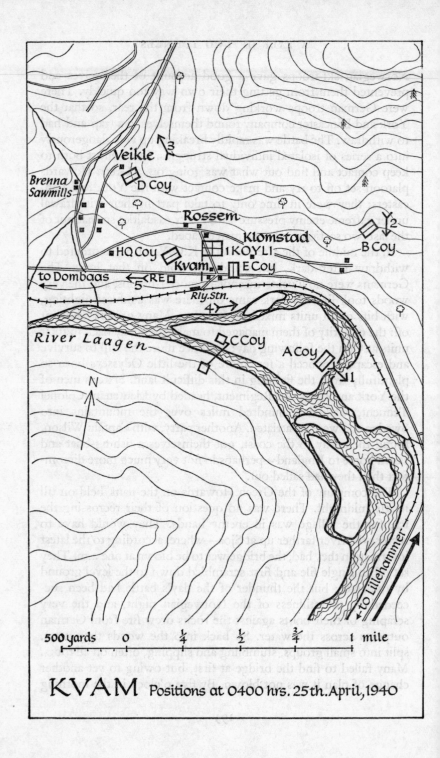

KVAM Positions at 0400 hrs. 25th. April, 1940

most of them were back with their main body—just about able to hoist themselves into the lorries that would take them back to Otta. While they were on their way the carrier platoon (needless to say it had no carriers) stayed behind as a rearguard, but at first light it was overwhelmed by armoured cars and only one man survived.

Now Otta was the last place where a stand could be made before Dombaas. It fell to the lot of the Green Howards to hold it, and here they fought the action of the lifetime. It was a strong position—perhaps the strongest of all the positions where vain stands had been made by one unit and another all the way up from beyond Lillehammer. It was, the official historian comments, not unlike some little North Riding market town in their native Yorkshire. The main road is here across the river from the village, with which it is connected by a bridge. There is flat ground on this side: on the opposite side the wooded hills rise sharply. The Germans were advancing on both sides of the main river, both along the road and the railway.

It was a position that needed at least two battalions to hold it. But the K.O.Y.L.I. had already been withdrawn to Dombaas to recover from the heavy fighting of the previous days, and the York and Lancaster, who were posted on the right flank of the Green Howards facing across the little tributary, had already been severely mauled. In effect, the Green Howards would have to stand the main impact of Group Pellengahr, with its seven infantry battalions, its motorized machine-guns battalion, its tanks, its artillery and its ever-present air umbrella. It was here, above all things, that the discipline, the confidence and the training of the regular soldiers told: against these things the inexperience of the mass of the German troops, which their own High Command had feared, was thrown up for the first time in sharp relief. The Green Howards' veteran C.O., Lieutenant-Colonel Robinson, noticed that they had no idea of taking cover, that they recoiled sharply from determined opposition and once they had recoiled, seemed uncertain what to do. But these things in themselves were not enough. Even the few anti-tank guns the brigade had once possessed had one by one been put out of action or lost in withdrawal. The three-inch mortars had had to be jettisoned. There were no anti-aircraft guns—for all of the few Bofors were now done for and, cruelly, the first heavy ack-ack battery to be sent to central Norway had the very evening before put into the bomb-harried waters off Aandalsnes, only to be sent to sea again because there was no possibility whatsoever of unloading them.

Helpless, therefore, in terms of long-range weapons the Green Howards watched the enemy deploy on the other side of the river, as armies must have watched their adversaries in the days when guns were but pop-guns or when the range of fire was no more than a flight of an arrow.

At seven in the morning the recce planes came over absolutely, as always, on timetable. They were followed by the bombers, which came in low to machine-gun after they had dropped their loads, and this went on virtually all day. Almost at once the German artillery came into action: against both this and the aircraft there was no reply. For more than three hours there was a tremendous rumble and thunder in the valley, but in spite of its appalling impact it was no more than noise, and there were very few casualties indeed. It was not until half-past ten that perhaps one hundred and fifty infantry with tanks and armoured cars came up the road on the west side of the river opposite the town: here C Company were posted—by coincidence near a monument commemorating the defeat of a party of Scottish mercenaries who, in 1612, had been the last troops from our own islands to fight in Norway. C Company held their fire. They held their fire until the Germans were no more than four hundred yards away and when they did fire every bullet told, so that the Germans withdrew with heavy casualties. It was an hour before they attacked again. This time fire was held until a hundred yards: again it was deadly and again the Germans withdrew. There was yet one more attack which was nearly four hours in coming and again this was repelled, but all this time the Company was under constant bombardment both by artillery and planes, and by the end of the afternoon it had stepped up to such a pitch that it was withdrawn to join the others on the opposite bank.

Meanwhile, on the east bank, the rest of the battalion had waited for the Germans until after midday: the little river lay before them and once more, with determination, they had found it possible to dig. Then a spearhead of light tanks appeared, moving up a track that ran parallel with the railway, making for the railway bridge. The first was knocked out by an anti-tank rifle—a remarkable feat, as anyone who ever handled that unlikely weapon will know, and only once more to be accomplished in this campaign. Immobilized, the tank blocked the track. Then infantry came up: under the cover of their artillery, they launched rubber boats on the river, and the Green Howards gleefully shot them up, so that not a boat survived. But more infantry were seen working round this flank: a patrol was sent urgently to summon reinforcements for it (there was no signals equipment to get a message back) and was never heard of again. So the line was shortened and in spite of the bombs and the shells that rained down upon them, in spite of the machine-gunning from the air, the dug-in troops dominated the crossing. There was, in the words of the regiment's history, 'great execution' among the enemy. At last, at five o'clock, came orders for withdrawal that night—first to the little wayside station of Rudi, thence to Dombaas.

But night was long in coming, and long before it was dark the Green Howards were being pressed so strongly that men inferior in training or determination would have broken or fled. At last, at a quarter to ten, the bridge was blown. It was blown not very expertly with borrowed naval material by the brigade's little detachment of Sappers: unable to gauge the strength of their explosives, they used too much, and instead of being merely breached, it rose gracefully into the air and settled back on its abutments. At the same time the whole battalion, except for C Company, withdrew under fire from their three-inch mortars. The Germans appeared to think the fire a prelude to attack and—astonishingly—broke contact. They never renewed it.

But while the rest were on their way back to shelter in the woods by Dombaas, C Company went up the hillside in search of the platoon which had been lost earlier in the day. There was no trace of it; but by the time they abandoned the search, the Germans had realized that Otta was deserted and moved in. The company withdrew in small groups along a steep hill track, crawling on their hands and knees over ice and bare rock—all through the short night and for many hours beyond. Then they set off, on top of their long climb and their day's fighting, to march to Dombaas: when they rejoined the battalion next day not a man was missing and not a man was minus his rifle. The list of individual 'citations' in the regimental history is very long. So was the casualty list, but the Germans had recoiled decisively from the first really effective opposition they had encountered. Is it idle, once more, to wonder just how little extra support, equipment and weight of seasoned troops it would have needed to drive them back and change the whole course of Hitler's offensive in the West?

But it was not to be. There would not be another attack in central Norway. There would be no stand, awaiting reinforcements, at Dombaas. While 15 Brigade had been fighting the last phases of the long battle along the Gudbrandsdal, the War Cabinet, by another of those lightning changes of mind, had determined on complete withdrawal. At Namsos the saviours of Norway were to sneak away like thieves in the night, keeping the Norwegians in ignorance of our intentions until the last possible moment. Here, south of Aandalsnes, it was characteristically left to Paget, the commander on the spot, to break the news to General Ruge. With the evacuation, quite dramatically, came the thaw.

How was Paget to break the news to Ruge? Ruge trusted him. Ruge regarded his one brigade as the spearhead of the force which was to stop the German advance at last, recapture Trondheim, give the Norwegians breathing space to organize their scratch forces into a real army with the help of British arms and equipment and recapture Norway. Now Paget had to face him and tell him that it was all a pipe dream—tell him that Britain had no more troops or any equipment to send, that the Prime Minister's promises had been no more than frothy words in the mouth of a politician, that Britain had broken her word and that the greater part of Norway was to be abandoned to its fate.

There have been many accounts of this meeting, not all of them accurate. The official history says that Ruge at first refused to accept the decision—but this is not wholly correct, for in this moment Ruge showed the greatness and the strength of his character and behaved with a degree of moderation and understanding which very few men in his position could have compassed.

It was a glorious day of Norwegian spring when the meeting

took place at the Norwegian farmhouse headquarters on the hill-side—one of those days of joy after the long winter of which exiled Norwegians all over the world speak with a nostalgia that is near to pain. In the prelude to the meeting there was that element of near-comedy which would have made so many happenings in Norway funny if their tragedy had not been so deep. When the telegram with Paget's evacuation orders was received at the base it was sent up with an officer on a motor-cycle—in itself a rare aid to communication in Norway. Paget ordered the officer to ride ahead of him to Ruge's headquarters while he followed with his chief of staff by car. He missed the Norwegian headquarters and shot away into the distance so that Paget found himself without his telegram. Eventually the officer reappeared, very flummoxed, and Paget and Ruge walked down to meet him. Paget asked for the telegram: the officer was momentarily foxed in his confusion, and then at last remembered he had put it in his boot. With some loss of dignity it was extricated.

'General,' said Paget, 'you are so much more experienced than I. I have received this telegram from my headquarters. What would you do in my position?'

The Norwegian read the telegram and for the moment was utterly bewildered. The light had gone out of him. At last he spread his hands.

'Why?' he asked. 'Why, when your troops are undefeated?'

There was a long pause, and then Ruge excused himself and left them. Minutes passed—ten minutes, a quarter of an hour—while those who waited were ill at ease with each other and forbore to talk. Ruge, in fact, was walking alone upon the hillside, turning over in his mind the bitter plight of his country, turning over his course of action and what he would say—but also, by almost superhuman process of fairness, turning over the plight of his allies and the predicament of the officer waiting below him, who had orders which he must carry out.

At last he reappeared.

'What can I do to help?' he asked.

It is difficult to conceive the load that must have fallen from Paget's mind at this moment. Had Ruge exploded with the bitter-ness of his feelings, as he might very well have done, the British general would have had to take everything he said—knowing all the time that both he and his men were undeserving of blame, that the responsibility rested with the incompetents back at home. Had Ruge done no more than wash his hands of the British and all their works, Paget would have been faced with the impossible task of getting his forces back to Aandalsnes without so much as a vehicle to help them or any of the other things for which they were wholly dependent upon the Norwegians they had been supposed to help. The Norwegian gunners would never have fired their last rounds to cover the retirement of the last British units from Dombaas—the bridge would probably have remained unblown, they would have been overwhelmed by the Germans on the march through a country alien if not actively hostile. Now, at least, the Green Howards and the K.O.Y.L.I. and the survivors of the York and Lancasters, the remnants of the Sherwood Foresters and the Lincolns and all the rest who had come thus far out of the valleys of damnation would reach the sea and might live to fight again.

There was little Paget could say to General Ruge and little they could do. A telegram indeed was sent to London insisting that Paget could hold on if only he were reinforced. But it was a forlorn hope. The Government had already turned its back on central Norway and—almost thankfully one cannot help feeling— was now concentrating all its attention once more on its beloved dreams of Narvik, the iron ore, the railway and the Swedish mines. It would talk of preserving a part of Norway for the Norwegian people—oblivious of the fact that to the majority of Norwegians Narvik and the Arctic provinces were barely Norway at all, but more like some sparsely colonized possession in the distant north. They would talk of the immense advantages to the Allied cause—including the cause of the Norwegians—that would come from the capture and holding of Narvik; still oblivious until the thing happened and the truth was forced upon them that Narvik could not be held while the rest of Norway was abandoned.

Now it was one thing to decide on evacuation and another to get the troops out. Moreover, getting them in without great losses had been a near-miracle, in face of the Luftwaffe's domination of the fiords and coastal waters. Dangerous then, these waters had now become deadly to the Navy's ships as the air attacks increased in intensity day by day and the Stuka dive-bombers joined in in increasing numbers and with increasing effect. Unflinchingly throughout these days the anti-aircraft cruisers and the sloops alone, relieving one another as ammunition ran out, guns became unserviceable or damage forced retirement, had stuck to their job of providing air defence close inshore; and their job was sheer martyrdom. Their four-inch high-angle guns were no adequate answer to heavy concentrations of bombers in level flight—they were no answer at all to the dive-bombers. The guns were too unwieldy, their rate of fire too slow. Nor could any ship afloat have carried in its magazines sufficient ammunition to last out more than a couple of the long days at the frantic rate they were consuming it: as it was, the cruisers and sloops were reduced on more than one occasion to firing practice shell for their own consolation rather than for any effect it might have on the enemy. No gun barrel or recoil mechanism had ever been devised that would remain serviceable for long under such continuous and unrelenting use. Amazingly, only one of these ships—the sloop *Bittern*—became a total loss, although *Black Swan* also got a hit below the water-line that reduced her to the same plight as *Suffolk*. But all of them suffered damage and casualties, major and minor, and their crews were tired beyond human endurance.

Misguidedly, another kind of ship had been sent to operate in the fiords—the Navy's anti-submarine trawlers. On the face of it, it was a good idea to send these sturdy little vessels to fetch and carry on a coast where transport by water was so much easier and more direct than by land, and where they could deal at the same time with any submarines that happened to be about. For various reasons they proved quite unsuitable for the first job, while as to the second, their asdics were useless in these waters—and there was a dearth of submarine targets anyway. For the rest, they were sitting targets for the Luftwaffe. Most of them were armed only with a few obsolete rifle-calibre Lewis guns, though some boasted a single Oerlikon. They lacked even sufficient speed to take evasive action effectively. And they were harried and murdered. In spite of all manner of expedients—camouflage, sheltering under overhanging cliffs, mounting their own and borrowed guns ashore—eleven out of twenty-nine failed to return and barely one of the remainder was left serviceable. Their story has been vividly told by Captain Macintyre in his oddly named book, *Narvik*; they were fought with the same courage as all the Navy's ships were fought and the skipper of one of them—Lieutenant-Commander Stannard—carried off yet another of the Navy's Victoria Crosses in the Norwegian campaign. But as on shore and in the air, heroism might win medals but was not enough to win a war, or even cover an evacuation with any certainty.

Difficult enough, then, the problem of getting ships in through these suicidal waters to re-embark the troops. Difficult, for that matter, to embark them, with the little ports in ruins, most of the quays little more than charred and splintered timber or rubble, the roads to them choked with the aftermath of bombing or littered with abandoned stores. The retreating army still had to be got there. On the Namsos front the problem was not so difficult, for there was relatively a short distance to travel. But on the Aandalsnes front there was the whole distance between Dombaas and the sea—more than fifty miles as the crow flies, nearly a hundred by the road and the railway, both narrow, both now increasingly cratered by bombs, both a continuous landmark for the Luftwaffe, both under the unremitting inspection of the recce planes which flew unhampered back and forth, for ever on their clockwork schedule.

As to the Norwegians, they must fend for themselves, and those who would escape from their country to carry on the fight for its liberation beyond the seas must do so through their own guts and initiative rather than through any help the British could give them. Already a large part of them had, in any case, been cut off beyond hope of extrication. On Paget's front there were still some four thousand of them on the right side of the German lines, and Paget had given their general an undertaking (which he kept) that he would cover their retirement. Thereafter it would be demobilization—and such reprisals as might in the course of time follow at the hands of the occupying Germans. It would be the same for Colonel Getz's troops and such others as were still in arms on the Namsos front: these would hear of the departure of the British only after the thing was done, for Ruge and King Haakon, the only Norwegians in the confidence of the British, had no means of warning them.

At Dombaas, therefore, Paget, having made his peace with General Ruge, faced his first problem of getting his surviving units back to the sea. What follows has in later years been dubbed by General Sir Cameron Nicholson (who was there, as Lieutenant-Colonel Nicholson, Paget's Chief of Staff) 'a Tale of Two Tunnels, or War without Means'. The Navy would somehow get ships for Paget into Aandalsnes on the night of 30th April/1st May and 1st/2nd May. The embarkation would at the best be a hurried and hazardous affair. The men alone could be picked up: such stores and heavy equipment as there were would have to be abandoned—though God knows Britain was hard pressed for these things and was to be pressed harder—and this included the first consignment of 15 Brigade's motor transport which had, improbably and too late to be of any significant use, been brought in and got ashore. Such men as could not be got there or got aboard would have to make do, like the Norwegians. Time, therefore, was short enough; but Ruge could not expect to get the last of his men clear before the 30th, and thus reduced the margin even more.

The K.O.Y.L.I. were already in Dombaas: Paget pushed them forward south of the little town, and the troops beyond them were brought in by road and rail, the bridges behind them being blown as they retired. This part of the valley, the Rosti Gorge, is wild and difficult and the river was now in spate with the thaw—at least the German tanks and heavy artillery would be delayed, though not the Luftwaffe. The Green Howards and the York and Lancasters came in according to plan; but the Germans, though obviously following a little more cautiously after their treatment by the Green Howards at Otta, were none the less close on their tails. Just as, farther south, they had appeared to move with ease in country where 148 Brigade was pinned down on the road, they worked round the demolitions in the gorge, moving on foot up the railway track with their heavy gear in handcarts and helped by supply-dropping aircraft. They came, in fact, too fast and ran unawares not merely into the British defensive positions but into the fire of the four Norwegian field guns which Ruge had generously given to cover our retreat. Thus halted, on the wrong side of the swollen river; they once more took to the water in rubber boats, and a company of the Green Howards which had been rushed up to support the K.O.Y.L.I. once more had the pleasure of shooting them up.

It was to be the last contact. That evening the last of the Norwegians passed through on time and after dark the 1st York and Lancasters climbed thankfully aboard a train in the shattered sidings of Dombaas, to start their precarious railway journey to the coast. The train was stopped short not far from Lesjaskog by an irreparable break in the line of which we shall hear more: they were able to finish the trip by road. It was no haven for which they were heading. That night—the night of 29th/30th April —the Germans carried their raids on Aandalsnes and Molde on into the night, and long before they reached their destination they could see the flames of the little town where, surprisingly, there was still something left to burn.

At this very time units of the R.A.F. were attempting to bomb enemy-held airfields with their short-range machines and *Glorious* and *Ark Royal* to operate off-shore, to give some cover at least to the evacuation. But the light raids were without noticeable effect on the concentration of air power and the vulnerable carriers were forced away to sea. The Luftwaffe was now so well established in Norway that it would have taken very much more than these pin-pricks to diminish the might of its attack. The woods were burning, too. There was complete chaos and disruption both in Aandalsnes itself and in the tiny sister port of Molde across the fiord, which now, for the time being, housed not merely King Haakon, his cabinet and precious bullion, but also General Ruge and the remains of his headquarters as well. No transport or ship-of-war could hope to enter these waters and stay long unscathed.

None the less, while the York and Lancasters completed their journey and made for what shelter they could find in the woods, the cruiser *Glasgow* braved the air raids to enter the fiord: her mission was to take aboard King Haakon and his party and General Ruge and his staff, for transport either to England or where they themselves thought fit. The whole area around the quay was in flames as she approached Molde and the quay itself was smouldering. Her fire hoses were rigged and she came alongside cascading water like a fire float: Ruge, this night at least, refused to go. His mind was burdened by the fate that had befallen seven-eighths of his countrymen—burdened even more by

his grief for the brave men who had fought their good fight unflinchingly, falling back day after day and selling dearly every mile
of ground. Now they must go into captivity. If they went he
would go with them.

There was no time to argue or persuade—*Glasgow* might be hit
or take fire from the general conflagration any moment. King
Haakon and his people were hurried aboard, bearing with them,
at least, not merely Norway's little store of gold but Norway's
integrity and her will to continue the fight wherever free Norwegians could get together. At sea they decided to make for
Tromsö, away beyond the Arctic Circle, more northerly even than
Narvik, in Norway's last unoccupied provinces to which the
way had been barred by General Fleischer's grim stand and the
Navy's disruption of the reinforcement plans of the Germans in
Narvik. *Glasgow* took them most of the way: for the last part of
the journey they transferred to a Norwegian vessel.

Back at Dombaas their last day on the Norwegian battlefront
dawned for the troops who were still there and who had given the
German advance-guard a second surprise blow the previous evening—the K.O.Y.L.I., the Green Howards, the remaining bits and
pieces from 148 Brigade that had not gone down the line, the little
detachments of sappers, gunners, marines and others and the
brigade headquarters. It was a day of great anxiety for Paget,
because it was obviously touch and go whether the contact would
stay clean broken or whether his last units would have to stage a
fighting withdrawal. It was probably a day of great anxiety for the
Germans too, because they had as yet no idea that an evacuation
was taking place and were desperately anxious to deal with the
remains of the British troops who, in these last rounds of the fight
and in spite of their still obvious deficiencies, seemed to have
acquired a second wind.

In the first of Cameron Nicholson's two tunnels—one of a
series of tunnels at Dombaas which had been good friends to 15
Brigade—the train was assembled on which the salvation of the
majority of the troops left there depended. It was a precious train
because it embodied most of what remained serviceable of the
rolling stock at Dombaas, but it was a train open to criticism by
conventional railway standards—consisting, as it did, of two
engines plus a passenger train, plus another engine, plus a goods

train, all coupled together. Odd though it was, it would take the K.O.Y.L.I., the Green Howards and the rest of their spare ammunition and a detachment of the Norwegian ski-troops who had stuck to their job of guarding 15 Brigade's flank. In spite of all the noise and confusion, brigade headquarters made a very precise job of it all. The train was paced, the hiding places of the troops in the woods were paced and it was made quite certain that, when the train emerged from the tunnel with the coming of dark, each man would find himself in the correct place to get aboard as it stopped at pre-determined points. This would deal with all except for the rearguard and the brigade staff, who would travel by road. For safety's sake there was a guard on the train crew.

Long before dark the Germans re-appeared and began to press on towards the town. They were held in check both by the rearguard and by the four Norwegian guns.

Colonel Robinson, the Green Howards' C.O., thought that the Norwegians' marksmanship left something to be desired by his standards: perhaps it did, but the effect of this, the first heavy artillery the Germans had come up against all the way from Oslo, was very noticeable on them, and it was a tremendous act of comradeship that Captain Zeiner Gundersen (whose name deserves to go on record) should shoot away his little stock of shell to cover the retirement of the erstwhile defenders, who had left the Norwegians very little to be grateful for.

Long before it was dark, also, the train made a false start—perhaps through a misunderstanding or because the train crew could no longer stick it out—and appeared out of the tunnel puffing vast clouds of steam and smoke, to everyone's consternation. It was got back, and the long wait went on: it seemed that it would never get dark.

As evening came the last of the units began to fall back on the town. The Germans followed cautiously, still not imagining that the battle was ended, and were pretty well entering the Dombaas tunnels as the train steamed out the other end to pick up the troops: not without further consternation brought on by the unfortunate engineer, to whom it was second nature to blow his whistle as he opened his throttle. The pick-up of the troops worked perfectly and soon they were on their way.

Now for the whole period of the bombing of Dombaas the railway had been continually damaged and repaired, so that, even as General Ruge claimed, it had virtually never been out of action. It was reliably reported that the break at Lesjaskog had been dealt with, though it would probably be the last to be repaired: Major-General Robinson is quite certain in his own mind that a recce was made ahead of the train and is convinced that what followed was due to sabotage—but it is only fair to say that he is also much more convinced than the majority of his former colleagues that the Fifth Column played an appreciable part in this stage of the campaign. Be all this as it may, the line was breached and the train came unstuck.

Riding on the leading engine (perhaps not without a certain grown-up boy's pleasure in spite of the perilous circumstances) was one Captain Robert Thomson, a staff officer of 15 Brigade: like most of the brigade headquarters, he had found precious little staff work to do and spent most of his time at the front. The train had stopped not far from Lesja to pick up the last detachment of the Norwegians and was gathering speed: from the footplate he watched the track faintly unrolling in the dimness. Then suddenly there was no track, only a sort of shadow. The next moment there was a most appalling lurch and crash as the engine fell on its side, the first coach telescoped and the whole train was reduced to a zig-zag of derailment and confusion. Surprisingly (since most of them were asleep), only eight men were killed and thirty seriously injured. Thomson remembers the cursing and momentary confusion as the men were got out of the train into the snow, still waist-deep by the track, and somehow or other formed up on the road to march. While all this was going on the rearguard came by in their vehicles—packed to bursting point and certainly with no room to spare. There was, however, an officer riding a motorcycle with no pillion seat. Perched on the rear mudguard Thomson was sent to find General Paget and report what had happened.

Some miles up the road and already very sore, they came up with a Command car with a staff officer beside it. Paget came out —imperiously they were waved to stop; it only then occurred to Thomson that he was black from head to foot through rolling about on the upturned engine, with a few touches of blood, and the pair of them looked precisely as though they were in full flight.

'Brigadier's compliments, sir,' he said to Paget, 'the train has been wrecked and the men are marching.'

Paget retired and there was a consultation.

'What are you going to do now?' he asked Thomson, returning.

'Go back, sir,' answered Thomson, surprised.

The General appeared satisfied.

'Tell them to go on marching,' he said, 'and'—as the pair got back upon the motor-cycle and turned it round—'one more thing.'

'Sir?' said Thomson.

'Clean yourself up, boy!' said the General.

'Sir,' said Thomson, and went.

The troops were very tired and many of them were shaken or had minor injuries from the accident. The snow at the point where the accident happened was still deep, for it was two thousand feet above sea level and the going was bad. None the less, the order to keep marching was the only one that could be given for, by ill-luck, they had been caught out on a plateau without a tree or vestige of shelter, and dawn was near. Ahead of them—seventeen long miles ahead—was another tunnel, at Verma, and this was their nearest cover from enemy aircraft. If they could not get there in the dark they must get there by daylight: they might as well be bombed on the march as sitting, lying or standing. And there was now another break in the line just before the Verma tunnel that ruled out getting another train back to pick them up.

So through the waning night they plugged wearily on, with the glow of the burning train diminishing behind them. Daylight came—with daylight came the recce planes, right on timetable. They were bombed and machine-gunned, not yet in very great strength or with much effect. Mileposts encouraged them falsely, for Norwegian miles are much longer than ours. At last, near nine o'clock and in full daylight, the anxious watchers at the tunnel saw the long, straggling snake of men come clearly into view against the snow. They were dog-tired and barely able to walk, but they beat the inevitable full-scale bombing attack to the tunnel and—as always in these endless stories of retreat—came in with their personal arms and equipment intact.

All day they lay low in the tunnel, while diving aircraft tried to bomb the entrances and block them. There was little space, for also sheltering in the tunnel was the train brought from Aandalsnes to take them on at nightfall: it was an uncomfortable neighbour, for there was no ventilation. There were also no rations. And there were constant alarms about the enemy advance: Marines and a company of the Green Howards were sent out to hold them, if there should be need. Towards dusk the banked fires of the engine's furnace were stoked up to raise steam and an unbreathable fog of smoke added to their troubles. To cries of 'pass down the car, please—plenty of room outside' they staggered out, coughing and spluttering, but their ordeal was nearly at an end. Night came. The train pulled cautiously out. They climbed aboard and Paget watched them as they steamed away. At Aandalsnes the ships were already waiting.

The previous night, about the time their ill-fated train was leaving Dombaas, *Galatea, Arethusa, Sheffield* and *Southampton*, with six destroyers, had braved the passage through the fiord to Aandalsnes. Mercifully it was a quieter night—the Germans still had no word of the evacuation. And a small concrete quay was still intact, though the wooden ones had gone: from this one thousand, eight hundred men who had already arrived were picked up, together with small parties from Molde and a few other points. They were away by daylight with only a handful of bombs to speed their departure: it had not yet dawned on the Germans that the cruisers were carrying the saviours of Norway home. And their luck lasted them all the way to Scapa Flow, where the troops were transhipped to *Lancastria* for passage to the Clyde.

Now it was the turn of the remainder, and after this night there would be no more ships at Aandalsnes. Already there were signs that the lull was no more than a passing one. During the afternoon the bombing attacks again became so heavy and the strain on the two anti-aircraft cruisers spending their last day of purgatory in the fiord so severe, that for the first time they had to put to sea at night. Admiral Layton was heavily attacked on his way in with two more cruisers and five destroyers. He was ready by eleven o'clock: meanwhile one destroyer had gone to Aalesund to pick up the last naval detachment from there and another to Molde for General Ruge—for he had been persuaded at the eleventh hour not to give himself up but to join his King in northern Norway.

Cameron Nicholson's last memories of the Norwegian campaign are of standing on the quay in the eerie near-darkness with the remains of Aandalsnes smouldering and flickering around them. With him were Paget who, as always, would see his men off himself, Colonel Beichmann and some others. Beichmann had been faithful to his allies and to Ruge's bargain with them. General Massy's official report speaks of the road transport used in the final stages being 'wheedled' out of the Norwegians: nothing could be more unjust to the Norwegian or the British commanders or the relationship between them—the Norwegians gave what they could ill spare but gave it with an astonishing lack of bitterness, while for his part, it was not in Paget's nature to 'wheedle' anything.

Nicholson remembers Admiral Layton pacing the quay in an agony of apprehension for his ships in the fiord. Every other moment he looked at his watch—time and time again he repeated that the men were late and that he must get his ships out of the fiord by daylight.

But at last they came—one thousand, three hundred of them, to be packed into the destroyers alongside the quay and ferried out to the cruisers. They were tired, unkempt and ravenously hungry after lying low in the Verma tunnel all day with hardly so much as a bite to eat, but their spirits were extraordinarily high and in spite of the fact that they were being harried along to make as much haste as they could, there were arguments as to who should be last.

When the one thousand three hundred had been embarked Admiral Layton made haste to get his ships under way, leaving behind *Auckland* with the two anti-aircraft cruisers to pick up the expected rearguard of some two hundred and forty men. In his haste and in the confusion of the last hours it was not realized that the whole of the main force had not been embarked, and shortly after another seven hundred and fifty men, whom everyone thought were accounted for, appeared. They were crammed into *Calcutta*: shortly afterwards the expected two hundred and forty arrived at the quay in good order but in great haste. They were positively whistled aboard *Auckland*, so that from first to last their embarkation took no more than seven minutes.

By two o'clock they were gone, and already the uneasy night sky was beginning to lighten slowly with the first touches of the early Norwegian dawn. There would be no more battles in the Gudbrandsdal: the thunder would depart from the valleys and whatever else was coming to the Norwegians in the grim years of the occupation ahead, at least they would be spared the ruthless bombing and gunning of their towns and villages as soon as the sight of the khaki battledress of their would-be defenders was seen in them. For what was left of the Norwegian Army—save for those who would get away to freedom by land or sea (and these were not a few) there was only the inevitable capitulation and disbandment, which followed everywhere within a matter of days. In the Österdal and to the west of the Gudbrandsdal, where Colonel Dahl's forces had been cut off after the disaster at Tretten, the fight against the invaders had already ceased; and for the rest, General Hvinden-Haug signed his terms on 3rd May. But the ancient fortress of Hegra held on for another two days. Its founders had built it in other times as a bastion facing towards the Swedish frontier. By superhuman efforts its antique but massive guns had been lifted and remounted so as to face the foe of a later day advancing from their rear. The guns were served until there was nothing left for them to fire and very little food remaining in the fortress: then and then only did Major Holtermann hoist the white flag of surrender, beaten but undefeated. Thus from his countrymen he earned for himself the title of the Hero of Hegra: he got away, to command the Norwegian troops in Scotland, and survived to be presented after the war, as a mark of signal honour, with the massive key of the ancient stronghold which he had so stoutly defended.

There were Norwegians who did not surrender, just as there were men of 148 and 15 Brigades who did not return home. They lie in many places, but most of all near Kvam and at Nord Sel, near Otta. At Kvam a great monolith of stone is the Norwegians' memorial to their countrymen who fell in the vain attempt to stem the German advance along the valleys from Oslo: the British war graves are nearby in the churchyard—in the centre a great cross and sword, around them rose bushes tended by

Norwegian schoolchildren. At Nord Sel the Norwegians still put flowers on the graves of the Green Howards on the anniversary of their great battle. May they rest there as long in peace as the monument to the seventeenth-century Scottish mercenaries who had preceded them in those parts—around which C Company of the Green Howards made their unforgettable stand at Otta.

So much for Sickleforce—which had started off as the southern limb of the pincer movement on Trondheim, switched to an impossible defensive action far from its base, all but became a second 'Hammer' and finally petered out. What of the five thousand four hundred men of Mauriceforce—lying uneasily in its defensive positions near Namsos since the German defenders had struck out desperately from Trondheim to force it into headlong and nearly disastrous retreat? Carton de Wiart had spent his last days in Norway in glowering inaction. He knew that evacuation was imminent and unavoidable. He was convinced there was no action of any importance he could take that would not lead to the speedy annihilation of the men under his command, who could not hope to bring off another escape almost unscathed a second time. He took no part in the abortive plan for a concerted counter-attack by the Norwegians and the Chasseurs Alpins. He was asked, however, to consider sending all or part of his force up into the mountainous region north of Namsos, where the next phase of this story will presently take us, to form a temporary defence around the little port of Mosjöen—an insurance of sorts against the inevitable German advance from the south before fresh troops were put in to hold it and block the way to all-important Narvik. This he refused to do. The road, difficult in the winter for infantry, was now almost impassable in the thaw. He sent a couple of staff officers to explore the way by car and when they came back to report that it had taken them twelve hours to cover forty miles his determination became adamant. If his troops had not had the arms and equipment to defend themselves adequately against the Germans around Trondheim, let alone to take offensive action, there was no logical reason why things should be any better for them farther north. It would be the same story all over again but this time extricating them would be quite a different matter.

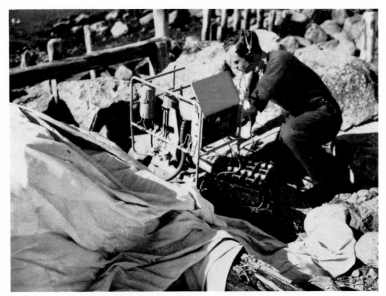

A radio post in use on the shore of Namsos Fjord.

A bomb that hit the railway between Namsos and Snaasa but failed to explode.

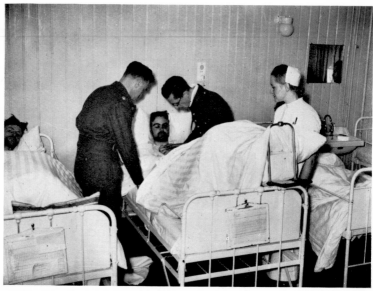

British wounded in Namsos hospital, the only building still standing in the town.

Incendiary shells setting fire to woods near Kvam.

He is severely criticized for his refusal by General Massy who points out that the Germans seemed to have found the way easy enough, but then General Massy, however good his intentions or however fair he tried to make his judgement, was in England, had not experienced the gross inequality of the battle on the ground in Norway and had not seen the *blitzkrieg* in full cry. In making his decision General de Wiart had one unassailable advantage—nobody, by the wildest stretch of imagination or invective, could call him a coward: after the event, with unclouded judgement and with all the facts in our possession, there can be very little doubt that he was right and his superior officer wrong.

In the event, a small detachment of French were shipped around the coast as a temporary holding force: the rest of General Audet's units were partly got away before the main evacuation, while the remainder were the first to embark when the evacuation ships came in, for he had besought Carton de Wiart not to leave the Chasseurs till the last.

Now the plan had been for the first of the evacuation ships—in this case cruisers, destroyers and three French transports—to arrive at Namsos on the evening of 1st May and to do the lift in two nights. In other words it would start a day later than the Aandalsnes evacuation—itself a dangerous decision, because although the Germans did not spot the evacuation of the other forces it would obviously not take them long to find out what had happened. But if by any chance they did not find out for themselves before 2nd May, they and the world would get the news from the British Government itself; for Mr. Chamberlain was being hard pressed for a statement on the Norwegian campaign and for all sorts of complicated political reasons he could not postpone it beyond that date. In the statement it would be necessary for him to announce the evacuation from Aandalsnes—before even that was complete and certainly while all the troops involved were still on the high seas. In short, not for the first time in this campaign or for the last time in the Second World War, the lives of men were to be placed second to political necessities. This was bad enough for Mauriceforce—but the weather took a hand in matters as well as Mr. Chamberlain. Approaching their rendezvous off the coast in the late evening of 1st May the warships and transports ran into a dense bank of fog which, in the absence of normal aids to navigation, made it impossible to hazard the ships. Carton de Wiart had no inkling of this because there was no sign of the fog at Namsos. He had already got his dispersed units out of their concealed positions and was concentrating them for embarkation when the news reached him: all his plans had to be put rapidly into reverse and the troops beat the German reconnaisance planes back to their hiding places by only a very small margin indeed. And here they passed the day while both Carton de Wiart and General Audet pondered the obvious impossibility of getting all their men away in one short night and Mr. Chamberlain made his announcement in the House.

It was a fair specimen of the terms in which politicians attempt to dress up in words the tidings of an undoubted military defeat. In face of the fact that by our wrong thinking and confusion we had not merely betrayed our new allies but also let slip the chance of striking a blow at German prestige which would have had enormous repercussions, he declared that the Norwegian campaign 'had only concluded a single phase'. He went on to say that it was too soon to strike 'the Norwegian balance sheet'—a miserable metaphor which conjures up a picture of a small, mean business man poring over his ledger rather than of a Prime Minister of a great nation conducting war. The same line of thought was to be repeated a few days later when he said that the Norwegian campaign was paying good dividends. Only a few days of power were left him, for at last the passionate indignation of Parliament and the country was to drive him from the power he had wielded unwisely and held too long—this little Prime Minister who talked in terms of account books, this pedestrian Prime Minister who talked of people missing a 'bus—but it would be too late to save Norway. He laid stress likewise on the way in which the supplies to Germany of iron ore through Narvik had been interrupted—without mentioning the fact that with the melting of the ice in the Gulf of Bothnia the iron ore could now for the rest of the season be shipped direct from Sweden in any case, and clearly showing that Narvik had been uppermost in his thoughts all the time.

Mercifully, the fog had cleared by the following evening and the cruisers, destroyers and transports came in on time. In his memoirs Carton de Wiart later gave full rein to his admiration for the efficiency with which the Navy ran the embarkation of the whole force from the one tiny quay which survived, and, in the face of the impossible, was on its way out of the fiord by two o'clock in the morning. The sky was already beginning to lighten, but the destroyer *Afridi* waited for the small rear party which had stayed to blow the last of the bridges and was steaming at top speed in the wake of the main convoy half an hour after it had left.

But it was too much to hope that, with all the obvious warning that had been given to the Germans, Mauriceforce could get away scot-free. The Navy had no illusions about the peril they were in. It was already abundantly clear that the light bombing raids on the German air bases had done nothing to check their activities. The Namsos area was completely out of range of any shore-based aircraft we had, and the aircraft carriers had already been driven off the scene. To make matters worse, the only air escort of any kind laid on for the convoy was a solitary Sunderland flying-boat which was useless for counter-attack against dive-bombers, and R.A.F. coastal command had not been told about the convoy at all. When the German reconnaissance plane came over on schedule for the last time at half past four it expected to find the convoy and did; and immediately it whistled up the bombers from their bases. It was, however, more than three hours before the first attacks came in—but when they came, they came in deadly earnest. For two solid hours they continued without intermission, while the anti-aircraft cruiser *Carlisle*, steaming at the tail end of the convoy, vainly tried to fight them off. A few aircraft, indeed, were brought down but the defences were saturated and once more it was only because the dive-bombers were not yet so expert as they afterwards became that the transports were not sunk. They did get the French destroyer *Bison*, setting her on fire and puncturing her fuel-oil tanks, so that the sea around her blazed as well. The British destroyers took her survivors aboard and then sank her by gunfire. In doing so they inevitably fell astern of the rest of the force and were out of range of such protection as *Carlisle*'s guns could provide for most of the rest of the two hundred miles for which the bombing continued. Shortly after two o'clock *Afridi* was hit by two bombs and mortally damaged. Among her dead—over one hundred of them—when she capsized not long afterwards were many of the survivors of *Bison* and of the rearguard she had taken aboard: so the

Hallamshire Battalion suffered the last of its casualties in the sorry tale of Mauriceforce.

Although the bombing went on until half past five, when the convoy was far from the Norwegian coast, there were miraculously no further casualties. Mauriceforce reached Scapa Flow on 5th May, eighteen days after it had left. It was Carton de Wiart's sixtieth birthday: he was able to celebrate it with a glass of champagne which he accepted gratefully, for it was a drink to which he was particularly partial. It had been, he afterwards wrote, 'the dullest campaign in which I had taken part'—which is another one of those understatements to which he was as partial as he was to champagne.

Colonel Getz and his Norwegian forces—still waiting for their orders for the counter-attack which would never come and for the British arms and ammunition they had been promised—knew less about the evacuation of their allies than the Germans. They received news of it, in fact, when Mauriceforce was already at sea—in a brief note from Carton de Wiart and a long letter from General Audet containing many fine and conciliatory phrases about the necessities of war. Suddenly he, too, was faced with surrender, though one slender, ill-equipped battalion of his forces was able to get away to the north, where it was to play a brief part in the futile attempts to delay the German advance by land on Narvik.

Getz had throughout been impatient and distrustful of his allies and cynical about the show they had made. He was by nature an impatient and energetic man. Now he reacted with great and unconcealed bitterness. After making his surrender terms with the Germans, he retired to his hunting lodge, to take no further part in public affairs or any part in the Resistance. In his bitter solitude he set down on paper his story of the campaign on his front, exposing stage by miserable stage the follies and shortcomings of his British and French allies as he had seen them. Ill-advisedly, he allowed this book to be published from enemy-occupied Oslo—blinded by his anger to the fact that he was providing the Germans with a magnificent weapon of propaganda which they eagerly used to the full. Because of this many people in his own country, as well as abroad, became convinced that he was a fifth-columnist and are so convinced to this day; and the inaction of his forces during the brief days of the fighting to the north of Trondheim has been interpreted in this light.

Only those who knew Getz closely and are most qualified to speak of him are able to say how absurd and impossible this accusation is. General Ruge and General Beichmann have both been numbered among his unswerving defenders, and their evidence must override the opinions of those less fitted to judge. It was not given him to strike the blow he burned to strike for Norway, and the bloodless liberation of his country gave him no second chance. Now he is dead, and it is owing to his memory that his name should be cleared.

CHAPTER II

THE DRIVE FOR THE NORTH

IN some ways what follows—the story of the encirclement and final capture of Narvik on the one hand and the remorseless advance on the other of the Germans up the almost trackless country between central and northern Norway—is a mere epilogue. Although the Allied military forces alone around Narvik were in the end to total nearly twenty-five thousand men and although far greater supplies of war material were shipped there, it cannot be pretended that it bore any relation to the defence of the great area many hundreds of miles to the south of it in which the majority of the Norwegian people were now irrevocably under German occupation, with all the miseries that was to bring in its train. Yet there was the fiction that part of Norway was still in Allied hands, and there was the reality that the Norwegian government was still on its native soil beyond the Arctic Circle, living out a strange dream-like existence under the midnight sun. There was also the undoubted fact that German supply arrangements for their beleaguered garrison in Narvik were still in a state of complete collapse and that their forces to the north and east of the town were now being hard pressed by General Fleischer's Norwegians, who really fought the most constant and determined campaign of the whole Norwegian war.

To his disillusioned and completely bewildered people far away in Trondheim and beyond King Haakon strove to keep up the pretence that all was not lost. Perhaps if he had reacted bitterly and violently, as Getz and others did, further disillusionment might have been spared and the British people, for their part, might have anticipated by a few days or weeks the violent awakening that was to be theirs before the end of May. It is understandable that he should have done his best to hearten his now captive people: in the course of the next few days he issued this proclamation:

'We still have strong positions in the north of Norway and with the help that is now planned we shall continue the reconquering of the country.

'It is the numerical and technical superiority of the enemy on land and more especially in the air which has forced us to withdraw. We have reasons to believe that conditions will soon change.

'It is not war the Germans are carrying on in Norway; it is murder and arson. But the morale of the people is unshaken and unshakeable.

'I and the government are firmly resolved to resist until the country has been liberated.'

Later still he declared:

'This part of the country, which perhaps for years past has not been noticed as it deserved to be noticed, has given evidence during these days of its ability and dignity to represent a free and independent Norway. It is my belief that, with the help of the Allies, we can here reorganize our defence and so win back the liberty of the whole nation.'

And he went on to beg his people in the occupied areas not to lose heart, but to go on believing and hoping in the conviction that for the generations to come they would one day be able to rebuild their country.

But, in spite of it all, the world was aghast at what had happened. To people at home in Britain, particularly, the news of the evacuation was utterly and completely incomprehensible. Before another year was up the pattern of landing in a threatened country, defeat and evacuation, was to become all too familiar to them: now it was not. Nothing had been done to prepare them, nothing had been done to give them the slightest inkling of the real character, size or strength of the forces that had been put into central Norway. Reverses had either gone unreported or been referred to only in the most guarded and misleading terms. As late as 29th April, when the battle was over, the evacuation had been decided on and Sickleforce and Mauriceforce were preparing for embarkation; the official communiqué read like this:

'The British are in touch with the enemy north of Steinkjer. Enemy patrols were repulsed with losses. Several prisoners were captured. A British raiding party yesterday ambushed a German detachment, killing and taking several prisoners.'

This came on top of reports of British air raids on German bases, which were not untrue but none the less totally misleading because they gave no hint of the slender strength in which the attacks were mounted, stories of the 'huge minefield' in the Skagerrak and so on. To the Norwegians, over whose homes the flame and thunder of the *blitzkrieg* had passed, the defeat of the mighty British Allies was much more easily grasped in spite of their bewilderment than in an island yet to know the weight of the Luftwaffe and yet to feel the stigma of defeat in almost every quarter of Europe on which the British had set foot. Only Churchill glowered, frustrated and ill at ease, but still bound to bolster the government of tired men to which he owed allegiance —and around him the little band of men who craved for action and bloody adventure in the face of the enemy, Sir Roger Keyes and the rest.

What now was the situation and what could we do? Nearly a fortnight previously, after *Suffolk* had been bombed and badgered all the way home from her attack on Stavanger, Admiral Forbes had put forward a scheme for at least stabilizing the situation at the level it had reached—by blockading Norway from the sea, holding the communications to maintain and reinforce our troops in the north, and so both consolidating our hold there and keeping up a constant drain on German resources. This, indeed, was the most that the bold and bloody-minded Navy, forced out of southern Norwegian waters, could now hope to achieve. But even this was impossible of execution for it took no account of what was going to happen elsewhere. By the beginning of May his forces were already being whittled away under the threat to the Low Countries and the imminence of Italy's entry into the war. In the first week of May Admiral Edward-Collins's cruiser squadron, with *Galatea* and *Arethusa* that had done such splendid service, was to be withdrawn to Sheerness and eight destroyers to Harwich. *Berwick, Glasgow* and more destroyers were destined first for Iceland, then for refit and duty in home waters. Before long another eight destroyers were to be withdrawn to Harwich and another nine to the Mediterranean, together with the battling anti-aircraft cruiser *Carlisle* and three of the anti-aircraft sloops. Admiral Layton's squadron, with *Manchester, Birmingham* and *Sheffield*, was to follow, and long before the final assault on Narvik could take place the Commander-in-Chief was to find himself bereft not merely of destroyers to do all the fetching and carrying jobs that had been their lot on the coast of broken-up islands and manifold fiords, but even without sufficient to screen his big ships.

In any case it could never be a question of the Norwegians and ourselves merely holding on to the territory that remained beyond the Arctic Circle. The situation could not remain static. The Germans could not and would not allow it to remain static: still at a loss to understand why their isolated forces in and around Narvik had not been mopped up long before, they were as desperately anxious about them as they had previously been about their isolated garrison in Trondheim—and now that Trondheim and the whole of central Norway were secured, they did not intend to lose a moment in relieving them. The Luftwaffe was now free to concentrate on Narvik, on the shipping in the fiords, the bridges, on the naval and military bases at Skaanland and Harstad, every place on land where there were signs of troop movements or troops billeted. Nor was there still any opposition to them in the air, apart from what *Ark Royal* and *Glorious* could provide from off the coast—in the intervals of being forced out of effective range, of having to go home to fuel or repair damage or for other purposes. The effects of the release of the Luftwaffe from central Norway became apparent immediately after the evacuation. For the moment it was a matter of attack by the long-range high-level bombers only: this was bad enough and made movement on sea or land even more difficult than it had been before; but the moment the German land forces, following up the thaw, could secure landing grounds farther north than Trondheim, the deadly Stuka dive-bombers could follow, and then there would be trouble indeed. For then, once more, the pattern of the situation round Trondheim would be reproduced all over again—the ships with steam on their engines all day dodging and pumping out anti-aircraft shell from rapidly deteriorating guns, the smaller craft being harried and murdered, the troops on land skulking from the all-seeing eyes of the recce planes and the missiles and machine-gun bullets of the bombers.

Yet, in the middle of all this, in the face of this inevitably developing situation, there was a fantastic and silly paradox. In Narvik, subsisting side by side with the civilian population on stinking fish eked out by parachuted supplies and supplies brought in by flying-boat and over the Swedish border, the Germans hung on in deadly anticipation of the final assault that was going to drive them into the mountains and over the border into Sweden, if they could get there. It is true that the daily anticipation had gone on long enough for the edge to have been worn off it, but it was there none the less. With the passage of time the command headquarters itself had been withdrawn eastward from Narvik town and the local command had devolved successively on officers more and more junior as the eggs were withdrawn from the basket. From day to day the Norwegians listened to the blast and crump of demolitions as the harbour works, the iron ore loading plant and the railway were put out of action, against the time when the Allies should gain possession of them: the tools of prosperity, which the people of this place had so hardly won for themselves after years of hardship and endeavour, were being blasted away before their eyes in a war which was none of their making.

Out upon the mountains to the north of the town and the fiords General Fleischer's reorganized and ever-stronger forces pressed relentlessly upon the shrinking perimeter of the German defences. By 1st May, in spite of straffing from the air, in spite of cold, hardship and lack of encouragement from their allies, a movement had been set up which was to go on continuously until the withdrawal of the Allied Forces suddenly left the Norwegians alone and in an impossible position.

Narvik was a nut to be cracked. It was a nut that was rotten at the core and could have been cracked already without difficulty. The nutcrackers—the Allied forces, virtually inactive all this time apart from skirmishes—were poised for the cracking, yet were remaining poised, awaiting a build-up that would make them more like a steam-hammer to be used to crack this nut. And the government at home, freed from the distraction, the minor irritation which the all-important campaign in central Norway had appeared to them to be, were now lavishing everything on the darling Narvik project—in so far, that is, as the scarcity of almost everything needed for the prosecution of the war allowed them to lavish. When Lieutenant-General Auchinleck finally left England to take over the command from Mackesy, his orders showed that thinking in the War Cabinet had gone right back to the days of Plan

R.4. The object of His Majesty's Government in northern Norway, they declared, was to maintain a base from which we could deny iron ore supplies to Germany via Narvik, interfere as far as possible with iron ore supplies to Germany via Lulea and—a bad third—preserve a part of Norway as a seat of government for the Norwegian King and people. It was all wrong and it was all in vain, because Norway was already lost and time in Narvik had, in fact, run out. But the build-up continued.

Some of the things in the build-up could have been spared, unless it were assumed that the steam-hammer would stand poised for ever—pioneers, field bakeries and garrison elements of all kinds. Lord Cork was, in fact, constrained to send some of these home because of the excessive congestion they caused in the restricted area of the base and the difficulty of protecting them from bombing. Others were more to the point. On 27th April the three battalions of French Chasseurs refused house-room by Carton de Wiart at Namsos arrived, to be followed immediately by General Béthouart; and although this officer was surrounded by staff and moved with a certain majesty, he quickly proved to be a bold leader and a much more congenial companion for Cork than General Mackesy. His troops, however, laboured under the same deficiencies of training and equipment as the other demi-brigade which had served at Namsos. They were short of mules and short of snowshoes—they were also short of trained skiers: the Scots Guards' history declares that they brought four hundred pairs of skis but only three men who could use them and the Irish Guards' account makes a similar statement. Whether the similarity of the two statements is confirmation or merely the turning of gossip into history it is difficult to decide: in other respects the accounts are carefully compiled. But it has to be admitted that whatever else they lacked, they showed plenty of ardour and offensive spirit, fought well and did not shrink from sacrifice.

The Chasseurs were followed by two battalions of the Foreign Legion, the same who had embarked from France with ceremonial parades and garlands. If ever there were troops who displayed at the same time all the virtues and all the vices of the French as a fighting nation, these were they: in spite of the fact they did well enough and were the first troops to enter Narvik, it is difficult (for this writer at least) to write about them wholly in deadly earnest—what can you do with a unit whose regimental march invites you to have a bit of sausage? Their achievements are related in a book by Captain Pierre Lapie, which is one of the most bombastic, exaggerated and infuriating documents that ever came off a press. One reads at great length about the celebration at sea of their regimental day, the Camerone, about the Colonel's hiccups, about the disorderliness of their disembarkation, their chaotic lack of discipline, their hilarious disregard of any sort of decency in their relations with the civilian population. One feels, amid the deadly earnestness and peculiar horrors of modern war, that they were conducting a sort of private buccaneering campaign both for the amusement of themselves and such of the audience as were able to see the joke. There are endless references to years of comradeship, campaigns under the scorching desert sun and much more that belongs purely to the pages of *Beau Geste*: yet these battalions had been formed less than three months previously and many of the men were recent and even raw recruits—especially Spaniards in flight from their fascist oppressors, and exiled Poles denied their own ravaged country. One cannot suppress just a sneaking thought that if these were the troops who actually captured Narvik ('the first victory of the war') then Mackesy's reluctance to capture Narvik was as misguided as Lord Cork had always maintained. None the less, not everything about them was comic. They brought with them twelve field guns, the first to be landed by the Allies in Norway, and ten light tanks: the only other tank unit—the British 3rd Hussars, who were also part of the build-up—had to operate without their tanks, and a battery of field gunners was followed, some days later, by its twenty-five pounders.

Four battalions of Poles completed the expansion of the force—grim men, these, anxious to hit back at the Germans anywhere they could find them, as they had every right to be. Though they were styled Chasseurs de Montagne they had no experience of mountains or mountain warfare—but some of them, at least, had seen the *blitzkreig* in their native land. Like Carton de Wiart, they knew what to expect and the throb of a Junkers engine held bitter memories for them.

These reinforcements were all very well. The tools of the trade of war were needed as much as the men to use them—the whole

course of the campaign in central Norway had shown that the
stoutest of men were powerless without weapons and equipment.
Water transport was needed—more than ever now that the air
raids were making the owners of the civilian 'puffers' more
reluctant to hazard their craft every day: there was an enthusiastic welcome, therefore, for eight landing craft which were
unloaded on 29th April. They were experimental, crotchety,
subject to all sorts of bugs and teething troubles but (in Lord
Cork's expressive and stilted language) they 'started a career of
remarkable usefulness'. Less useful (though it would have been
otherwise if the base had not been thoughtfully placed on an
island) was a large consignment of trucks—most of which were
oiled and cleaned daily, only to be pushed into the sea when the
evacuation came. Bren carriers were a different story: although
most of them went down in *Effingham*, three survived, as we shall
see, to do great service in a very grim moment.

But the tools Lord Cork had agitated for most of all were tools
to put up some opposition, at least, to the enemy in the air—anti-
aircraft guns and fighter aircraft. He had become as insistent in his
demands for these as Carton de Wiart had been from Namsos—
made them, in fact, his almost invariable counter-demands to the
constant urgings from London for the capture of Narvik. At last,
towards the end of April, twelve Bofors guns arrived—limited in
their use but welcome. On the last day of the month he was
promised another forty-eight Bofors and sixty 3·7s—far less
than he had asked for to cover his scattered forces, but with them,
at any rate, the men could begin to feel they were hitting back and
some rudimentary defence could be spared with difficulty for the
civilian population at Tromsö and elsewhere. On 6th May the
guns began to arrive: they were speedily in action. The sending of
two anti-aircraft cruisers was a more doubtful blessing: as elsewhere, they would bring relief to the land forces largely by
attracting attention to themselves.

But fighters . . . where were fighters to be based? With the
terrible object lesson of Lesjaskog fresh in the minds of everyone,
there could be no more frozen lakes. Cork had been scouring the
countryside for possible landing grounds since his earliest days in
Norway, but with three feet or more of snow on the ground it
needed some sort of second sight to see what was possible and

what was not. Under the snow at Bardufoss was a Norwegian airfield, said to have been used by Gladiators: there was another to the south, at Bodö, and the Germans already had eyes on this, too, as an objective to be captured and so help in bringing the Stukas north. The Fleet Air Arm got busy on clearing Bardufoss and another possible site was marked out at Skaanland, near the naval base. Not until the last day but one of April did the thaw, which had come suddenly to central Norway some days earlier, begin to make itself felt beyond the Arctic Circle. Now, perhaps, serious work could start, though the period of the thaw itself, with the whole lower-lying part of the country a quagmire, would be the most difficult of all. So on 4th May another of those civilian flying-boats which in the couple of years before the war had pioneered the Atlantic service, only to be shot up doing jobs for which they were never intended, brought Wing Commander Dick Atcherley to prepare for the coming of two R.A.F. Squadrons already earmarked for the fighter defence of the Allied forces —263 Gladiator Squadron, which was now blooded by its violent experience at Lesjaskog and this time was to have its own ground staff and equipment, and 46 Hurricane Squadron, a crack unit from the east coast, already experienced in battle. A young man with a considerable past and a distinguished future was this Atcherley: ten years or less before, as a Schneider Trophy pilot, he had been as fabulous a figure to the youth of his time as the first astronauts were to be to a later generation, and he was to survive to be an Air Marshal with a handle to his name.

Atcherley had brought with him no 'gen' (to use the language of his own Service) from the Air Ministry—there was none to be had, on climate, conditions, or anything else. He did bring with him an unshakeable determination that what had happened at Lesjaskog was not to be allowed to happen again and an equal determination not to allow himself to be governed by the operations of nature in the matter of snow, thaw or things of that sort. He was positive that nature could be interfered with and in fact he was right: Bardufoss was ready on time and was operative as long as aircraft were there—Skaanland was less lucky. And once started, for the brief period left to the Allies in Norway, flying operations went almost without a hitch.

He started with a good omen. Arriving (inevitably) to find an air raid in progress and buildings on fire, he was greeted by cheering troops: the departure of the Germans had coincided with the appearance of his totally unarmed flying-boat. It was coincidence, but it did a lot for morale. He found Cork and Mackesy not talking much, Fleischer (to whom he went with a pencilled note from Ruge for credentials) resentful and unco-operative, but such survivors of the Norwegian Air Force as were in the district eager and helpful. And he got down to the job. It is a thousand pities that Atcherley or someone like him could not have been let loose in central Norway, for then many things that happened would have happened otherwise.

By the time of Atcherley's arrival there had been a lot of movement around Narvik, though none of it added up to the capture of the port, which the War Cabinet in London were still wearily demanding, or even its attempted capture. General Béthouart, as we have already seen, arrived with a breath of that offensive spirit which Cork had once owned to but had lost in the course of many frustrations. He had immediately proposed a landing directly opposite Narvik at Öyjord,* an attack from there up the Rombaksfiord on Bjerkvik, the western extremity of the German line and—after an advance down the eastern side of the same fiord, an assault across the water, covered by artillery bombardment, on Narvik itself. General Mackesy promptly vetoed this. He was already, with the prospect in sight of the thaw for which he had waited so long, putting his own ponderous, World-War-I-type plan of encirclement into effect. He had brought the Irish Guards once more over to Bogen, on the next inlet westwards from the Rombaksfiord, from whence they were to advance on Bjerkvik along the road across the base of the Öyjord peninsula. He had shipped the South Wales Borderers across the main Ofot-fiord to Ballangen, a long way from Narvik and separated from it by two fiords, but at least on the right side of the water—and thence moved them farther along the coast, over the first of the fiords between them and their objective, on to the Ankenes peninsula. Here they were, for the first time, within firing distance at least of German patrols, and they sat down to a sort of investing operation. He added a battalion of the Chasseurs to help them.

* Pronounced 'Ay-yure'.

The other two battalions of the Chasseurs he gave to General Fleischer, to help the movement of the westernmost of the two brigades into which the Norwegian forces had now been reorganized—the first direct reinforcement the Norwegians had received from the Allies in more than three weeks of grim Norwegian battle and Allied inaction. Painfully and determinedly now the Norwegians were pushing the Germans back towards Bjerkvik in a series of small, desperate encounters as bitterly fought as any of the bloody little actions in the valleys of South and Central Norway—only now it was the Norwegians who were pressing and the Germans who were in retreat. The cold was still bitter at night and the French suffered severely from it, but they stuck it out. The Scots Guards—whose defensive rôle had been so sneered at by Fleischer and so irksome to themselves—were withdrawn to the base at Harstad: they had another fate awaiting them, which would make them wish they had never complained of boredom.

At the same time Fleischer's easterly group—now entitled 6th Brigade—pressed in from the north on the bulge in the German front at Lapphavgen and clawed their way up on to a one thousand-five-hundred-foot plateau where the Germans had established defensive positions which General Dietl's orders bade them to hold at all costs. The hardships of the attackers were extreme, even for men accustomed to the country. There was still great cold, but almost perpetual daylight—little rest, no hot food, no cover except for snow-holes. The approaches to the plateau were too steep for horses and every scrap of ammunition, equipment and food had to be painfully carried up in rucksacks. They were thin on the ground, with battalion fronts up to four miles, isolated—their only communication through telephone cables precariously laid in the snow and desperately unreliable. They lacked engineer stores of all kinds, for all this equipment had fallen into the hands of the Germans at Elvegaard. Yet they pressed on unflinchingly and presently joined hands on the plateau with the left wing of the other battle groups. The German salient was being flattened out.

The Earl of Cork's one and only attempt to stimulate a similar show of action on his own front petered out once again in the thirsty sands of argument and opposition. Perhaps it was the arrival of General Béthouart which had conjured up in him the ghost of the fire-eating little admiral who had once arrived in those parts to take Narvik forthwith by storm: perhaps it was the thaw, perhaps it was the constant and querulous demands from London or perhaps it was all three. At any rate, he gave orders for preparation for a direct assault on the town by two British battalions, to take place on 8th May. The Scots Guards once more prepared themselves for this assault in meticulous detail and with tremendous labour. Two companies of them embarked in the netlayer *Protector* for an advance base along the Ofotfiord. They slaved for thirty-six hours without sleep, manhandled by sheer sweat well over two hundred tons of stores and by 4th May had, in their own words, 'everything ready to assault Narvik except the means of getting there'. On this day a recce was made in the cruiser *Aurora*, their officers (for the Guards thought of everything) wearing naval caps to avoid giving the Germans the slightest hint that anything was afoot. At this stage opposition against Cork's plan brewed up throughout the whole of the British command, and the representations they made to him were so strong and so determined that he felt he could not possibly carry on in face of such united opposition. It is true that he was the commander of the combined forces and was in a position to give orders: earlier on, in spite of his command, he had realized that it would be folly to insist on carrying out plans with Mackesy against him—how could he now carry on with virtually every senior British Army officer against him and some of his own naval staff as well? The objections were complex and some of them based on deficiencies of which Cork was very well aware, such as the shortage of landing-craft, the restricted size of the landing area, the almost perpetual daylight and the enemy command of the air. He could not but concede their validity. Wearily, therefore, he referred the whole matter to superior authority in London for decision, and received a reply which in effect passed the responsibility for the decision back to him. He must have half expected such a reply because by the time it arrived he had already made up his mind to put off any further action until the arrival of the new miltary commander, General Auchinleck, who was due to embark on 7th May in *Chrobry* and would not arrive until the 11th. In any case, he had further problems on his hands. The fact that time was running out was being emphasized by the Germans' obvious intention to continue their advance up the coast from central Norway.

In theory the way from central Norway to the Narvik area is beset by what, in old-fashioned military terminology, used to be called natural barriers—faith in which persisted in some quarters of British military thinking for at least the two earliest years of the war—until, having at last appreciated, for instance, the fact that the Japanese were capable of operating in what was alleged to be impassable jungle we found that we were able to operate in it ourselves. In this particular case sufficient warning and sufficient demonstration had been given by the Germans farther south that with proper equipment and training they could move with tolerable ease in winter mountain conditions which pinned our own troops down. None the less, the country north of Namsos is formidable indeed. For one thing, there is well over three hundred miles of it. For another it is a region of very high mountains, in many places well over two thousand feet above sea level, and parts of it are extremely high—they are snow-bound right through the year. It is very narrow—over much of it the Swedish border is barely forty miles from the sea. It is cut by many lakes and by long, narrow fiords that sometimes sever the narrow strip almost completely. There is one valley route by road—a narrow road, running often through deep defiles and interrupted at several points by ferry passages up to ten miles long. And in 1940 the single narrow line of railway stopped altogether at Grong, the railway junction for Namsos with which we are familiar. It is sparsely populated—for the excellent reason that over large tracts of it there is nothing on which even a Norwegian could subsist. The only inhabited places along it which justify the name of anything larger than village are Mosjöen,* on the Vefsenfiord, ninety miles from Namsos by sea but a hundred and fifty by road; Mo, sixty miles farther to the north at the head of the long, narrow Ranfiord and only a few miles from the Swedish border; and Bodö.† The latter is the largest of the three, but itself houses no more than four thousand souls—a picturesque town of parallel streets which have grown one by one inland from the little harbour which is its livelihood. At both Mosjöen and Mo there is

* Pronounced 'Morshern'.
† Pronounced 'Boder'.

sufficient level ground to make small airfields just possible: at Bodö there was a landing ground, used in the summer, and at the time of which we are writing about to be cleared by the thaw. In theory, access to this narrow coastal strip should have been easy for the Navy by virtue of its superiority at sea: in practice German air supremacy denied the Navy these coastal waters as effectively as those farther south had been denied, and the maze of narrow passages—the selfsame Leads with which the whole story started —was suicidal to ships denied the sea room to take avoiding action under air attack.

We have seen how Carton de Wiart had stubbornly refused to move 146 Brigade or any other part of Mauriceforce into this area to delay the German advance farther north. By doing so he saved them from the purposeless fate that befell the forces which were, in the event, put there. One battalion of the Chasseurs was, however, it will be remembered, carried round to Mosjöen by sea on the evacuation of his troops, as a temporary holding force— for any good a lightly equipped battalion might be able to do against a whole German Army Group. Almost at the same time, C Company of the Scots Guards was sent from the Narvik front to Bodö, at the other end of this difficult region, with the idea that they might at least hold the airfield there against German paratroops when the thaw came. Attempts to prospect for air-fields (supposing aircraft could have been spared and got to them) at Mosjöen and Mo were quickly scotched: two more Empire flying-boats carrying a R.A.F. reconnaissance party were bombed to bits in the Vefsenfiord within less than one hour of alighting, proving that the Germans were keeping a wakeful eye on the situation.

Lord Cork was as alive to the need to protect the force round Narvik from German attack by land through this uncompromis-ing country as the War Cabinet at home. On 4th May he rashly asked for instructions about it, and the War Cabinet promptly obliged him by putting it under his command. This brought him greater responsibilities rather than greater glory: it certainly brought him no reinforcement to his ships for the purpose, nor did it prevent them being whittled away, as they were about to be.

None the less, the War Cabinet had their own plan for the defence of this area—or at least, for the delaying of enemy advance through it. To it the genius who presided over the nomenclature of forces gave the name Scissorsforce: it was to cut the road to the north. There was never any possibility of it doing anything of the sort, and it was a counsel of defeat from the beginning.

As far back as 18th April, when Sickleforce and Mauriceforce were still intact and only starting their operations, recruitment had begun of what were called Independent Companies: one cannot help feeling that somewhere in the War Office, at least, there was consciousness, for very good reasons, of impending disaster. Churchill suggests that these companies were akin to what we afterwards came to know as commandos; but the rôle in which they were employed was very different from that of commandos, for—essentially lightly equipped and self-contained units—they were used in an attempt to stop the advance of a massive opposing army fully equipped with the heaviest of weapons and supported in the air. By their very nature they were an acceptance of the fact that it was impossible to provide either defence or support for them: they were to be mobile and therefore, in theory, in less need of air support than conventional units, but although they were mobile they had no transport. Employed, as events fell out, in country cut up by water in one way and another to an extent that made it remarkable even in Norway, they had no water transport either, although when they were dispatched to that country, they had attached to them a group of deep-sea trawlers which were outstandingly unsuitable for use on that coast.

The companies were all volunteers, drawn from various Territorial brigades and each was a little under four hundred strong with twenty officers. Their establishment included sappers and signals personnel, their weapons were small arms supplemented by a Bren section of four guns to each company. They were spared the massive Arctic kit which had been such a useless burden to the other forces although they did have some Arctic clothing. They were, however, equipped with snowshoes, though they cannot have received any lengthy training in using them, and a five-day emergency ration of pemmican for each man—though equally there is no evidence that they had been given the experience in training of subsisting on it. There is no evidence either (nor, once more, can there have been time for it) that they were trained in the kind of tactics called for by the rôle in which they were employed, which was to delay the advance of German forces in any way they could. This is where they were a counsel of defeat, because their very employment implied the supposition that the Germans could not be stopped, but only retarded. The name Scissorsforce, therefore, was a complete delusion, for the force had neither the means, strength nor equipment to cut the road to the north and was most certainly not qualified in numbers to stand against the Germans face to face. Five companies in all made up the force: in other words it was not even the equivalent of an ordinary infantry brigade.

It has been suggested that in their original intention the Independent Companies had been merely a sort of nucleus for 'raising the country' against the enemy. Certainly if they were going to obtain any sort of transport, local co-operation was essential; but whoever thought they might be able to subsist on dependence on such co-operation and for that matter whoever suggested they could 'raise the country' could not have gone into matters very closely, because the part of the country in which they were employed is one of the most sparsely populated parts of Norway, so that there was little to raise and little to get co-operation from. There was not even much co-operation to be got from the Norwegian Army, because the only Norwegian unit left free in the area after the desertion and surrender of the forces farther south was the one weak battalion which had escaped that way in not very good shape (for a variety of reasons including a railway accident) and the kind of isolated fighting groups which crop up here and there throughout this campaign.

When the campaign in central Norway ended with the pushing of the Allied forces into the sea, the triumphant relief of Trondheim and the junction of the two German Army Groups pushing up the parallel valleys from the Oslo region, the Germans paused —but paused for a very brief space indeed. They consolidated and amalgamated their forces and sent some of them home. Less massive but more specialized forces were required for the next job, which combined rigorous country with a narrow front. And to be their spearhead in the further advance, they sent in a new and truly formidable formation, their Second Mountain Division, which was one of the most specialized, highly trained and efficient units in the whole German Army. The units sent home could well be used on the Western Front—where the great offensive that would turn Norway into a minor theatre of war was only a few days from its beginning, first on the Low Countries and then on France.

With the reorganized forces they would now push up by land to the threatened garrison, only holding on at Narvik through the dilatoriness of the Allied Command. They would step up their air supply arrangements to Narvik: in the coming days it was soon to be noticed that the seaplane and supply-dropping traffic to the Narvik garrison and the forces beyond it increased very rapidly. And at the same time the air attacks on the Allies sitting around Narvik would be increased to a pitch that would make life impossible instead of merely intolerable. As soon as the advance of the land forces put them in possession of the few small airfields on the road to the north, they could enormously increase the effectiveness of their attacks: there was certainly the airfield at Bodö and presently Wing Commander Atcherley, on a dangerous survey by destroyer and Walrus amphibian to the south, was to report that there was a prepared landing field at Mo, which the thaw was rapidly clearing, and possibly others.

Admiral Cork's forces on land and sea soon felt the weight of the increasing offensive. Casualties on land were still few, though the buildings in use as a naval barracks at Harstad were destroyed and the historians of the Guards Brigade describe the base as being steadily battered to bits. The ships were not yet quite so hardly put to it as they had been in central Norway, for the waters in which they operated were at least wider and gave more room for manœuvre; but the Polish destroyer *Grom* was sunk, a British destroyer had a very narrow escape, the cruiser *Aurora* had one of her turrets damaged beyond repair. *Enterprise* survived one hundred and fifty bombs in one afternoon and was 'riddled with splinters'. Temporarily Skua fighter-bombers from *Ark Royal* damped down the attacks, but the Germans soon became wise to the shortcomings of this unsatisfactory aircraft; and in any case, *Ark* had to go. And the anti-aircraft ships soon found themselves once more having to put guns out of action through wear in the barrels and the recoil mechanisms.

Scissorsforce—the five Independent Companies—was therefore

about to be thrown into an operation for which it was no better fitted than the units that had fought in central Norway. The three battalions of the Guards Brigade, relieved by Polish and French troops, were to be thrown into a vain attempt to bolster Scissorsforce when it inevitably collapsed. And so the trained troops who could have done tremendous service if they had been properly employed in the earliest stages of the campaign were to be frittered away. Norway was already lost and Narvik, the War Cabinet's darling and obsession, not yet conquered. The offensive on the Western Front was poised. This was the situation in Norway in the first week of May.

One other thing happened in the course of this week—although, in common with so many other things, it happened too late to save Norway. The people of Britain and the Commons in session rose against the government of old men who had lost the peace and were now losing the war. It is part of history at large rather than merely part of the Norwegian campaign, but it was stimulated by the Norwegian campaign, is inseparable from it and in a very special way is one of the credit items on its dismal balance sheet—to pursue Mr. Chamberlain's metaphor. It was only the partial awakening of the British people; the full awakening was not to come until after Dunkirk. But had not Britain awakened just in time sufficiently to oust the old men on the verge of the great battle in the West, the miracle of Dunkirk might not have been possible, the Battle of Britain might have been lost before it started, the long road first to survival then to victory might have been closed for ever. The United States might never have had time to poise, re-adjust and equip itself for the coming struggle and Hitler might never have been driven into his foolhardy Russian adventure. The whole course of world history might have been changed. To this extent, therefore, the agony of Norway widened the narrow margin whereby the world triumph of the Nazis was staved off.

The first reaction in Britain to Mr. Chamberlain's announcement of the evacuation of Aandalsnes was bewilderment: with the evacuation of Namsos and the inevitable growing awareness of what had really happened in central Norway it changed to anger. By 7th May, when he rose to make his second statement in the House, country and Commons alike were seething. Interruptions grew steadily as his speech progressed: unsteadied by them, yet still incapable of viewing the whole thing as more than a political debate and an issue of political power, he appealed for the support of his friends in the House. And when he sat down, his friends rose against him on all sides.

Speaker after speaker flayed the unpreparedness of the government, the sloppy thinking, the cumbersome machinery, the delays and vacillations. Outstanding among them, Admiral of the Fleet Sir Roger Keyes—a slight figure (how many of the Navy's great men have been slight figures!) with the gold insignia of his rank on his arms and the six rows of medals on his breast proclaiming his authority—kept the House tense and silent as he damned, stage by stage, the 'shocking story of ineptitude'. It was, he said, repeating the story of Gallipoli step by step. From the Conservative benches his old friend and colleague, Leo Amery, flung at the Prime Minister Cromwell's bitter words to the Long Parliament: 'Depart, I say, and let us have done with you. In the name of God, go!'

Chamberlain survived the two-day debate, but only just survived. In the day that followed it he attempted to form a National Government, but his leadership was contemptuously spurned and on 10th May, Churchill was summoned to Buckingham Palace to receive at last the power of action for which he had craved. On that same day Hitler invaded the Netherlands, Belgium and Luxembourg by land and air. The 'Phoney War' was over: the real war had begun.

In the face of the vastly greater battle which had now commenced, the twilight struggle for the possession of Narvik receded: 'a sense of doom', to quote one contemporary writer, hung over it. But the tragedy still had to be acted out, and some of it is grim in the telling.

CHAPTER 12

'I RELY ON THE GUARDS'

IT is quite plain that the Earl of Cork had no illusions about the Independent Companies holding the German advance and cutting their line of communication between Trondheim and the north. Even before the arrival of General Auchinleck he proposed that to bolster them the whole of 24 Brigade should be withdrawn from the area round Narvik and their place be taken by the Poles and French. He could indeed have had still more troops to add to the latter—there were five more Independent Companies being recruited at home and these might be sent to Harstad to complete their training: there was also the demi-brigade of Chasseurs which had been evacuated intact from Namsos and had now been re-equipped. Cork did not avail himself of these troops for the same very good reason that had prompted him to send some of the base details home—he had no room for them in the restricted and bomb-battered island that was his base; and it must be admitted that the idea of any sort of training going on under these conditions was optimistic.

The Irish Guards were therefore withdrawn by stages from around Bogen on the north and the South Wales Borderers prepared for withdrawal from the Ankenes peninsula: the Scots Guards, who had already been withdrawn to the base (less the company who had already been sent south to Bodö) were re-assembled at Skaanland. Transport on land was now for the moment even more difficult and exhausting than it had been previously—the thaw was in full swing, turning everything into slush and water. With the new troops in position, he at last went ahead with the plans for the assault on Bjerkvik which both General Béthouart and himself had been endeavouring to get mounted ever since the latter's arrival on 28th April. General Auchinleck was now on the high seas on his way to take over from General Mackesy, and with any luck he would arrive to find the assault ready to take place. If successful, the capture of Bjerkvik would at last join up the Allied Forces with Fleischer's Norwegians who, supported by the Chasseurs, were pressing the Germans hard on top of the plateau while their left-hand brigade group was bearing down on the salient and squeezing them out towards the Swedish border like toothpaste from a tube. Many German dead and wounded were brought in to Narvik town in these days. The Norwegians were shocked by the callousness with which their comrades treated them and by the scant burial they gave their dead. One gets the impression that in spite of the supply dropping and in spite of the dribble of reinforcements and material through Sweden, a feeling of despair was growing among the Germans of a much more serious sort than the panic which had momentarily afflicted them during *Warspite*'s bombardment. This was virtually to be the only occasion for years on the European front when the Germans were seen in defeat or near defeat. We know now that on 6th May General Dietl had considered evacuating Narvik altogether.

But on 4th May the regrouped German forces in the south started their northward advance from Grong, the town near Namsos where the uncompleted railway ended. And it was on the very same day that the first of the Independent Companies was landed at Mo—by good fortune and the skill of the Navy once more in one piece. In the four succeeding days the others followed—two companies to Bodö, two companies to Mosjöen. It was near Bodo that Colonel Gubbins, commanding Scissorsforce, set up his headquarters, not far from where C Company of the Scots Guards had already established themselves. The naval officer in charge of the unsuitable deep-sea trawlers which had been sent out at the same time for coastal transport, Lieutenant-Commander Fell, soon realized the mistake that had been made: laying up his own craft, he set about collecting a force of Norwegian puffers, to be commanded and partly manned by his own petty officers and ratings. In its brief but remarkably useful existence this unorthodox command became known as the Gubbins Flotilla, and many a man still alive owes his salvation to the initiative of a comparatively junior officer.

The last of all the companies of Scissorsforce to set foot in Norway were (it is difficult to understand why) those closest to the advancing enemy, at Mosjöen. They landed on the night of 8/9th May—although it must be borne in mind that night in these latitudes did not now mean darkness—and by the time they got there the Germans were already well on the way with their aircraft scouting ahead of them and doing a little desultory bombing for good luck. The one very makeshift Norwegian battalion—four hundred strong and therefore hardly a battalion at all—had already gone south to meet them, and Gubbins, who had landed with his most southerly troops, sent his No. 5 company south to join them at Fellingfors, twenty-five miles south of the town. The last information placed the enemy a hundred miles away; but No. 5 Company and the Norwegians had scarcely had time to establish themselves before the infantry, tanks and guns of the Germans were upon them. In the middle of the thaw they had advanced one hundred and thirty miles in four days with as much apparent ease as they had previously advanced over the snow-bound country of southern Norway.

British and Norwegians together beat a hasty retreat to a posi-tion a few miles to the north, which the troops in rear of them had been preparing in the precipitous valley: the familiar pattern of the Gudbrandsdal was already beginning to assert itself, with the only difference that the Allied troops were even thinner on the ground. None the less, they applied themselves to their rôle of forcing the enemy to buy his advance dearly, and the following morning—the momentous morning of the 10th, when Britain was waking to the news of the *blitzkreig* on Holland and Belgium and Churchill was waiting for his historic summons to power—they shot up the Germans' screen of scouts, cycling up the road, and killed fifty of them. It was both a momentary success and a momentary lapse into carelessness or over-confidence on the Germans' part. But by midday they were building up on both the road and the uncom-pleted railway line with their inevitable accompaniment of machine-gun, mortar and artillery support, and for the light forces to attempt to hold them further would have been sheer suicide. It was withdrawal again.

But the next withdrawal would be a long hop. Oddly enough in this cut-up, mountainous country, Mosjöen and the country between it and Mo, fifty-four miles away, offer no natural defensive positions. But roughly half-way between the two towns is the biggest of the breaks in the road north, where the traveller, in peacetime at least, must leave the road and take to the ferry. For here the long, narrow Ranfiord meanders in from the sea towards Sweden, and perhaps twenty miles from its mouth, sends a side-shoot to the south. At the junction with the main fiord is a little village, Hemnesberget, at the western end of what is as near an island as makes no odds; at the eastern end of this same near-island is Finneid. And south of the two of them is an irregular patch of water for all the world in shape like a caveman's drawing of a jumping animal, poised on front legs and kicking its back legs out. Where the front legs touch the ground the road from Mosjöen comes to a dead end, and the traveller may take passage either to Hemnesberget or Finneid, as he pleases. It is a tricky place, and Colonel Gubbins sent orders to the solitary company in Mo to guard the passage for the Norwegians and himself.

But the Germans had no intention of letting them get to Mo unmolested: for the second time they gave a convincing demon-stration of the fact that while Britain might rule the waves, the *Herrenvolk* ruled the coastal waters of Norway. Just as they had chopped at Carton de Wiart's strung-out forces round the Trondheimsfiord, they proceeded to chop No. 1 Independent Company, now holding the crossing at Hemnesberget, as ordered. A small force of three hundred Germans set out by sea from Trondheim in a little vessel escorted by two Dornier flying-boats. The vessel was *Nord-Norge*, and there was a cruel touch of coinci-dence in the choice, for she was owned by the citizens of Narvik—an answer by them to the fact that the main coastal steamers in peacetime went straight from Trondheim to Tromsö without calling at their town—and had been their pride and joy.

The sailing of *Nord-Norge* was detected by the improvised Norwegian coast watch which was soon to give such signal help to the fighter squadrons operating from Bardufoss—but there were no ships near enough to the spot to deal with it. Less than a week previously the Admiralty had been planning to put a division of destroyers to patrol this part of the coast, but the destroyers were simply not to be found: in other words demands elsewhere were so great that British command of the sea off the Norwegian coast was now a mere fiction, in addition to the Luftwaffe having

long since virtually put it out of bounds except to ships there of
dire necessity. The nearest two ships were the anti-aircraft
cruiser *Calcutta* escorting a convoy and the destroyer *Zulu* at
Skjelfiord. After a furious chase these two met and sank *Nord-
Norge* at the mouth of the Ranfiord in the evening as she was
returning, her mission completed; but the sinking of the poor
little steamer which had once meant so much to Narvik could not
undo what had been done, for the Germans were ashore at
Hemnesberget and the Independent Companies and the Norwegians were in deadly danger of having their escape route cut.
As always, once on the ground the Germans proceeded to build
up. They had started with three hundred men and two mountain
guns: the two Dornier flying-boats added another forty men with
machine-guns and mortars and the following day a regular air
ferry service was bringing in men, guns, ammunition and equipment from Trondheim, so that before long they had six hundred
and fifty men at their disposal. In numbers alone, therefore, they
were already more than half the strength of the three Independent
Companies and all the Norwegians put together but they were
already superior to them in the fire they could put down—and it
goes without saying that the Luftwaffe was already overhead in
force. Mo, in fact, was already being bombed.

Immediately, Colonel Gubbins had to abandon Mosjöen, even
more quickly than he had intended. He was lucky enough to be
able to lay hands on a small Norwegian steamer which picked up
the two companies at separate points on the coast: they had but
little to leave behind them, but this included their only anti-
aircraft weapons, a section of Bofors guns which had been left
them by the French. Partly in this steamer and partly in two
destroyers, to which they were afterwards transferred, they were
got to Bodö. Some reinforcements which had been collecting at
Mosjöen for the undermanned Norwegian battalion likewise got
away by sea, although only as far as Mo. As to the Norwegian
battalion itself, this retreated along the road to the point where it
was cut by the long ferry passage at Elsfiord—from whence they
struck inland and so made the difficult march around the water to
Finneid at the inland end of the near-island which is the Hemnes
peninsula. So they also got to Mo, but such heavy equipment as
they had was perforce abandoned and both their fitness and their

morale were further undermined by the long, arduous and hurried march.

This left the troops of No. 1 Company, who had originally been hurried south from Mo to hold the passage for the units retreating from Mosjöen, in sole contact with the enemy: in a fighting withdrawal through the village streets of Hemnesberget they retreated on Finneid and there stood for a little in company with a few Norwegians who had stayed there. The Norwegians gallantly counter-attacked the following day, but the tremendous fire power of the Germans forced them back.

By 12th May, therefore, the Germans had already made a considerable bound up the coast towards the relief of their threatened troops in the north. Mosjöen had gone: whether or not they would be able to establish an air base there had yet to be seen. Mo, unless something drastic happened, was about to go and there certainly was the landing ground upon which Atcherley had already reported, within very easy flying distance of Narvik. It so happens that the Germans did not use this, for their rapid advance to Bodö made it unnecessary. The Guards Brigade was still partly at Harstad, partly at Ankenes, and transport earmarked for its intended move included the troopship *Chrobry* and the cruiser *Effingham*. *Chrobry* was just arriving with General Auchinleck, his staff and a quantity of stores, and *Effingham* was needed for the bombardment of Bjerkvik which Lord Cork, after a final postponement of two days, was at last at this moment about to take by storm.

Auchinleck had had an uneventful passage. He disembarked at Harstad with the urgency of his instructions still ringing in his ears, while in his pocket, so to speak, were those orders which started off with iron ore, dealt briefly with preserving a part of Norway for its King and government, dealt with some details of command and returned in their conclusion to iron ore, with the suggestion that he might find it possible to ship home any ore already on the quays at Narvik and investigate the possible resumption of supplies from Gällivare. He himself had formed a slightly different series of conclusions about priorities, in which the establishment of the air base and the provision of fighter cover ranked very high.

Auchinleck made straight for headquarters. The base was

(as always) under air attack and he was rapidly to discover that its state of organization left something to be desired, but he was not concerned with such matters just for the moment. Here he found Mackesy, but not Lord Cork, who was already aboard *Effingham* at Skaanland together with Béthouart and about to sail for the preliminary bombardment of Bjerkvik, where the assault was due to take place the following night. Auchinleck's published report makes no comment on the fact that Mackesy was not with the other two generals about to supervise personally this operation—which was, after all, the long-delayed first stage to the long-delayed capture of Narvik. No comment is necessary: the stated fact is enough and there is no need to press it. Mackesy's ponderous offensive plans were in ruins, he was about to be superseded and he was no longer in effective control. The position of a commander in these circumstances is always difficult and sometimes painful—Auchinleck was to taste the bitterness of it himself in the Middle East in years to come, though circumstances were then different and history, on the whole, would vindicate him. It is superfluous to add that neither in his actions nor in his subsequent report on them is there any hint of a realization that he was embarking, with energy, drive and enthusiasm on an operation for which the time had run out: his horizons were limited to achieving what he had been ordered to do, and there is nothing surprising about that. Only in later years would it be possible for the whole business to be seen in perspective.

He next took himself to Skaanland, where he joined Cork and Béthouart on the cruiser and remained aboard throughout the operation. Although it was a decisive success, with no more than thirty-six casualties, it was attended by many hazards—the principal of which were the shortage and unreliability of the landing craft, which meant putting the men ashore in comparatively small parcels, and the ever-present danger of air attack. It was for the latter reason that midnight was chosen for the start of the attack, for though there was light throughout the twenty-four hours at Narvik, it would be dark on the aerodrome at Trondheim: in the event there was low cloud as well, and so for once there was no enemy air intervention at all. The same conditions, however, held up supporting aircraft from *Ark Royal* off the coast until the main objective had been won—after which they were able to come in and bomb enemy communications. The guns of *Resolution, Effingham, Aurora* and the destroyers supplied the initial bombardment instead in a more traditional fashion. On the credit side, likewise, the Foreign Legion had their light tanks: five of them were successfully put ashore—to achieve, in fact, the first tank landing from the sea in the history of war—and there is no doubt that their influence was considerable, if not decisive. For the first time—indeed for the one and only time in Norway— the tables were turned. And once more one speculates, endlessly and fruitlessly, on how much difference a mere handful of the lightest of tanks, as well as the means to achieve the smallest res- pite of attack from the air, would have made in central Norway.

By the afternoon of the 13th, Bjerkvik was in Allied hands. A whole month after Admiral Whitworth's devastating attack, which had seemed both to him and to Lord Cork the obvious preliminary to a direct landing in Narvik, the first real step on the road to the town had been made. The Germans had now been pushed away almost completely from the northern shores of the fiord, Elvegaard—still with many of its stores intact, including a hundred machine-guns—had been recaptured and contact made with the Chasseurs Alpins, who were now the active left flank of General Fleischer's eastern battle group. It is odd how persistently Auchinleck's dispatch speaks of the Norwegians' 'assisting' the Chasseurs, or the Anglo-French forces in general. One would have thought the boot was on the other foot. After all, Fleischer and his men had been fighting for many weeks a battle in which the Allies had only just intervened. Also it was their country— although this tended, from start to finish, to be overlooked.

How to exploit his new positions and speed the capture of Narvik itself was only one of the problems awaiting General Auchinleck when he arrived back at the base. There was first a hurried consultation about the situation developing to the south. While the capture of Bjerkvik had been proceeding smoothly, the Scots Guards had been packed into the much-bombed cruiser *Enterprise* and rushed away to Mo. At the conference—from which Mackesy was absent owing, we are told, to illness—it was decided to send the Irish Guards after them, albeit not to Mo but to Bodö; showing that however much Auchinleck was later to insist on the holding of Mo, he was convinced in his own mind

The Verma tunnel. Lt.-Col. Robinson on extreme left.

that it could not, in fact, be held. Then there was the work on the landing ground at Bardufoss to be pushed on with every ounce of haste that could be put into it. Group Captain Moore had come out with Auchinleck to take charge of the air base, but he was as determined as everyone else that there was to be no second Lesjaskog, and it was not disputed that there would only be another disaster if the fighters were flown in before Bardufoss was fully ready for them to operate from. It was not merely a matter of providing the vital air cover for the culminating assault on Narvik: it was a matter of the survival of the base and the ships around it, for with every day that passed the more the picture began to resemble the picture around Namsos and Andalsnes in the days immediately before the evacuation. As usual the ships presented the easiest targets and got the worst of it—in the next twelve days twelve warships, transports and storeships were sunk, including the anti-aircraft cruiser *Curlew*, and it can be considered pure good fortune that the losses were not higher.

Then there was the whole of the base to be taken in hand and somehow reorganized into working order, for the more Auchinleck saw the more he realized what a sorry state it was in. There were more personnel and stores crammed into it than it could possibly hold in any sort of good order and yet the stores of essential ammunition and equipment were low. The French were running their own base separately, but had hardly any personnel to deal with it, and storeships had been awaiting completion of their unloading for sixteen days or more. There was an utter shortage of water transport and relations with the civilian population, whose help was needed for this and other purposes, were in a sorry mess—partly because they had never been properly organized through the civil power and partly because the civilians themselves were completely bewildered by the Allied goings on while their own troops were fighting in the mountains and the Germans holding on to Narvik by the skin of their teeth. All this would have to be sorted out and a second base area established to relieve Harstad: the General had his eye on Tromsö, where the Norwegian government was, but the Norwegians would demand air protection for Tromsö before the billeting of Allied troops there turned it into a target for the Luftwaffe. Auchinleck, formally taking over from Mackesy, worked hard and fast and had got his reorganization well on the way by the time the orders came to abandon Norway altogether. This was a matter precisely of eleven days from the capture of Bjerkvik and a great deal was to happen in that time.

The Scots Guards landed at Mo on the afternoon of the 12th, while the last preparation for Bjerkvik was still being made. They had had a most unpleasant passage. First of all there had been an embarkation via puffers with 'too bloody much luggage'. They had been bombed on the way down the coast and bombed all the way up the fiord. They had been very seasick. The bombing in the fiord was particularly unpleasant because it was too narrow for the ships to manœuvre; as a result of this experience it was decided that even anti-aircraft vessels would only enter the fiord again under the very direst necessity, so that further supplies would need to be landed on the coast and transported by what-ever means could be found over eighty miles of road, of which twenty-three could take only single line traffic. By the same token the seaward flank of any troops here would be exposed to further German landings on the Hemnesberget pattern—just as the land-ward flanks would be exposed as always to attacks by ski-troops.

There was a break in the bombing while they actually got ashore; which was just as well, for the disembarkation was by puffers again, starting with a climb in single file for the whole battalion down a twelve-foot ladder. There was a great deal of rush and excitement and some equipment was lost, as it always was under these circumstances, but the losses at this stage were not serious.

Immediately after the disembarkation, while the men were still suffering from the effects of seasickness and their strenuous efforts, they had to set off on a seven-mile foot-slog to Dalskubben, and thereafter dig themselves in. Though there was no darkness, the night was cold and they had neither sleeping bags nor blankets: no fires could be lit and so there was no hot food. It was a fine preparation for a battle and it is quite remarkable how, in the course of this whole campaign, things were so organized as to put even the best trained, prepared and equipped of troops at a disadvantage. Even their Brigadier, who had landed with them, was at a disadvantage. He had been wounded while making a recce at Ankenes, where he had been trapped between German machine-gun and mortar-fire in a church tower, and had not properly recovered. In the course of the next couple of days the unfortunate man was invalided home, just as his brigade was at last in action, and Gubbins was promoted to command the brigade as well as the Independent Companies.

Here, then, were the Scots Guards, rushed hastily in to prevent Scissorsforce, which had failed to snip the road to the north (as it was bound to), from becoming unhinged altogether. Here, in fact, in not very good order and minus their C Company, which was still at Bodö and had been ordered to stay there. With them, three Independent Companies, two already mauled, and the remains of the Norwegians—also in bad shape. They had also a troop of artillery with four twenty-five-pounder field guns, three Bofors guns and a party of Sappers, which was admittedly more than had been the lot of the troops in the central Norway campaign, to whose situation their own was already becoming remarkably similar. Even the same little maps, with the ominous black arrow showing the German advance from the south, begin to reappear in the official history at this point. They were defending against a force which included the German 2nd Mountain Division, a front which called for at least a brigade, though they were certainly not equal to a brigade in strength; albeit they were under the happy delusion that the other two battalions of 24 Brigade were on their way to join them, which was not the case. And these, in large part, were the troops who should and could have taken Narvik a month before!

On the face of it, however, the position of the Irish Guards was a strong one, and Lieutenant-Colonel Trappes-Lomax set out his dispositions to make the most of it. On his right flank was the fiord and the river in spate, crossed by two bridges with a good field of fire. On his left were hills and deep, soft snow, more hampering than ever in the thaw. Things were less satisfactory here: the field of fire was masked by trees and in addition to the difficulty of finding good points for covering fire, he had no spare men to put in them. There was no means of discovering what was happening on the other side of the hills, and it was only when disaster finally descended upon them that they realized that the Germans had, in fact, been collecting in force in the valleys beyond and building up for a carefully planned attack. Even one

solitary recce plane would have yielded this simple piece of information to the battalion. As it was Trappes-Lomax had absolutely
no means of getting information and he had to take the chance.

During the two days that followed they stayed in these positions with their heads down under the bombs and machine-gun
bullets of the Luftwaffe, while first the Norwegian battalion and
then the Independent Company in front of them, rolled up by the
Germans, withdrew through their lines. The build-up of the
Germans through Hemnesberget was going on steadily all the
time, and equally steadily there were reports of German units in
increasing numbers in the area north of Mosjoen. By the 15th—it
was almost the last decision he made before handing over—
Brigadier Fraser became convinced that Mo could not be held by
the forces at his disposal with the weapons and air cover available to them, and he reported accordingly. His opinion was confirmed by the Norwegian commander in the area, Lieutenant-
Colonel Roscher Neilsen. If anything, they were already in a
worse position than any of the troops in the Gudbrandsdal had
ever been because their only line of communication—by sea—
was for all practical purposes cut by the German Air Force and
their supply route or retreat route (according to whether they
were to stand or retreat) was as good as cut by the formidable
country between themselves and Bodö. Much of the latter lies
above the permanent snow line—very difficult for any means of
surface travel and utterly naked to observation from the air. In
spite of this, the order was repeated that a stand must be made at
Mo.

Whether there might have been second thoughts about sending
the Irish Guards to Mo instead of Bodö after all will never be
known because of the fate which now overtook that battalion.
It was embarked in *Chrobry* as soon as she could be got ready, and
after sitting under the rain of bombs for some time, they set out
for Bodö at half past six in the evening of the 14th. *Chrobry* had
steamed many sea miles between the bomb splashes in the course
of this campaign and carried her burdens unscathed in and out of
a number of difficult places. She had been a fortunate ship, but it
would not have needed an expert in the mathematics of proba-
bility to work out the fact that her little stock of luck was running
very low. She set off with an escort of an anti-aircraft sloop and a

destroyer, with a German reconnaissance plane in respectful attendance. Lieutenant-Colonel Faulkner had ordered his officers and men to get what sleep they could: from the information at his disposal it seemed to him quite possible that they would have to go straight into action on landing and he wanted them to be fresh. *Chrobry* was a large and comfortable ship; and so sleeping they were when three Heinkels descended upon her a few minutes after midnight and on their third run straddled her with a salvo of bombs that immediately crippled her and rapidly turned her into a blazing inferno. In those moments every senior officer in the battalion was wiped out, but the tremendous discipline of the Guards held and those who witnessed the scene that followed have more than once likened it to the almost legendary sinking of the troopship *Birkenhead*. While the after part of the ship blazed, stacked ammunition exploded and the enemy aircraft zoomed unchallenged around the spectacle, the battalion fell in company by company and platoon by platoon in the forward part, each man with his arms and his personal equipment. With them was their Roman Catholic chaplain, steady and calm. The escort ships, *Stork* and *Wolverine*, put alongside, for most of the troopship's boats were already useless, and the Guards proceeded aboard them in what appeared to the ships' companies to be an outrageously leisurely fashion. One naval officer remembers how he shouted and cursed at the troops, urging them to hurry, without any effect—until a young Guards Second Lieutenant came up and said a word to them. Then they hurried: they would obey only their own officers. None the less, their leisurely proceeding was deceptive. All the survivors—six hundred and ninety-four men—embarked in sixteen minutes and were soon on their way back at full speed to Harstad. It took them seven hours, and they were bombed all the way.

They had lost a great deal of equipment and there were not enough reserve stores at the base to make good their losses—outstandingly there was a shortage of Bren guns, the only automatic weapon at that time on their vocabulary. The discipline and training of the men had proved themselves, but organizationally this splendid unit was a wreck: the remaining officers would have to be parcelled out to do the senior officers' jobs as best they could and all the intense personal threads which are woven so deeply into the fabric of a unit like this were disorganized and broken. Unused when its use could have achieved tremendous results, the battalion had been frittered away. It was to have a respite of best part of a week to re-equip and reorganize as far as the circumstance allowed: its only function in the campaign thereafter was to cover the withdrawal of the Scots Guards.

The very same day that the survivors of the Irish Guards were landed once more at Harstad, the German attack broke on their comrades of the Scots Guards before Mo. The attack began in the evening—with the usual combination of dive-bombing, machine-gunning, mortaring and artillery fire. And it continued without respite for the whole of the light, unwinking night. The Bofors guns brought down two aircraft: they could have brought down ten times the number and there would still have been aircraft to spare. The following morning both the bridges were demolished, for the Germans were seen advancing up the coast road in great strength—there were estimated to be at least one thousand seven hundred and fifty of them. Under a curtain of heavy fire they set about attempting to repair the bridges, but the Guards were accurate in their returning rifle-fire and the German casualties were heavy enough to make them desist. What would happen now was inevitable—it was a matter of German textbook tactics: they would desist from a frontal attack and work around the flanks. There was in this case only one flank they could work around on land and so it could be fairly certain that the suspect left flank, where no covering fire had been possible, would soon be in trouble. At this point the field telephone wires from headquarters to the company on the left were cut by shell-fire and so there was no means of finding out.

At seven o'clock in the evening, however, an exhausted Norwegian boy of twelve stumbled into the command post. He had been told by his father to run as fast as he could, and he had done his best. The news he brought was that German parachute troops in Norwegian uniforms had landed up the valley, were now advancing down it and were very close. The news was all too true, but there was more besides. Within the next couple of hours the whole of the German force which had been collecting over the hills, invisible to Trappes-Lomax and his men, arose and descended on the left flank. The rifles of the Guards were at a discount in the woods, where the German tommy-guns were far more effective. Trappes-Lomax pushed in a platoon from his right flank for reinforcement, but by midnight the left flank was virtually surrounded and more parachutists were coming in. B Company were now ordered up to help, but by two o'clock in the morning it was clear that the end had come.

By this time the third battalion of the brigade—the South Wales Borderers—had also met with disaster. They had been got ready for embarkation immediately after the sinking of *Chrobry* and the return of the Irish Guards to Harstad. The cruiser *Effingham* was now available: the French were sufficiently well established at Bjerkvik no longer to need the support of her guns, and on the evening of the 16th the Borderers went aboard her—better equipped, in this evening of the campaign, than any British unit that had yet fought in Norway. They had Bren carriers and the only three British light tanks, belonging to the troop of Hussars already mentioned. At four a.m. on the morning of the 17th they sailed for Bodö—with one destroyer only but, surprisingly, without the customary escort of German aircraft.

What happened now, however, was directly due to the danger of air attack. Instead of following the normal route through the Leads, *Effingham* took a less familiar way outside. German aircraft would, perhaps, not expect to find her there, and indeed, they did not. She hurried on the whole day unmolested, and shortly before eight in the evening was within sight of Bodö itself, steaming at a good twenty-three knots. Then suddenly there was a great, jarring shock and a lurch to port that sent everyone and everything loose aboard reeling. She lurched back again on to an even keel and was brought up standing in her own length. Her unfamiliar route had run her on to the Faksen shoal, and she was as fast as if she had grown there. Once more there was no panic, and the Borderers assembled in good order at their boat stations. But it was quickly apparent that *Effingham* would not be got off the shoal where ill-luck had stranded her, even assuming she would float if she could be got off, and there was nothing to be gained by the troops staying there, a sitting target for the bombers. The destroyer took off the troops and Marines, leaving their irreplaceable heavy equipment behind, and set off back to the base. The Navy set about salvaging what they could from

Effingham and did succeed in recovering three Bren carriers, which were worth their weight in gold. But the tanks were lost.

The re-equipping of the Irish Guards, incomplete though it was, had cleared out the stores in Harstad. There was little left for the Borderers. The only thing to do was to skin the base units for them and this was done, but it still left them woefully deficient in mortars and signals kit particularly. There were, of course, no replacements for the tanks. The battle on the Western Front, which had already reduced Norway to a minor theatre of war, was taking on an ugly look. Holland had surrendered on the 16th: this same day, the 17th, Brussels fell and the Maginot Line was broken. Clearly there was no hope of fresh stores and equipment from England.

For that matter, General Auchinleck had just received a signal from home which, in addition to stating in plain terms that he now had as much as he was going to get, questioned for the first time the wisdom of holding Narvik after it had been captured. This is perhaps the only outward hint for the moment that in top official circles in London there was about to take place one of those changes of opinion that had taken place over the direct assault on Trondheim. It was not quite so rapid or so violent and there was better reason for it, since it stemmed less from a lack of desire to finish the job in Norway than from the appalling news which came every day from Belgium and France. Here the German offensive, outflanking the fabulous Maginot Line—a larger illustration of the same movement the Germans had already carried out so many times on a small scale in Norway—was acquiring a speed unprecedented in twentieth-century warfare and a momentum which was going to take more stopping than any opposing army seemed capable of. Churchill himself, who for most of the third week in May had been demanding the final capture of Narvik in plain terms, had by the 20th been driven to reconsider the whole future of the Norwegian campaign: before very many days were up he would be debating not how Arctic Norway could be established as an enclave of freedom, but rather how Norway might be used by the Germans to assist in the invasion of Britain.

The Norwegians were no more in the confidence of the British Government over these discussions than they had been in the discussions over the evacuation of central Norway. Perhaps it could be fairly said that there was no time to take them into our confidence in the press of events: certainly there was no machinery for doing so. Sir Cecil Dormer, the British Minister, after a brief visit to London, had returned to King Haakon's centre of government at Tromsö: he, however, was much more concerned than anything else with the relations between the Allies and the civil power in Norway and in particular the relations of the military forces with the civilian population, which were tending to get worse rather than better. On the 23rd, in fact, Lord Cork journeyed to Tromsö to discuss these matters, among others, with the King and his ministers. The control of military operations lay completely with General Ruge, who was not in Tromsö at all, and the machinery for liaison with him was virtually non-existent. He had never ceased to demand the appointment of a new military attaché to replace King-Salter; but no military attaché had been appointed and certainly there was never again the accord with the Norwegian command that had been achieved in the Gudbrandsdal in the brief days first of King-Salter's presence at Ruge's headquarters and thereafter of Paget's close collaboration with him. By his side now Ruge had the iron-willed and bitter General Fleischer—at least as bitter as Getz but with a record of achievement against the invaders which gave far greater authority to his words than Getz had ever been able to claim. He could point to the Allied troops in their thousands virtually idle around the Ofotfiord while he and his half-trained men, helped only in the later stages of their battle by French reinforcements on their seaward flank, had first halted the German offensive to the north and then in the face of the most gruelling hardships and shortages turned their advance into a slow retreat that the help of more fresh troops and more powerful arms might have turned into a rout. His demand had been for twenty thousand rifles—to the very end he received no more than one thousand. He was completely intransigent on any demands from the British forces for co-operation from the Norwegians, civil or military, and made it plain that his intransigence would continue until he had evidence of some Allied will to fight. This extended to the disciplining or evacuation of civilians in the battle area, to the supply of labour for airfield construction at Bardufoss and

Skaanland, only wrested with the greatest of difficulty. And it could not be denied that at this very moment in the mountains the German front had everywhere collapsed, that the Germans were withdrawing inch by inch towards the Swedish frontier. Yet—and herein lay the greatest and most justifiable cause of Fleischer's resentment—the defeated enemy could not be mopped up. The two Norwegian battle groups had been fighting without remission for three weeks. They had had little rest, for much of the time no hot food, no cover except for snow-holes, little communication with their rear, the most appalling labour bringing up their supplies. The thaw was now in the hills and was magnifying the difficulties of movement. They could not pursue, they could only stand exhausted to consolidate for a little space and try on their own (for want of positive help from their Allies) to mount one more offensive that would at last scatter and drive the Germans over the border.

Ruge and Fleischer, therefore, were far from thinking about the abandonment of Narvik—although after the betrayal in central Norway it would probably not have surprised them to know it was being discussed. They were thinking instead of how an offensive could be mounted beyond the Arctic Circle that would drive the Germans back first from the north, then from central Norway, then from the Oslo plain. They were thinking not of how the German advance through Mosjöen and Mo could be delayed, but how it could be reversed. They were demanding that the Allies should at last prove the sincerity of their professions once and for all by throwing their men, their ships and their equipment into an offensive that would prove them to be allies in deed as well as name.

It was this uncompromising attitude of mind which led, from first to last, to Norwegian rejection of what became known as the Mowinkel Plan. Mowinkel was a former Norwegian Prime Minister who had led several left-wing coalitions during the confused period of Norwegian politics in the late twenties and early thirties, until, in 1933, he resigned and was replaced by Johan Nygaardsvold. After the invasion he had rejoined the cabinet, had been one of the delegation appointed to meet the German ambassador in the fruitless negotiations of 9th April, and was now with the government at Tromsö. In concert with the Swedish

Foreign Minister he had produced a scheme for the neutralization of northern Norway, whereby the Swedes would garrison and assume responsibility for it, and in particular for the railway and the ore-loading plant at Narvik. The Chamberlain government had been inclined towards it: the Foreign Office had certainly favoured it. Churchill had stoutly rejected it. The Norwegian government as a whole had had little sympathy with it and the Norwegian military leaders had refused to consider it.

It is probable that the Germans would have accepted the Mowinkel Plan. It would have suited their book to have the Narvik headache removed by diplomatic rather than military action at a time when they needed all their forces for the Western Front. It would have suited them to have the Norwegian forces neutralized and their unreliable but exasperating allies removed from the theatre of operations. It would certainly have suited them to have the Swedes in control of northern Norway; for the Swedes had shown little inclination to oppose them or even resist their demands for collaboration, and once both the Norwegians and Allied forces were out of the running, would not have been able to resist them at all, however much they might wish. The Mowinkel Plan could then be conveniently forgotten or torn up, as the Munich Agreement had been torn up, as sundry other pieces of paper had been torn up and as the treaty with Russia was going to be torn up. In the meantime direct ore imports from Sweden would recommence any day, now that the Gulf of Bothnia was free of ice, so there would be nothing to be lost for months to come. If anyone lost iron ore through the neutralization of Narvik, it would be the Allies.

The Mowinkel Plan never got any farther. Norway would fall to the Germans, but at least she would be spared the humiliation of Czecho-Slovakia.

But things were going on down the Ofotfiord that at last (albeit too late) gave promise of the sort of action Fleischer had been over-long clamouring for. In the first place General Béthouart had mapped out the attack on Narvik which he had been itching to carry out since the beginning of the month: his plans had been approved both by Auchinleck and Cork and the assault would take place in a matter of days. In the second place the carrier *Furious*, repaired and re-equipped, was at sea. She was on her way to relieve *Ark Royal*, and in her hangars she carried the eighteen Gladiators of 263 Squadron, returning to the battle under very different conditions from the conditions of Lake Lesjaskog.

Atcherley's determination that there was to be no more fighting from a scratch landing ground that doomed the R.A.F. to failure and Moore's equal determination not to bring the squadron in till everything was ready for it, had been upheld to the bitter end. It must have been difficult for them to sustain their determination under the endless blitz by the unopposed Luftwaffe, the harrying of the ships, the ever-growing destruction and confusion at the base. But they stuck it out, and it paid off. The Gladiators, and the Hurricanes that were to follow them, were to wipe out the memory of Lesjaskog and to make all the difference to the closing days of the campaign. They were going, few though they were, to restore freedom of movement by sea and by land; and the imagination boggles at what might have been the story of the evacuation had they not been there.

How long it would have been possible for them to continue to operate at the pitch that was forced upon them—how long it would have been before the pilots were reduced to exhaustion and the airfield defences saturated—is a matter for thought, but by a narrow margin the point was not reached. The landing ground at Bardufoss had been made sound. There had been clearing, digging, blasting and rolling and an immense amount of hard physical toil by hundreds of men, Allied and Norwegian—for in the end Fleischer had relented and even lent a reserve battalion to help in the work. It had but a single runway, but it was well laid and drained, so that even the waters of the continuing thaw failed to swamp it. It had guns for ack-ack defence, heavy as well as light. It had shelters for the ground staff and dispersal points for the machines. It was stored and properly equipped. It even had a mess—short of supplies, especially of drink—but a mess which would give relaxation to hard-pressed men: it was in a Presbyterian church and there is no evidence that the R.A.F. dishonoured it.

Far away to the south of Narvik, alas, something else was happening, and no one would be able to do much about it: the Scots Guards, the one Independent Company that had been at Mo and the Norwegians, were on the run. If, in the offensive spirit that

had been restored to the Allied forces since the arrival of Auchinleck, in the illusion of permanence that came from the reorganization of the base and the imminent arrival of the fighters, a warning
was needed that time at Narvik had run out, this was it.

We left the Scots Guards, in the early morning of 18th
May, caught in the trap the Germans had sprung upon them—
the direct result of their inability either to guard their mountain
flank or recce beyond it. Caught with them were the remains of
the Norwegians and the Independent Company. B Company was
cut off on the flank and at first they were convinced it was lost:
this made them two companies short, for C Company was still at
Bodö. There were already more than seventy wounded—few of
them, fortunately, seriously, owing to the short effective range of
the German tommy-guns and the damping effect of the snow.
And the only available transport was five broken-down local
lorries, which could carry little and were obviously not going to
get far.

Withdrawal, therefore, meant immediately the abandonment of
all the men could not carry—everything, in other words, bar a
minimum of rifle ammunition, one day's rations and the wounded.
In one stroke they were reduced to the normal conditions of
British forces in Norway in retreat: it was the story of the Sherwood Foresters, the Leicesters, the K.O.Y.L.I. and the Lincolns
all over again. In this condition they fell back and made a brief
attempt to stand at a precipitous ridge, but failed. At nine o'clock
Gubbins ordered the evacuation of Mo. The dumps and the
bridges were blown and at three in the afternoon they were clear
of the town—by such a narrow margin that the Germans were
entering it a few minutes later. Thus the latter had accomplished
yet another great bound forward in their advance by land to
relieve General Dietl's troops round Narvik: the black arrow
moves again up the little maps.

There was now an immediate threat to Bodö, with its airfield
rapidly thawing. To hold Mo had been essential—to defend
Bodö was vital: the holding of Bodö was a cardinal point in all
the plans for the capture of Narvik and the consolidation of the
Arctic. If Mo could not be defended, how could Bodö? If the
Guards had not been able to stand at Bodö with all their kit and
equipment intact, what chance had they of standing without it?

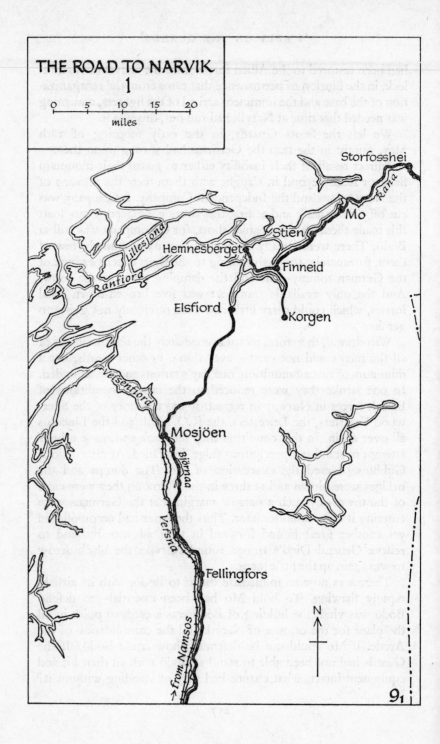

THE ROAD TO NARVIK
1

0   5   10   15   20
miles

Storfosshei

Rana

Mo

Stien

Lilleslona

Hemnesberget

Finneid

Ranfiord

Elsfiord

Korgen

Veisenfiord

Mosjöen

Björnaa

Versna

Fellingfors

N

from Namsos

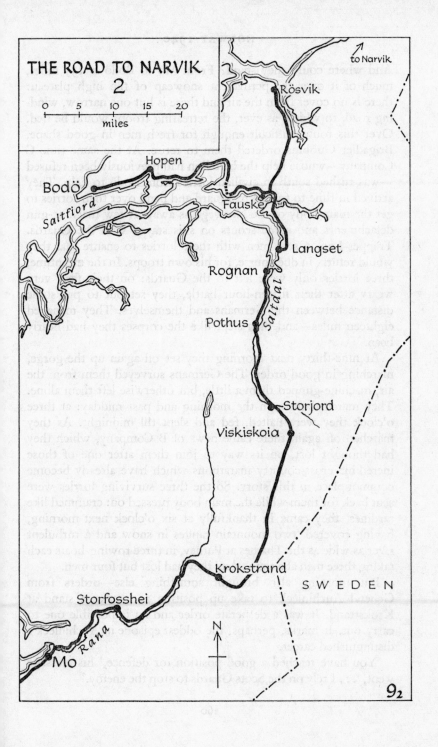

THE ROAD TO NARVIK
2

0   5   10   15   20
miles

to Narvik

Rösvik

Hopen

Bodö

Saltfiord

Fauske

Langset

Rognan

Saltdal

Pothus

Storjord

Viskiskoia

Krokstrand

SWEDEN

Storfosshei

Rana

N

Mo

9₂

And where could they stand? From Mo to Bodö is 135 miles, much of it over the permanent snowcap of the high plateau: there is no cover from the air and there is but one narrow, winding road, to which, as ever, the retreating troops would be tied. Over this route, difficult enough for fresh men in good shape, Brigadier Gubbins ordered them to retire. At the same time C Company—whose help the battalion had previously been refused —was rushed south in civilian lorries from Bodö to help. They arrived in time to form a rearguard and hand over their lorries to get the main body of the Norwegians away. A few machine-gun detachments and some scouts on skis stayed with the Guards. Trappes-Lomax sent men with these lorries to ensure that they would return, in due course, for his own troops. In the meantime, three lorries only were left to the Guards: on their feet, very weary after their fifteen-hour battle, they set out to put some distance between the Germans and themselves. They managed eighteen miles—and then slept like the corpses they had nearly been.

At nine-thirty next morning they set off again up the gorge, marching in good order. The Germans surveyed them from the air, machine-gunned them a little, but otherwise left them alone. They marched through the morning and past midday: at three o'clock they were halted, fed and slept till midnight. As they marched off again there came news of B Company, which they had thought lost, on its way to join them after one of those incredible cross-country marathons which have already become commonplace in this story. So the three surviving lorries were sent back for them while the main body pressed on: crammed like sardines, they came in thankfully at six o'clock next morning, having covered 'two mountain ranges in snow and a turbulent river as wide as the Thames at Putney, in three rowing-boats each taking three men at a time'. And they had lost but four men.

But morning also brought something else—orders from General Auchinleck to take up position and make a stand at Krokstrand. It was a desperate order and an impossible one to carry out. It marks, perhaps, the oddest episode in Auchinleck's distinguished career.

'You have reached a good position for defence,' his message went, '. . . I rely on the Scots Guards to stop the enemy.'

It may have looked a good position on the map, but the reality was very different. It may have been a good thing to appeal to the regimental pride of the Guards, but it was hardly fair to do so in circumstances under which they had little chance of upholding it. It is not clear whether the General knew how much of their kit and equipment had been lost; if he did know, his order is more difficult to explain than ever. It is true that he amended it to permit a fighting withdrawal if the safety of the force was threatened—but this was meaningless, for the safety of the force could not be threatened much more than it already was. And the event showed that he did not intend even this measure of withdrawal without his direct permission. Fighter support is said to have been promised. It did not materialize till later in the retreat: the Gladiators had not yet arrived.

The Guards obey orders. They obeyed these—as well as they could and stopping short of meaningless suicide. At midnight on the twentieth—very tired indeed, short of ammunition and rations—they reached the indicated position and proceeded to dig themselves in in such fashion as they could. Then they waited: it was, at least, relief from the march. They waited for the broad, black arrow marking the German advance on the map to catch up with them. With morning (a matter of time on the clock rather than actual dawn, for it was already light) the German planes came over on their reconnaisance as true to timetable as they had done in the days of Mauriceforce. All day they waited for the attack, which did not come. There was no doubt that the attack would come, and it was quite certain that the Germans were preparing it with as much thoroughness as they had done at Mo.

CHAPTER 13

ANTI-CLIMAX AT NARVIK

WHILE the Scots Guards watched and waited at Krokstrand, the aircraft carrier *Furious* arrived off the coast.
It was calm weather, with poor visibility, but, with the carrier
steaming at speed, the biplanes of 263 Squadron, led by a naval
Swordfish, cleared her easily. They had no illusions as to what
might lie ahead of them: they desperately and very genuinely
hoped that the squadron might, perhaps, have more of a fighting
chance than it had had in central Norway. The weather thickened
over the coast and the first landings at Bandufoss ended in
disaster: two of the precious machines hit the mountainside and
were wrecked. The remainder landed successfully at the second
attempt: the runway held and was to hold throughout the take-
offs and landings of the following days. For those who had
laboured, schemed and planned throughout the back-breaking
and nerve-straining days and weeks before there was the tremendous relief and achievement of seeing that the impossible had
been accomplished, that everything worked. For the pilots, on the
morrow there would be the fighting chance for which they had
asked. For the tired crews of the ships and the troops for ever
keeping their heads down there would be relief and a little
freedom of movement. For Cork, Auchinleck and Béthouart—
for the Foreign Legion, with their untidy, buccaneering but stout
enough concept of valour, and the Poles, burning with hate
against the Nazis—there would be cover for the assault on Narvik
at last. For bitter, restless Fleischer and for Ruge there would be
the reality of Allied action in place of the procrastinations and
postponements of the previous weeks. Yet there was to be one
more postponement. In the mood of optimism conjured up by the
safe arrival of the Gladiators, Béthouart's attack was fixed for the
night of the 24th/25th—but the decision having been made,
caution once more supervened. The Hurricane squadron was also

at sea in *Glorious*: as a matter of fact it had been at sea for a long time, waiting for news that the other landing ground at Skaanland was ready to receive it. It would now come in on the 26th: would it not be well to hold up the attack till air cover was more certain? It was put off till the 28th—before which time the evacuation had already been ordered, so that it would be more of a hollow victory than ever; and it would be a victory with no fanfares, for it would coincide with Belgium's capitulation to the Germans in the West.

The Gladiators were fully operational from the moment of their arrival and flew their first sorties the following morning. Thereafter brief intervals of bad weather alone kept them on the ground until the last phase of the evacuation was over, more than a fortnight later. Efficiently serviced and enterprisingly flown, the relief which they and the Hurricanes that followed them brought almost beggars description. Both on land and in the anchorages the picture was completely changed. The bases were relieved from the continual strain of attack challenged only by inadequate ack-ack guns. Movement became possible. The nagging certainty that every plan and every disposition would be spotted and reported from the air was removed. So few planes could accomplish this: the Germans were immeasurably superior in numbers and the Gladiators, at least, had not the speed to out-distance their fastest bombers, though they were more manœuvrable: for the Stukas, of course—the deadliest, but the most vulnerable of the German aircraft—they were more than a match. The very sight of the roundels on the wings of the British machines was a boost to morale on the ground and afloat. So few planes for so great a result: once more one comes back to the inevitable question of how little it would have taken to stem the tide in central Norway. And without any slight to the pilots who were to fight their glorious and historic Battle of Britain in the high days of the coming summer, it could be truly said that these were the first of the few.

Officially the Gladiators claimed twenty-six enemy aircraft, the Hurricanes, in their shorter time, eleven. The true figure is probably higher—Atcherley is convinced that it might have been sixty or more all told, though in any case, the mere figures of aircraft destroyed are no criterion. Each pilot had to seek his quarry, very much more after the primitive fashion of the air battles of the First World War than the practice of the second, for interception conditions were difficult and information terribly incomplete. Radar gave no better results than it had farther south, ground-to-air communication was unreliable: the mountains, as always, were the friends of the enemy and so, too, was the Norwegian sun, so that pilots called the process of acclimatization to it 'getting Norwegian eyes'. Two allies the R.A.F. had. One was the coast watch which the Norwegians had set up in the days of neutrality—an almost scratch organization which, like so many scratch organizations the Norwegians had flung together in their emergency, worked better than it had any right to. Its avenue of communication was the civilian telephone service, which ran right through the German lines and which the Germans, for their own purposes, had allowed to continue in operation—it was still possible to telephone from Narvik all over Norway. It was, of course, hopelessly insecure and was taboo for military purposes, but the telephone girls devised a simple but intelligible code which the Germans do not seem to have suspected: the very word 'Fliegalarm', which prefaced the information, they appear to have taken for a civilian air raid warning. Through the code at least could be given location, direction, height and type of plane; and as the Germans invariably flew up the coast they were nearly always under observation, and sometimes up to a couple of hours' warning could be given of an attack. With the help it gave, Atcherley was able to set up in the improvised operations room at Bardufoss a rudimentary plotting system—no more than a map on a desk, a civilian telephone and a series of discs and arrows cut out by hand. Primitive though it was, it was a tremendous advance on the horrors of Lesjaskog.

The R.A.F.'s other friend was the remarkable regularity of the Luftwaffe's habits. It has already been noticed how the recce planes worked to a timetable, and punctually at that—they became known at Bardufoss as 'the milk train'—and many of the other German air movements were equally predictable. 'If you went at the right time,' says Atcherley, 'you bagged an aircraft.' It sounds easy—much easier than it was.

The R.A.F. felt bitterly about the Swedes—on watch, as the Norwegians had been, for violation of their borders, but on watch, in the pilots' conviction, in a partisan sort of way. The Swedish border was near, and pursuit of a German adversary often took them over it. The pilots were positive that the R.A.F. alone got the flak—and the protests. How much of this is fact and how much pardonable assumption is virtually impossible to say. The Swedes alone know the answer and understandably they are not anxious to discuss it. At this distance of time it seems pointless to revive old bitterness by pressing the point too far.

Now had time not run out in Norway and had the Luftwaffe been the only peril threatening Cork's and Auchinleck's forces, the triumphant opening of Bardufoss and the appearance of the R.A.F. in the skies might have been a harbinger of better things. But this tiny force of fighters could do little to dam or even slow up the appalling threat of the German army group's advance on Bodö, now about four thousand strong with tanks and artillery— against which the Guards, faithful to orders, were about to make the stand Auchinleck had demanded. While they waited for the Germans to attack, the lorries, which had taken the Norwegians and the Independent Company across the snow cap, returned: with them came the three Bren carriers which had been salvaged from *Effingham*, and these were a prize indeed, though they were no match for German tanks. There is also said to have been one three-inch mortar in the action that followed, though it is not clear where it came from. Behind them there was not a man or rifle nearer than Rognan, at the beginning of the Saltfiord, which has Bodö at its seaward end—best part of fifty miles in a direct line and much more by the single narrow road. Here were the Norwegians, the Independent Company that had been at Mo and the two Independent Companies from Bodö. On their way there were the hastily reorganized and more or less re-equipped Irish Guards, who, with one field-gun battery, had at last left Harstad (in an air raid, as usual, for the Gladiators had not yet come in) the previous day. The prospects for Bodö were not bright.

In the very early hours of the 22nd the German recce plane came over. It was shot down by accurate rifle-fire. Then, as always, came the first German bicycle scouts: eight of them were killed and the remainder captured by a second lieutenant in one of the carriers, now at the start of seventy hours of continuous action. A good start, but no basis for extravagant hopes:

almost immediately afterwards the main attack came in supported by aircraft with both machine-gun and cannon fire, with the usual rapid penetration on the flanks, exposing the Guards, in their hastily prepared positions, to enfilading fire. After several hours of stubborn resistance it became quite clear that the Guards had neither the means nor the numbers to 'stop the enemy'. They could either retreat and hope to fight again or stay where they were and be slaughtered—neither course would make any significant difference to the German advance. Could it not, therefore, be said, that the safety of the force was endangered—the very contingency specified in Auchinleck's orders as being the occasion for a fighting retreat? On this point, Lieutenant-Colonel Trappes-Lomax felt in no doubt at all, nor did he see any good reason to sacrifice good, trained fighting men (of which there was a scarcity) for no useful object.

With a perfectly clear mind, therefore, about what he was doing—not intending to disobey orders but acting in what he conceived to be the spirit of them—he that night withdrew his troops in the lorries across the snow cap, which is, in fact, the watershed between the two rivers that emerge in the Ranfiord at Mo and the Saltfiord at Bodö. Second Lieutenant Anderson stayed behind with his carrier and continued as rearguard the action in which he had been valiantly engaged all day. The Germans did not follow up immediately, although if they had flung their whole force upon the retreating battalion it is clear that they could have turned the retreat into a rout and annihilated the Guards. The Guards' regimental historian speculates on the reason why: perhaps, he suggests, they thought the Guards were going to fight till the end and that, therefore, they had all the following day to deal with them—so that they could afford to rest their troops in the daylight and twilight that passed for night. We, too, may speculate, and remember once more that every time the Germans came up against determined resistance by trained troops, even inadequately armed, they either recoiled or at least hesitated. Had the whole of the Guards Brigade been there instead of merely one battalion, and had it had a measure of support weapons with a few aircraft, the story, even in these dying days of a lost campaign, might have been as different as the story of Otta could have been with just that 'little more'.

Beyond the snow cap the Guards halted at Viskiskoia—in other words, they were still not much more than half-way on their long fighting retreat from Mo to Bodö. The men were clearly near the end of their tether. They were exhausted and there were signs of some demoralization due to fatigue, loss of kit, the succession of rearguard actions and, above all, the continuously harassing effect of air attack and air surveillance. None the less, Brigadier Gubbins ordered that this position was to be held for four more days, until the 27th, although the only reinforcements available for them were No. 3 Independent Company which had come in from Rognan, and the field battery, which had sailed in from Harstad with the Irish Guards—this latter without its vital signalling equipment and therefore unable to provide accurate gunnery. Likewise, there were still a few Norwegian ski-troops who could, after a fashion, watch the flanks. On the face of it the position was another one of those positions offering great possibilities for defence when looked at on the map: the road crossed from the east to the west bank, the bridge was easily demolished. But when the Germans—having discovered very quickly that the Guards had gone from Krokstrand—came up hot-foot in pursuit the following afternoon, the reality was very different and the tired troops were once more called upon to stand in the face of air attack, mortar-bombing and the pressure of infantry both much more numerous and much fresher than themselves.

In the middle of this battle Trappes-Lomax was called away to battalion headquarters to receive a message: he came back to tell his officers that he had been sacked for disobeying the order to stand at Krokstrand and was to report back to Harstad forthwith —Major Graham, the second-in-command, was to take over the battalion. The news got around: its effect on the already tired and partly demoralized men was very bad indeed and might well have been disastrous. 'This crushing blow,' says the regimental war diary, 'took place in the middle of an enemy attack, and it is hardly to be wondered at that the morale of both officers and men was still further shaken by the loss of a commanding officer for whose personality and ability everyone had the highest respect, and in whom everyone had the greatest confidence.' Personal ties are very strong in a regular battalion, especially in such a regiment as the Scots Guards. Trappes-Lomax was one of three officers who had served the regiment since 1917: he was not only, as the diary says, regarded with immense respect, but had only in the last hours and days added to it by the way in which he had carried the battalion through a gruelling retreat with very few losses and surprisingly few casualties. When he died in February 1962 one of his old comrades wrote these words in *The Times*:

'Trappes appreciated every situation during that enforced retreat with calmness, patience and accuracy. He was right where others were wrong time and time again. Our gratitude to this man of fine mind and transparent integrity does not lessen as the years go by. Now that he has gone, we salute his memory with devotion.'

This was the man General Auchinleck sacked because in his view he had not carried out an impossible order. What was Auchlinleck thinking of? Can he really have supposed that the unsupported and lightly-armed Guards could stop a whole German army group? Can he really have supposed that Trappes-Lomax retreated for any other reason than because he could hold the enemy no longer? Can he really have thought that it was either wise or proper for this fine battalion to be slaughtered to a man without holding up the enemy advance in the slightest, instead of being saved to fight other battles at a time when Britain's shortage of fully-trained troops was both very great and very well known to people like himself? What subsequently happened over this matter is buried somewhere in confidential reports that have never seen the light of day: some retraction may well have been made, for Trappes-Lomax did not suffer in the end and two years later appears in the *Army List* as Brigadier, General Staff.

In his subsequent campaigns and especially in the Middle East (where he fought a more successful rearguard action, the credit for which was for a long time to be denied him), Auchinleck was by repute most considerate to his subordinate commanders. Was his treatment of Trappes-Lomax the only time he ever treated a subordinate commander in this high-handed and uncompomising way—and was it, on reflection, an object lesson to him which he remembered with profit for the rest of his distinguished career?

The battle continued very bitterly. Before the afternoon was out the light forces on the flanks had been driven in and once more the position was rapidly becoming untenable: certainly there was not the slightest possibility of it being held until the 27th. The injustice done to Trappes-Lomax was underlined by the fact that that evening at six o'clock Gubbins himself ordered the battalion to withdraw farther down the valley. They did so in good order in spite of their fatigue and their shaken morale, safely evacuating all their casualties with them, and once more halted at a place called Storjord, where a little tributary joins the main river and there is once more a bridge. The moment half-light became day on the morning of the 24th the recce plane came over and the enemy once more started their overwhelming attack, which was none the less held until the late afternoon. By now the Irish Guards had come up the valley to Pothus, thirteen miles away, and were taking up positions through which the Scots could retire. Thankfully, therefore, they fell back for the last time in good order and round about midnight passed through the Irish Guards in Pothus woods. As they wearily trudged in, dirty, battered and unkempt, there was none of the usual banter between the Jocks and the Micks. Small wonder: the Jocks had 'marched nearly a hundred miles in a week, fighting rearguard actions, out-flanked and out-numbered and continually attacked from the air. They had lost everything but their personal weapons and what they stood up in'.

The picture of the battered Scots Guards passing through on their way out of the battle is perhaps symbolic. With the Germans completely in possession of Holland and Belgium, driving across France and already within striking distance of the Channel ports, the War Cabinet this day had decided that the campaign in Norway had become a luxury it could no longer afford.

The decision cannot really be criticized, in the light of the dire peril now facing the Allies elsewhere and the acute shortage of men, weapons and equipment in the West and on the Home Front. The German conquest of France and the loss of virtually the whole of the British Expeditionary Force's equipment in the retreat on Dunkirk—both completed in the early days of June—were to make the peril vastly more dire and the shortages infinitely more acute. But, in any case, the battle for Norway had already been lost with the evacuation farther south and the whole of the events of the last two chapters have been, as was said at the beginning of them, a sort of epilogue and a concession to the iron ore strategy. As a further concession to this strategy—there can have been no hope of prestige in it either in face of greater defeats elsewhere or in face of the fact that it was to be given up as soon as captured—the final assault on Narvik, now imminent, was to be allowed to take place before the evacuation. The ore loading plant and the railway were to be destroyed as much as possible so that, if we could not have the Swedish ore, the Germans would, at least, be denied it also. The first objective was superfluous and the latter a vain hope. The installations had already been gutted, both by German demolitions in anticipation of their own retreat from the place and by Allied gunfire: by the time the Allies entered it, much of the town itself was also in ruins. And in spite of this, the Germans, in the event, repaired the installations and got both the port and the railway into working order in time for the following winter, when the freezing of the Gulf of Bothnia again made the use of Narvik necessary.

But the evacuation was going to be an even more perilous business than the evacuations from Aandalsnes and Namsos— very much more so. True, there was air cover and would be more air cover with the coming of the Hurricane squadron, due in at Skaanland on the 26th. But there were now nearly twenty-five thousand Allied troops to be got away, not counting the unfortunate Norwegian forces in the north, who would have to be left to their own devices. The Navy was under tremendous pressure. It had lost still more ships in the fiords: in addition to the casualties already mentioned the battleship *Resolution*, which had replaced *Warspite*, had gone home with a bomb hole through three decks, the valuable depot ship *Mashrobra* had had to be destroyed and there was hardly a ship without damage of some sort. The process of milking the naval units around Norway for the more urgent needs of other theatres of war had gone on. And to cover the fleet of troopships which would need to be employed in the evacuation, two aircraft carriers, a few cruisers and a mere sprinkling of destroyers were now all that were available.

Neither the attrition of the Navy nor the extent to which it had been hounded away from the greater part of the long Norwegian coast have always been fully appreciated by those who have written about these closing phases of the campaign. Churchill himself in *The Second World War* says of the German advance through

Mosjöen and Mo that 'we, who had command of the sea and could pounce anywhere on an undefended coast, were outpaced by the enemy moving by land across very large distances in the face of every obstacle'. We did not have command of the sea off the Norwegian coast. Our loss of command had been demonstrated as long before as the sea-borne assault from the Trondheimsfiord against Carton de Wiart's troops and confirmed by the landing at Hemnesberget and the decision to keep naval ships out of the Ranfiord. It had been further demonstrated by the loss of *Chrobry* and by the grounding of *Effingham* in taking a passage where she might slip through unobserved. Command even of the fiords about Narvik had been held only in the nick of time by the arrival of 263 Squadron at Bardufoss, but the strength of the Navy in these waters was at a low ebb.

Neither the Navy's weakness nor its loss of command in Norwegian waters escaped the Germans. More than a week before the evacuation from central Norway they had already been debating the employment of what was left of their own navy to carry supplies and reinforcements to Narvik. With the passage of time and the deterioration of the Allies' situation at sea, their thoughts gradually turned from the mere relief of Dietl's troops to an attack on the British naval forces in the Arctic; by the time the Scots Guards were retreating on Pothus, Béthouart was preparing for his postponed attack on Narvik and the evacuation orders were being signalled from London, *Gneisenau* (now repaired), *Scharnhorst*, the cruiser *Hipper* and four destroyers—all they could muster—were being got ready for such an operation, which was eventually to be entitled Operation Juno. Though it was, in Chamberlain's kind of language, to 'miss the 'bus', it was still to add the final disaster to the Norwegian campaign; yet this much can none the less be said of it—that it kept these powerful surviving German units out of the Channel during the vital days of the evacuation from Dunkirk.

Before the fruition of Operation Juno and the evacuation of the Allied forces from Northern Norway, there are three stories to be told—the final phases of the grim retreat from Mosjöen to Bodö, the arrival of the Hurricanes to join the battle and the taking of Narvik, coupled with the final build-up of General Fleischer's unrelaxing and persistent campaign in the extreme north—the only operation which had gone on without intermission since the Germans had first set foot in Norway.

First, therefore, let us finish the story of the retreat on Bodö. Since it was a retreat, its end was inevitable, but its last few miles still had to be fought. For the moment the Scots Guards were out of the battle and deserved to be. Short of complete re-equipment they were not in a position to enter it once more with any effectiveness. The transport arrangements on this front were much less effective than in the withdrawal of 15 Brigade on Aandalsnes and their journey down the valley to Rognan, at the head of the fiord, was somewhat chaotic: none the less someone at least in the battalion appears to have had time to observe the scenery, for their war diary records it as being 'of astonishing beauty'.

The Irish Guards—the 'Micks'—were now in the battle instead of them. With them they had the three last Independent Companies—the one that had preceded the Scots Guards in the retreat from Mo and the two that had been stationed at Bodö. The Norwegians were able to contribute a machine-gun company and a couple of mortar detachments. Nearly the whole of the Borderers had also been got into the area in their partly re-equipped state: two companies had arrived at Bodo in destroyers shortly after the Irish Guards, and at this moment the remainder of the battalion was on its way down the coast in puffers. Nothing illustrates better than this the Navy's increasing shortage of ships, for puffers are not the most speedy of vessels and what was a trip of a few hours for a destroyer was a twenty-four-hours' voyage for them. The compensation for the tossing and wallowing troops was that the German aircraft paid no attention to them, apparently not suspecting what sort of fish these boats had in their holds. But the Borderers could not be pushed into the battle, for the line of communication had to be held, Bodö had to be held and the airfield had to be held. At this moment some hundreds of Norwegian civilians under the town's chief of police were braving continual air raids to cut, lay and cover with wire netting grass sods for a landing ground, in the hope that a few fighters might be spared to give a little relief in the battle and prevent the Germans from using the landing ground themselves.

The action at Pothus was yet one more repetition of the little play that had been acted time and again, first in the retreat along the Gudbrandsdal and more recently in the retreat from Mosjöen and Mo. The site, indeed, might almost have been a replica of that in which Trappes-Lomax and his men had fought their first engagement more than a hundred miles to the south—steep-sided valley, trees both restricting the field of fire and making observation difficult, a river and a bridge. The bridge, as always, was demolished (in this case not very successfully), the Guards proceeded to attempt to hold the crossing, while the enemy slowly built up pressure on the front and filtered in upon the flanks, so that in the end the defenders had to extricate themselves as best they could and withdraw. There were only two variations on the theme. One was that in the later stages of the action the Germans constructed a floating bridge to help them across the river—a much more successful expedient than the rubber boats which had been such a rewarding target for the rifles of the Green Howards. The other was the brief appearance of three Gladiators; and this deserves its own little place in the record, for it is the story of three brave men—Flight-Lieutenant Hull, Pilot Officer Falkson and Lieutenant Lydekker, a Fleet Air Arm armament officer who had volunteered to take the place of a sick pilot of 263 Squadron.

These three flew in from Bardufoss on the 26th and their first trial of the grass sods and wire netting was almost a disaster, for wheels were bogged as soon as they touched the ground and only skilful handling avoided wreck on the spot. They eventually found a dry patch, and while they were refuelling the chief of police and his gangs laboured furiously to lay snow-boards over the soft patches. In the midst of all this the Germans came over and began bombing, and everything seemed set for a repetition of Lesjaskog. One after another, however, the three machines took off, one to crash, one to land again on Hull's orders and the last—flown by Hull himself—to chase the Germans down the valley and do battle with them until his ammunition ran out. Taking off a second time over the snow-boards, Hull found the valley quite clear of enemy aircraft and proceeded to amuse and encourage the troops in the front line by doing aerobatics. Considering that it was the first time that these had seen a British fighter in action in Norway it is no wonder that they cheered and waved furiously for the pilot's encouragement.

But, as Hull himself says in his own account of the battle, it was a vain hope. The landing ground was so unfit for use that the machines were bound to be written off one by one—even if the Germans did not return in force to bomb it to pieces, which they were about to do, and the town with it. Certainly no more machines could be spared from Bardufoss to replace the casualties, even though the Hurricanes were due in this day. And the troops had already been forced out of Pothus and were withdrawing down the valley to the sea, where, with great difficulty, they were ferried across to the north side of the fiord.

When the Germans made their expected comeback next morning to start the concentrated bombing of the airfield, Hull and Lydekker took off. In the battle that followed Hull was hit and crash-landed. Lydekker was also wounded and his machine badly damaged, although not before he had given a good account of himself. Pursued by the Germans, he got his machine back to Bardufoss: it was nothing more than a flying wreck and never took the air again. So ended very creditably the air battle of Bodö in which three pilots in three obsolescent machines demonstrated once more what had already been demonstrated on the ground— that the Germans, having had things so far completely their own way, recoiled rapidly and paused for consideration when they suddenly found themselves faced with training, skill and daring. Had there been just a few more Gladiators, had they been there just a little earlier in the battle—who can tell what the difference would have been?

Once more, the Germans did not immediately follow up the troops retiring on Bodö, where Gubbins was concentrating them —no longer for the defence of the place as a bastion to protect the north, but in preparation for their withdrawal with the rest of the Allied forces. They had their own difficulties along the tenuous and difficult line of communication that now stretched behind them; the relief of General Dietl was a more important objective than the mere annihilation for its own sake of the scattered bodies of men making their way out of the valley and being transported in the inevitable puffers across the waters of the fiord. In any case, they had their own plans for Bodö, whose turn for the blitz that had descended on Namsos, on Aandalsnes, on Dombaas, Steinkjer, Molde and every town and village that had housed Allied troops or been a centre of Norwegian Resistance, was long overdue.

The destruction of Bodö took place on the evening of 27th May. Those who witnessed it say that the Luftwaffe—free once more of opposition—descended on it in a leisurely fashion out of a clear spring sky. One hundred and fifty machines took part in the operation: they systematically obliterated the pleasant little town street by street and building by building. Fires were soon burning everywhere. The civilian population had not been evacuated: now they were machine-gunned as they fled. The hospital was not spared: in it were many wounded British servicemen, especially from the Scots Guards, and the heroism and devotion of the Norwegian nurses is recorded with gratitude in their History. Recorded there, too, with a sensitivity unusual in regimental documents, is the story of the last broadcast from Bodö radio station:

'Over and over again from the blackened and smoking ruins of the township of the dead went out a recording of the great death hymn of Björnson and Edvard Grieg: "The mighty host of saints we see as a thousand mountains clad with snow".'

Over the distance of the years this picture comes clear, fresh and poignant as it was at the hour when the last of the German bombers had throbbed away into the clear sky; leaving behind the rubble, smouldering timbers and scattered small possessions of what had been not a great, imperial city, a port where navies rode in pride and rich men wielded dominion over half the world—but a small, poor place, where people of but modest ambitions had asked no more than to live in peace and happiness and earn their little living from the sea. It epitomizes the whole agony of Norway. It reduces to human terms the tragedy of the little nation that for a thousand years had sought neither conquest nor aggrandisement, but by ill fortune possessed two things needed for the survival of great powers locked in a struggle to the death —a sheltered passage down its inhospitable coast and an ice-free port for the export of iron ore. It is the final condemnation of those who proclaimed in grand phrases their will to save Norway —and bungled the job.

The original plan for the defence of the Bodö area had been to make a final attempt to block the enemy advance to the north at Finneid, near the eastern end of the fiord. It was a true defensive position with wide water on front and flanks and high mountains on its eastern side, stretching away to the Swedish border, which here is barely twenty miles away. It was a better defensive position than any in the whole campaign at which an attempted stand had been made. To help in its defence the Norwegians had concentrated once more the remnants of the troops who had been withdrawn from the south and added to these the reserve battalion which had been helping in the construction of the airfield at Bardufoss. To them, time for Fleischer to mount his final offensive against Dietl's battered troops was vital. Now, without being vouchsafed the reason why, they saw to their astonishment the British forces withdrawing westward along the fiord to positions that were palpably less good and, furthermore, did not cover the road to Narvik. These were, in fact, being withdrawn on Bodö (or rather on the place where Bodö had been) for the evacuation. Their astonishment was but little assuaged when they were told by their own headquarters of the British decision to evacuate the Bodö area—the main evacuation was, of course, a closely guarded secret known only to a relatively few senior Allied officers. The decision to evacuate rather than reinforce, with the peril to the north nakedly apparent, made no sense to them. They were out on a limb again. And they were not strong enough to stand on their own.

All their indignant representations could wrest from Brigadier Gubbins was a three-day postponement of the evacuation while they withdrew across the little neck of land from Finneid to Rosvik: here, at the mouth of the Leirfiord, the road to the north finally comes to its end, for the country between here and Narvik is some of the wildest and most formidable in the whole of Norway. The Norwegians considered it impassable for all practical purposes and in normal times the passage from Rosvik to Narvik had been by sea alone. They would, therefore, collect boats for themselves and make their way to the Lofoten Islands, which curve down the coast like a great, broken tongue around the beginning of the Vestfiord.

But in the course of these three days, Gubbins was withdrawing the British units progressively towards the tip of coast

An oil and petrol dump burning after a German bomber raid.

Sappers levelling the landing strip at Skaanland.

A Norwegian soldier guards petrol tanks at Harstad, set ablaze by
German bombing.

on which Bodö had been, at the very mouth of Saltfiord. The Germans were now on the move again and were following very close on the heels of the retirement, although they did not attempt to re-engage. So the Norwegians were cut off long before the time was up, and extricated themselves only with the greatest of difficulty and some losses. The last of the British troops embarked on 31st May—some bound direct for Scotland, some for Harstad, to melt away into the general evacuation which was by then being organized. As they embarked the advance German scouts were already entering the ruined town; and their general state is summed up by the fact that all that the Scots Guards, who had sailed for Mosjöen a well-equipped regular infantry battalion, took back with them was six thousand rounds of rifle ammunition. That they got away without further interference was due to two causes: in the first place, a handful of Gladiators and Hurricanes from Bardufoss maintained a patrol above them—in the second, the Germans were much more interested in the urgent job of relieving General Dietl than in mopping up the remnants of the brigade which no longer stood in their way athwart the road they must take.

For though they had come to the end of the road, the most difficult part of their march lay ahead of them, and here the country itself—impassable even to the Norwegians—would be a much more formidable enemy than the Norwegian and Allied troops had been. The Second Mountain Division were facing their most severe test, for their orders were to cross the mountain belt and so effect a junction with the Narvik forces by land. A way had been worked out and supply-dropping arrangements made for them with great thoroughness. It would be idle not to admire the boldness and realism with which the plan was made, as well as the fitness and determination of the men who undertook it, and it stands out in very real contrast to the ill-considered way in which the Allied troops in Norway had been ordered to achieve impossible objectives. The severity of their task is shown by the fact that a week later their most advanced units had completed only a third of their journey—by which time the urgency of the need had vanished with the main Allied evacuation.

It needed a desperate situation to inspire such desperate measures—and, for that matter, other desperate measures which the

Germans were considering while the last of the British troops at Bodö were being withdrawn: these included a glider attack on the Allied base area, while their great and valuable crack Atlantic liners, *Bremen* and *Europa,* rushed reinforcements north by sea. Ignorant as they yet were of the fact that the Allies were making no more than a gesture of victory at Narvik before withdrawal, that Fleischer—who had done all the real fighting and was within sight of success—was about in his turn to be left out on a limb, they regarded the situation of General Dietl as very desperate indeed.

By the end of the third week in May, it will be remembered, Fleischer's grinding offensive had pressed down the German front from the great elephant's-head shape, into which it had once swelled out north of Narvik, into a straight line which extended no farther north, roughly, than the latitude of the northern shore of the Ofotfiord and ran back towards the refuge of the Swedish frontier. The French landing at Bjerkvik had, moreover, forced the Germans away from the Herjangsfiord and the Ofotfiord—almost as far east as the mouth of the Rombaksfiord, the last narrow inlet into which Whitworth's destroyers had once pursued the surviving Nazi ships of war to their destruction. Narvik itself had become a salient, on the western side of which the Poles on the Ankenes peninsula faced the invaders grimly. The German headquarters was no longer, indeed, at Narvik at all, but at Björnfjell, beyond the head of the Rombaksfiord, and they were prepared to evacuate the town at any moment—having progressively completed a series of demolitions which would prevent the export of the iron ore that had started all the trouble. They were finding the obstinate and independent citizens of Narvik more difficult to control than ever: these, still living on their diet of stinking fish, seethed as they watched the destruction of all that had brought them their brief few years of prosperity and the amenities their prosperity had brought them—seethed and still wondered why the Allies did not come. By their uncompromising attitude and the numberless ways in which they contrived to make life more difficult for the Germans—the shape, as has already been said, of the Norwegian Resistance to come—they were laying up for themselves a dreadful retribution in the future; those who had been foremost in making things difficult were already marked men and would be wanted men when the conquest of Norway was secure beyond doubt.

But since the taking of Bjerkvik there had been no major movement of the Allied forces. Auchinleck was busy about his task of getting the confusion he had inherited into some sort of order, hiving off part of his overcrowded base to the proposed subsidiary base at Tromsö and generally organizing everything for permanent occupation, as he had been instructed to do. At the same time he, Cork and Béthouart were making their plans for the taking of Narvik and the final elimination of the German forces, which would leave both shores of the Ofotfiord, together with what remained of Norway to the north of it, safely in the hands of the Allies—and incidentally, also, of the Norwegians, whose country this happened to be. First planned for the 24th, the assault was postponed for the last time until the 28th for the sake of the extra protection the Hurricanes of 46 Squadron would given when they were settled in at Skaanland.

Now there was one thing, to begin with, that 46 Squadron had in common with some units of other services—it had taken them a long time to get to Norway. In fact, it had taken them even longer than most. They had been sailing around the North Sea and the Arctic Ocean for best part of a fortnight, but they had been ready for Norway for well over a month. They had been earmarked for central Norway in the days when the ghost of Operation Hammer was reviving and Cross, their squadron leader, flew in to prospect for an airfield on the day after the disaster of Lesjaskog—only to get back and find the operation had been cancelled and withdrawal decided on instead. They were a tough, enterprising and experienced squadron, who considered themselves very warlike—not without reason, for they had spent the whole of the previous winter (and an abominable one it had been) on the east coast, where they had had plenty of action with German seaplanes operating over the convoy routes, in what, by peacetime standards, would have been impossible flying weather. They were the flying counterpart of the Green Howards, tremendously high in their morale, tremendously confident. They were willing as well as ready to go to Norway instead of to France, for which they had been previously warned, for this was before the great German offensive had made France interesting to bloody-minded young men. As the years of peace lengthen—even the years of an uneasy peace—it becomes more and more difficult to remember that there were men who, without any false glamour or sentiment, thought danger a privilege and the chance of death high glory; yet such there were, and the coming months were to prove that their spirit was more closely akin to the true spirit of Britain than the querulous elder statesmen who fumbled with the opportunities of war and quailed at the sight of men in uniform.

When operations in central Norway petered out, 46 Squadron was re-allocated to the build-up in the north: on Thursday, 9th May—while Auchinleck was still on his way to supersede Mackesy, taking their Wing Commander with him, they left Digby, in Yorkshire, and flew to Abbotsinch, where their aircraft were dismantled and taken down the Clyde on barges to be loaded into the carrier *Glorious*. The pundits considered it impossible for these monoplane fighters, with their high wing-loading and correspondingly high landing speed, to be flown on to a carrier and doubted, for that matter, whether they could be flown off; though flown off they would certainly have to be, and off the coast of Norway, too. It was this thinking which had conditioned the choice of new fighters for the Fleet Air Arm, which was getting, instead of its own counterpart of the Hurricanes and the Spitfires, the Blackburn Skua, which was a compromise and a failure: naval pilots, who suspected that even the Admiralty could sometimes be wrong, were watching the fate of the Hurricanes with great interest and were overjoyed when they flew both off and, later, on without undue difficulty. The problem and the hazard were accentuated by the choice of *Glorious* for the job: *Ark Royal*'s flight deck was seventy feet longer, but her lifts had been made for naval aircraft with folding wings, whereas the old *Glorious* had been commissioned before folding wings were heard of and her lifts would take the full span of the Hurricanes. There was really, therefore, no choice and *Glorious* would have to do her best for 46 Squadron by flogging her old turbines into the wind to bursting point when the time for take-off came.

They sailed on Whit Sunday, 12th May: had it then been merely a question of crossing the sea and landing in Norway, ships would have been saved and a lot of agony at Harstad and elsewhere avoided, for they would have arrived in time for the peak of the German air offensive. But alas, there was nowhere for them to land in Norway: neither Bardufoss, which was intended for the Gladiators, nor Skaanland, which was intended for them, were ready or anything like ready, though sweat and tears were now being lavished on both. Skaanland, if only it could be got ready, had enormous advantages over Bardufoss, which was thirty miles farther away from the battle area, but its preparation was an even more difficult job: as at Bodö, the runways were constructed from vast numbers of grass sods, laid, rolled and covered with wire netting—a Herculean labour and, as events turned out, a vain one.

So on the 13th the squadron found themselves back in the Clyde, to sail again the following day and cruise well off the Norwegian coast for nearly a week. Presently they found themselves in company with *Furious*, carrying 263 Squadron, and eventually had the mortification of seeing the Gladiators take off on that sinister day of low visibility and cloud—to disappear from sight almost immediately on their way to their perilous landing at Bardufoss. For themselves, they went back yet again to Scapa, to refuel. At last, on the 26th, they were off the Arctic coast again, and the wayward genius of the Norwegian weather granted them a flat calm and good visibility—the latter a blessing, the former not, with no wind for the carrier to steer into. There was also another wayward genius, Captain d'Oyley Hughes of *Glorious*. He was a brave man, a submariner of the First World War and a peacetime amateur pilot, and was soon to meet a brave man's death, but he was also a man of strong ideas, which happened to conflict with those of Squadron Leader Cross, very much his junior but determined to run his squadron in his own way.

Still very conscious of the lessons of Lesjaskog, Cross was determined that none of his aircraft was going to be caught sitting on the ground. He therefore planned to take them in in three groups of six: the second would cover the landing of the first, the third the landing of the second, and by the time the third was ready to come in, the first would be refuelled and in the air, ready to protect them and the airfield in turn. D'Oyley Hughes demanded that they take off in groups of two. Sir Kenneth Cross remembers the argument to this day, and remembers the lecture he got about the presumptuousness of young men—but he stuck it out and got his own way. At last, therefore, the first six machines were ranged up on the flight deck and *Glorious* proceeded to steam as she had never steamed before. Cross, sitting in his Hurricane, saw an old Engineer Commander come staggering across the deck in the gale *Glorious* had made for herself. He climbed on to the wing.

'She's going faster than she's been since 1929,' he bellowed.

And the Hurricanes went.

They roared down the deck, came unstuck with nothing to spare and climbed. From the air the carrier looked like a great speedboat: she was doing something over thirty knots.

Cross landed first at Skaanland. There was not a German aircraft in the sky. Everything was perfect. His wheels touched the ground, he slowed. And as he slowed, he felt the tail of the Hurricane lifting, and knew his wheels were bogged. The machine stopped, hesitated and tilted gently on to its nose: the propeller blades smacked into the ground and bent.

Furious, he flung back his canopy and climbed out of the machine. Nearby stood an elderly airfield construction officer.

'What the hell sort of place is this to bring Hurricanes into?' demanded Cross.

The other man looked at him for a moment—then burst into tears. It was suddenly borne in upon the angry young squadron leader that these people had been toiling and scheming for days and weeks to do a job which needed months—toiling under impossible strain, for all bar the last few days under constant and uninterrupted air attack. They had finished the job, they had made an airfield, they had called the aircraft in—and now it was no good. Their labour had been in vain and they had worn themselves out, torn their nerves to shreds for nothing. Here was the first aircraft, and it was a wreck.

He couldn't feel angry any more—only sorry. In any case, there was a more urgent problem to cope with—the problem of the other aircraft coming in behind him.

The second Hurricane made a perfect landing. So did the third. The fourth caught its wheel fairings in the wire netting and turned a somersault. The fifth and sixth got in all right—but that was enough of Skaanland!

The second lot was now overhead and the third was somewhere

on its way. There was no ground-to-air radio in operation. Climbing back into his machine, he was luckily able, in those un-propitious radio conditions, to contact both groups and redirect them to Bardufoss—easier said than done, for the available maps were of even less use for flying purposes than for ground opera-tions. But they got there. Cross's bent propeller (which would have been a precision workshop job at home) was straightened with a hammer and the somersaulted machine set right way up: they joined the rest of the squadron at Bardufoss and shared it with the Gladiators for the rest of their short but hectic stay. Skaanland remained deserted, the pain and labour wasted, like so much else in Norway. From Bardufoss on the morning of the 28th, 46 Squadron flew its first patrol at eighteen thousand feet above Narvik and had flown nine patrols by a quarter past four. For this was the morning of the great assault, so long delayed that it must have been difficult for the frustrated Cork and the others involved to believe it was happening at last.

Narvik lies on a little tongue of flat land jutting out into the Ofotfiord: this little tongue is the end of the peninsula something less than ten miles long overall, formed by the Beisfiord, which runs south-east out of the Ofotfiord, and the Rombaksfiord which, in fact, is the last easterly continuation of the Ofotfiord itself. Across the Beisfiord the town faces the Ankenes peninsula and the water separating the two is about a mile at its widest; across the Rombaksfiord it faces Öyjord with a somewhat greater distance between. Behind the town and away from the relatively flat ground at sea level the mountains rise steeply to peaks of more than four thousand feet. The flat ground peters out very quickly away from the tip of the peninsula, so that both on the northern and the south-western sides the steep, broken rocks tumble to-wards the sea with only the narrowest of beaches between. There is a little more beach on the north coast than on the south-western coast, and it is along the narrow strip here that the railway skirts the edge of the Rombaksfiord, finally to curve around its end to Björnfjell and make its way from thence to Sweden. Thus all possible landing places are easily overlooked from above, and it was precisely the difficulty of blasting the enemy out of any fixed defences overlooking the town and beaches that had caused so many misgivings, so many deliberations and so many postponements in the weeks that had gone by. On the wider beaches about the town and the tip of the peninsula the Germans had sown mines.

The Foreign Legion were firmly in possession of the Öyjord peninsula, from which the Germans had been progressively cleared since the landing at Bjerkvik; the latter were now firmly dammed back by the linking up of the French with General Fleischer's right-hand battle group. The Germans, however, were still in possession of the area beyond the end of the Rombaksfiord—working around which, as General Mackesy had originally intended, would still have been a long, difficult and costly operation.

The Poles were on the Ankenes peninsula, where they had relieved the South Wales Borderers nearly a fortnight before, but they were not in complete possession of it and there had been a number of skirmishes between them and the Germans, who were still holding the inner shores of the Beisfiord in some strength.

From Öyjord, therefore, General Béthouart had determined to bring the attacking forces directly across the water on to the narrow beaches behind the town, from there work downwards and so take it in the rear. Three important things were needed for this operation. One was some protection, if not complete freedom, from air straffing while the assault forces made the water crossing —and this could now be given with reasonable assurance by the Gladiators and Hurricanes from Bardufoss. Another was bombardment to cover the actual landing and blast the enemy out of artillery, mortar and machine-gun positions covering the narrow beaches from above. This was less certain: it would best of all have been provided from the air on the German pattern, but there were no bombers available and now never would be. The second best for the operation was bombardment by naval gunfire, which was technically less effective because of the flat trajectory of naval guns; but a still graver handicap was that the depletion of the naval forces had left Admiral Cork without a single ship mounting more than six-inch guns and only one of these—the cruiser *Southampton*. For the rest the four-inch high-angle guns of the two remaining anti-aircraft cruisers, *Cairo* and *Coventry*, and the sloop *Stork*, backed up by the guns of the little force of destroyers, would have to suffice.

The last requirement was the most difficult of all to fill and was, in fact, so difficult that it presented the main hazard of the operation—sufficient shallow-draught small craft to get the troops and their equipment across the water, together with the Foreign Legion's light tanks, which had been so useful in the taking of Bjerkvik. There were but five of the landing craft still serviceable, and these were suffering from the troubles that had dogged them throughout. Puffers were too deep in draught and too slow and ships' boats were also very unsuitable for the job. All that could be hoped was that the landing craft could be used to put the first party ashore, where they would have to establish and maintain themselves while the craft went back for a second flight. Even on this hazardous scale, the whole of the landing craft would be needed for the assault across the Rombaksfiord, therefore the Poles would have to mop up the Ankenes peninsula and make their way round by land.

Thus, in spite of all the forces that had been poured into Narvik, there were still hazards and shortages in this final operation, which was really the objective and end-product of everything that had been sent to northern Norway—indeed in the eyes of Mr. Chamberlain's Cabinet, at least, it was probably the object of everything that had been sent to any part of Norway. But now there could be no further hanging back either for hazards or shortages: certainly no more supplies of any kind would now be spared for Norway, and inasmuch as the decision to evacuate the whole country had already been made, the assault must take place now or never. The last postponement had taken place. The forces were poised across the water on both sides of the peninsula. General Fleischer had come down from the mountains to see the Allies in action at last: he had added to the French forces a battalion of Norwegians and a small detachment of Norwegian military police, who would be needed for duties in the town when captured.

Shortly before midnight on the 27th/28th the civilians in Narvik—who had never given up hoping throughout the barren weeks and still maintained a look-out—saw ships steaming into the fiord. It was a calm night with only a little purple in the sky to pass for darkness—purple with a few small clouds, soon lightening again into the blue sky of day. 'A whole fleet' is how Mayor

Broch describes them: that description is, perhaps, a measure of the pitch of the Norwegians' excitement, because there was nothing like either the number or the weight of ships that had been seen in the attacks of early April. Still, here were the ships, moving at high speed in close formation with fighters overhead, and within minutes of the news flying around hardly a Norwegian was asleep or even in bed. Long since they had become accustomed to gunfire and to the destruction of their town: a little more destruction seemed a small price to pay for freedom and their people had already been prudently evacuated from the area around the waterfront. Yet even so the bombardment appeared to them the most tremendous they had ever heard. Once more Broch's description of it reads oddly, because the bombardments of other days, with the fifteen-inch guns of *Warspite* thundering in the middle of them were of heavier stuff. Conceivably it was the concentration, and in particular the concentration on the beaches and the seaward parts of the town, that made the impression. Broch talks of the overwhelming fierceness of the attack being beyond expectation or description. 'The night,' he says, 'was one continuous explosion.' From across the fiord the French field guns and the Norwegian battery manned by Fleischer's troops added to the bombardment and the official report describes their fire as heavy and accurate: in the same breath however it says that the broken ground and the birch scrub which covered it made observation difficult.

While all this was going on the men of the Foreign Legion, suffused with their old-fashioned ideas of military ardour and their antique buccaneering traditions, were embarking in the handful of landing craft around the corner of the Herjangsfiord, where they were concealed from the eyes of the German defences. Lest anything that has been written about them be misunderstood, let it be said that perhaps old-fashioned ideas and old-fashioned bravado were not wholly out of place—a little of both would not have come amiss to General Mackesy six weeks before. Presently the excited Norwegians saw the landing craft round the point and make straight across the water to the beaches behind the town. There was at this stage little German opposition and a complete absence of German air attack—as at the taking of Bjerkvik, the regularity of the Luftwaffe's operational timetable served the assault troops well. The landing craft hastily decanted the infantry on the beaches, according to plan, and went back for the tanks and more troops. There was now some German shelling across the fiord, which interrupted the embarkation of both these, but they were brought safely across. The tanks, however, did not frisk rapidly about, popping off their little guns as they had done to the discomfort of the Germans at Bjerkvik: they were bogged down immediately on landing and took no part at all in the battle. The same happened to a second detachment of tanks which was later put ashore on the Ankenes beaches: like the hulks of the grounded German destroyers at the end of the Rombaks-fiord, these remained as monuments to the battle during the occupation and, indeed, for some years after the war.

But in spite of it all, a whole battalion of the Foreign Legion and the Norwegian battalion as well were ashore by four o'clock and scrambling up the rough ground towards their objective, the heights behind the town, against opposition that was far less than had ever been imagined. Naval gunfire had had just the effect on the half-hearted and dispirited defenders that both Churchill and the Earl of Cork had sworn it would have, though General Mackesy and others had refused to believe them: shorn, furthermore, of the air support that was an essential part of their tactics, the Germans showed little inclination to stand and fight it out.

But just at this moment German aircraft appeared, and the British fighters disappeared almost within the same breath. Fog had suddenly come down upon Bardufoss, preventing the fighters from taking off, so that as one patrol departed to refuel their place was not taken by another. Restored to their unchallenged command of the air, the Stukas and Ju 88s descended on the cruisers and destroyers, which were forced away from their target area, zig-zagging in evasive action and throwing everything they had at their attackers: it was a timely reminder of the narrow margin by which the Gladiators and Hurricanes were keeping the Ofotfiord from turning into a replica of the waters around Namsos. Heartened by the appearance of the bombers and relieved from the covering bombardment of the naval guns, the Germans rose in the hills and counter-attacked, to drive the French and the Norwegians inch by inch back down the slope to the beaches. For a short while things looked very grim and were made more so by the fact that communication between ships and shore had broken down, so that the Navy, engrossed with the danger from the air, was unaware of the desperate need for support. The destroyer *Beagle* was only dispatched back to the beaches in the nick of time after the naval liaison officer with the land forces had set off down the fiord in a landing craft to report their predicament verbally. The *Beagle*'s guns halted the Germans: this time the French and Norwegians forced their way to the crest of the slope and held it, their numbers increasing all the time, in spite of two further counter-attacks. By eight o'clock the fog had cleared and the fighters were in the air again: this day, in all, the R.A.F. flew ninety-five sorties and the Hurricanes had the satisfaction of bringing down their first Junkers 88s. By mid-morning a second French battalion was ashore and the Germans were now out-numbered. Meanwhile the Poles on the other side had been battering their way down the Ankenes peninsula—first against opposition so bitterly determined that they were forced back by counter-attack beyond their original positions, but the opposition faded: by the evening they were around the tip of the Beisfiord and during the night made contact with the French.

From the town the last of the German garrison had melted away in small groups until none were left except the wounded in the Norwegian hospital and the dead in the cemeteries. They left behind them a shattered port and a township already half in ruins: over it hung the smoke of the Norwegians' last dump of coal, which had been set on fire by the blowing up of one of the Germans' gun positions as they left. Full marks go to General Béthouart for the fact that he halted his troops, so that a Norwegian detachment should be first to march into the streets of Narvik. First of the Norwegians was a young man, the son of the town baker, who was enthroned in a hastily decorated car and escorted in triumph to his parents. The Norwegian flag floated again over the city hall.

It was victory, but it was victory with an anti-climax. Anti-climax in the first place because even the Norwegians were so tired after all the excitement and after being up all night that they could hardly realize the Germans had gone at last—besides, they had waited so long and been so often disappointed that, like the realization of all hopes deferred, the taste of the reality was blunted by the long anticipation that had preceded it. The whole operation had taken but a few hours and had cost no more than one hundred and fifty men, in spite of the Germans having had time to prepare defences, mine the beaches and take all possible precautions against the onslaught of which the threat had been hanging over them since the second week in April.

But it was an anti-climax for other reasons. Not the least of these was one of which none of the Norwegians and only a handful of British officers were yet aware—that the town had been taken only to be given up—that now it was taken, the arrangements for the massive evacuation operation to follow must go ahead with all speed. It was to be a cruel and incomprehensible blow for them—cruellest of all for Fleischer and his battle-scarred men in the mountains, who now would arise in their weariness and make the final effort to drive the remains of the German forces the last few miles into Sweden and internment. Even the moment of triumph—the only military success on the Allied side in the whole of this misconceived and misfought campain—could not disguise the fact that the Germans were advancing up the difficult country north of Bodö and were firmly in possession of Bodö airfield, to make it serviceable and use it when they chose: nothing could conceal the fact that, apart from the little area round the Ofotsfiord and within range of the two fighter squadrons operating from Bardufoss, the Germans were firmly in possession of the whole of Norway and the whole of the Norwegian coast, against which British command of the open sea could avail nothing. Nor could anything conceal the fact that what was true of Norway was shortly to be true of the whole of Western Europe: this very day of the taking of Narvik, King Leopold of the Belgians had surrendered, the British Expeditionary Force was in full retreat on Dunkirk and soon that much greater evacuation would begin; so that Arctic Norway was indeed a luxury that could no longer be afforded.

What perhaps brought the greatest sense of anti-climax to the Norwegians was the fact that Narvik had been taken only to be cleared of its civilian population and subjected to a further battering. It was abundantly clear to the Allied command that, now it was in their hands, the town was due for the fate of Namsos,

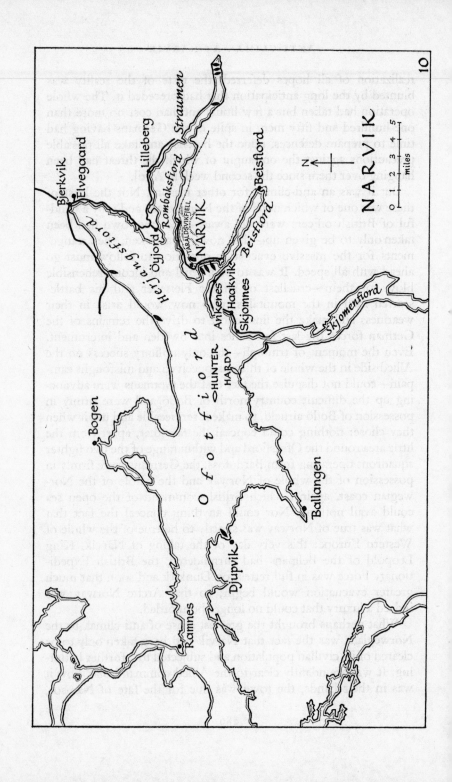

Aandalsnes, Bodö and the rest; and before the next day was many hours old a fresh fleet of puffers, chartered in the Lofoten Islands, was already on its way up the fiord to take aboard the first loads of women, children and old people and to distribute them in places of safety around the waterways and islands. Not many hours after that the first of the bombers arrived to carry on the destruction which German demolitions and British gunfire had begun. The Gladiators and Hurricanes could do a great deal, but they could not do everything, and their first duty was now the defence of the base area and the ships and the covering of the evacuation.

CHAPTER 14

FAREWELL TO THE MOUNTAINS

THERE was no rejoicing in England for the capture of Narvik. It went almost unnoticed in the shadow of the appalling news from France: the news releases strove to lighten the shadow a little with tales of enormous German casualties and assurances that the B.E.F. were 'in good heart'—but the latter phrase alone sounded like half an obituary. In the grey dawn of the last day of May, British troops were already standing up to their waists in the sea, waiting to be taken off from the beaches of Dunkirk: when the first shiploads of tattered, sleepless and hungry survivors began to come ashore at Channel ports, it could no longer be concealed that Britain and France between them had suffered the biggest military defeat in modern history. Small wonder that there was little attention to spare for a minor success away beyond the Arctic Circle, very far indeed from what had now become the main theatre of war.

Apart from the sober and restrained joy of Narvik—tempered as this was by partings with womenfolk and children and the jeopardy of precious personal possessions—there was little rejoicing in Norway either. What, in fact, was engrossing the attention of the Norwegian government at Tromsö very much more was the evacuation of Bodö, the last line of defence against the main German advance to the north, which could not be relied upon to be halted by mountains or other 'natural obstacles'. So great was Norwegian concern that on 1st June Allied observers at Tromsö for the first time feared that they would sue for a separate armistice without regard to British and French military necessities. Were they to do so before the evacuation of the whole of the Allied forces was complete, the whole operation would face disaster as certain as that which appeared to be threatening the troops around Dunkirk.

Quite apart from the possibility of the Norwegians deserting their would-be saviours, the evacuation offered hazards enough. For the twenty-five thousand Allied troops involved, fifteen large troopships were required—although, in the event, only thirteen were used. Sitting targets, these, vulnerable to attack by air, surface raider and submarine. For their protection there were available two aircraft carriers (themselves targets), three cruisers, the depot ship *Vindictive* (merely a token defender) and—most sinister of all—eleven destroyers only: these were little more than sufficient, on paper, to screen the carriers. Air cover, once Bardufoss had been cleared and the runways destroyed, there could be none but what the carriers could offer: home-based fighters were far out of range and Coastal Command's flying-boats, which alone could make the distance, were palpably so little use that they were not called upon. But before even these hazards could be faced, the force had to be concentrated and embarked; and as much of its equipment as possible must be taken with it, for the abandonment of everything the B.E.F. had possessed in France had left a desperate shortage of every sort of arms and equipment for the coming siege of Britain against a now unquestionably superior foe. And the movement of troops, armaments and stores—now scattered over a wide area from Tromsö to Narvik and beyond—into any sort of concentration that looked like a preparation for withdrawal would be noticed, unless the most stringent precautions were exercised and the most elaborate deceits practised.

So the greatest secrecy was necessary and this in turn meant, as it had meant at Aandalsnes and Namsos, that the Norwegians, except at the very top level, would have to be kept in the dark. In turn again this meant two things—that there was no possibility of evacuating any substantial part of the Norwegian forces to carry on their battle from beyond the sea, and that the bulk of them would be left to face certain surrender when the Allied troops had gone. Yes, the necessities of war now demanded that the little garrison of Narvik should be betrayed, that Fleischer's battalions, poised on the verge of victory for which they had striven so desperately and so courageously, should find themselves out on a limb in the very moment of impending triumph.

The evacuation of the Bodö troops presented no difficulties. It was already under way and was known. The opportunity, as we have seen, was taken of shipping some of them straight home: the remainder—the majority—were taken back to the base area, ostensibly for re-equipment. Likewise, some stores and storeships could be moved without comment for there was continuous movement of this sort within certain limits, and Cork had already taken the opportunity, within a few days of receiving his orders, of getting as much as he could of these on the way. For the rest, a general rumour was allowed to spread that units and equipment were to be moved in a considerable way to the new subsidiary base at Tromsö, and the overwhelming majority of the British and French personnel had no idea that they were actually leaving Norway until they were at sea—or if they had, commendably appear to have kept their counsel.

The problem of the Norwegians was, as it had been in the south, a bitterly insoluble one for the Allied commanders on the spot. It was one thing for the War Cabinet to insist that even the Norwegian government be kept in the dark as long as possible, and that thereafter the Norwegian forces be either evacuated with ours or given what could be spared to continue the struggle: of these two latter things the first was impossible for reasons already stated and the latter was bungled by a last series of vacillations that finally resulted in orders to Cork to leave substantial supplies of ammunition arriving after he had gone. Auchinleck and Cork certainly felt their position deeply; but it was felt most deeply, perhaps, by Béthouart, whose men alone had fought side by side with the Norwegians, and by the R.A.F.—Moore, Atcherley and Cross in particular. The R.A.F. had come into Bardufoss to be faced with the cynicism of Fleischer and the disillusionment of Ruge. They had proved their integrity by deeds, and relations between them and the Norwegians had become close and happy. They had entertained the Crown Prince in their mess and he had—unwittingly, to be fair to him—helped them to drink their last bottle of brandy. Now they were, after all, to be tarred with the same brush as the others. All they could hope was that in time the Norwegians would understand—as, indeed, they generously came to.

At last, on 1st June, permission was given for the decision to be communicated, under great secrecy, to King Haakon and his government. Under equal secrecy they in turn communicated it to

General Ruge: so the way was laid open for the withdrawal of the French and Polish troops from around Narvik and on Fleischer's western flank, and they were carefully moved into the concentration area. To Norwegians not in the know this proved to be no more mystifying, perhaps, than some other Allied movements had been in the past. For the rest, neither Fleischer's men nor the people of Narvik were in touch with or attuned to events in the world beyond their narrow field of struggle. Contact even between Tromsö and themselves was tenuous and blanketed both by the difficulty of communication and the need for security. The events in France and even, for that matter, the events around Bodö were shadows to them. In these circumstances the possibility of the withdrawals being linked with an Allied evacuation, especially after the capture of Narvik and the pushing of Dietl's forces into their last, small enclave, did not even occur to them.

King Haakon decided that he and the Crown Prince, together with the principal members of his government, must leave the country with the Allies, to remain in freedom, although in exile, a visible symbol of Norway still unconquered. They would carry with them still Norway's precious supply of gold which they had brought with them all the way from Oslo, far away in the south. To the British people they would, perhaps, be yet another government in exile, another national anthem to be added to the growing string played before news bulletins by the B.B.C.: to Norwegians the world over they would be a rallying point in the war that neither they nor the British would admit was lost. Of the military commanders, Fleischer would go with them, and Beichmann and some others, to organize the new Norwegian forces on land, at sea and in the air. Ruge would not go. This time his mind was made up. When the last of his fighting forces, with whom he was deeply and personally identified beyond the possibility of divorcement, surrendered, the great man would surrender with them. But he declined for himself the freedom to disperse to their homes which was vouchsafed to his men. He insisted on remaining in captivity as a symbol that Norway was still at war—and so remained until the war's end, first in his own country and then in Germany. He was proof against captivity, as he was proof against dishonour. No soldier ever served his country better than this sincere, simple and single-minded man. No man made a greater sacrifice. His reward was the honour which became his from that day until the day of his death, many years later, in a Norway once more undivided, happy and free.

The Norwegian government pleaded for twenty-four hours' respite to revive once more the ghost of the Mowinkel Plan. It was granted and the Foreign Minister, Dr. Koht, saw the Swedish Foreign Minister. The Germans were no longer interested and the Swedes were powerless to sway them: his journey, however, came near to sparking off the very disaster the Allied Command feared, for under stress, he told the Swedes of the evacuation plans. Fortunately for everyone—not least the twenty-five thousand troops and the King of Norway, shortly to be at sea—the confidence was kept. They further pleaded for a few more days for Fleischer to complete the rout of General Dietl: beyond his penned-in troops the Swedish border was literally in sight, the Swedes could actually be seen erecting new demarcation posts and flags and four trains were known to be waiting to carry the German internees away. But this could not be granted: Fleischer could not be ready before the 8th and the evacuation could not wait that long.

Astonishingly, the Germans remained in complete ignorance of the fact that the Allies were about to leave Norway. They remained in ignorance as the advance units of the Second Mountain Division struggled over the rugged mountains between Bodö and Narvik towards Dietl's troops, facing captivity or flight into Sweden. They remained in ignorance as the Luftwaffe chafed at poor flying conditions that held them off from the onslaught that was to complete the destruction of Narvik, obliterate the base and the ships at Harstad and eliminate Bardufoss. This onslaught started in earnest on 2nd June with waves of Junkers 88s, Heinkel III's and Stukas coming over in steady succession for the whole of the day. Each wave was escorted by the Me 110 long-range fighters, and the clear intention was to saturate the defences and put the R.A.F. squadrons out of business. But the R.A.F. fought a desperate battle this day. Flying no fewer than seventy-five sorties, they brought down at least nine enemy aircraft and continuously so broke up their formations that they either failed to reach the target area or dropped their bombs inaccurately. The following day and for all the succeeding days until the last one of the evacuation, the weather—which had so often been the only protection from the Luftwaffe—came to the aid of the hard-pressed Gladiator and Hurricane pilots, and mist and low cloud lay practically continuously over the base and the anchorages. This prevented observation as well as attack: without it, even the fighters might have had difficulty in staving off the discovery of the evacuation, more obvious as it proceeded.

The Germans remained in ignorance even as Operation Juno was finally put into effect on 4th June—the day of the virtual clearance of the beaches of Dunkirk—when the repaired *Gneisenau, Scharnhorst, Hipper* (still minus a great deal of her armour belt) and four destroyers were sailed from Kiel under Admiral Marschall. This operation, it will be remembered, was designed to take advantage of the weakened state of the British naval forces in the north—particularly their lack of any heavy units. And such was now the state of things that the German ships were certainly able to out-gun all the ships under Admiral Cork's command: they could not, however, out-gun Admiral Forbes's Home Fleet, which was still at large in the North Sea and which (although it had itself been weakened) included the old battleship *Valiant*, the battle cruisers *Renown* and *Repulse* and several cruisers. Admiral Marschall's orders were therefore very precise and he was expected to adhere to them. In the first place he was to attack warships, transports and bases in the Harstad area and in the Ofotfiord and do as much damage as he could—obviously the operation was envisaged as concurrent with the great air attack waiting for resumption as soon as the weather cleared. He had a secondary task—to carry supplies from Trondheim through the Leads to Bodö for the German forces there—but he must on no account disclose his presence by entering Trondheim before his first and much more important task was completed. In other words he was to disappear from Kiel and do his best to reappear on the doorstep of the British base and anchorages like an unwelcome bolt from the blue—which he certainly would have been. The only flaw in the plan was one which neither he nor the German High Command could possibly be aware of—namely, that by the time he reached the Ofotfiord the Allies would no longer be there, for the first phase of the evacuation was timed to take place on the very night before he sailed from Kiel, to continue for the following five nights and be completed in the night of 7th/8th. And for that matter the only flaw in the evacuation plans, which had been worked out with the meticulous detail typical of naval operations, was that the British, for their part, were unaware that the German heavy units were at sea and that by pure coincidence the whole of the evacuation ships—including the cruiser *Devonshire*, which was to carry King Haakon and his people away from Tromsö, were in the most terrible danger.

According to all the official accounts the German ships were undetected throughout the whole of their passage. This is not so. They were spotted by the Norwegian coast watch and were reported to Wing Commander Atcherley's scratch operations room in the same way that the German air movements were reported. The telephone girls described them as two German battleships. The report caused two reactions. In the first place it was thought very funny and in the second place it was assumed (pardonably but, one sees now, unjustifiably) that the Navy, who knew everything, knew all about these ships. Atcherley distinctly remembers that the last words said to him before he himself embarked after the fighters had been finally flown away were, 'Look out for the bloody battleships!'—and this, in fact, became a catch-phrase that was current for quite a time afterwards. In the event, of course, it was tragically unfunny but neither Atcherley nor others about him can justly be blamed for not realizing that they were the only people in possession of this piece of information, which was irrelevant to the particular job in which they were so completely engrossed.

With powerful and unknown German units at sea, an element of curious and quite coincidental similarity begins to appear between the last naval operations in the Norwegian campaign and those which had marked its beginning on 8th April. The similarity was about to become closer and the coincidence more curious. The Earl of Cork had appealed to the C.-in-C. Home Fleet to do what he could for the safety of the almost unprotected convoys that were about to leave, and Admiral Forbes had every intention of covering them. But on the morning of the 5th June— that is to say after the second night of the evacuation—the British Q ship *Prunella*, patrolling away to the north, reported two large and unidentifiable warships, hull down on the horizon and apparently steering in the direction of Iceland. This, if true, might mean one of three things: an attack on Iceland, to which British troops had been sent nearly a month before, a descent upon Ireland, which at that time was very much feared—or the main eventuality for which Forbes was ever on the watch as he had been on 8th April—a breakout by German raiders into the convoy routes of the North Atlantic. And his reaction to *Prunella*'s report was exactly the same as his reaction to the report of German ships at sea and steaming north on the previous occasion—without hesitation he sailed *Repulse* and *Renown* at high speed for Iceland with two cruisers and five destroyers, leaving only the battleship *Valiant* at sea and *Rodney* and a mere handful of destroyers in Scapa Flow. Thus the troop convoys were left naked to the world. What ships *Prunella* saw has never been established. They cannot have been German and they were certainly not Operation Juno.

The evacuation had proceeded in a most orderly manner that was different indeed from the hasty embarkations which had marked the end of the campaign in central Norway. The troopships assembled well off the coast—seventy miles according to General Auchinleck, one hundred and eighty miles in fact. The destroyers, as always, were the ships of all work for the parties as they moved—embarking them direct at Harstad itself and at other points from puffers which ferried them from the shore. Alternative embarkation points were earmarked in case the original ones were bombed or otherwise interfered with, and there was even a reserve of puffers to cope with accidents. The puffers worked in small fleets, each with an army officer in charge and two British soldiers as guards: once more, it is a pity that such essential organization of water transport, the lack of which had been such a handicap throughout almost the whole of the history of the island base, was only achieved at the stage of departure. Priorities were carefully organized—the last to go would be the men manning the ack-ack defences and the fighter pilots.

The weather conditions and the fighters and anti-aircraft guns between them kept air interference at a distance: mercifully, it was only on the last day of the evacuation that the weather cleared and the Luftwaffe once more descended on the scene in force, so that the fighters were continually in action for the whole of the last twenty-four hours of their stay. Had the weather not helped them, it is very doubtful whether, with all the guts in the world, they could have withstood continuous pressure for so long. As it was, the whole of the operation was completely unobserved by the Germans from start to finish and not one of the emergency provisions that had been made was put to use. On the first three nights fifteen thousand men were put aboard *Monarch of Bermuda*, *Batory*, *Sobieski*, *Franconia*, *Lancastria* and *Georgic*. These sailed from the rendezvous at sea on the night of the 6th/7th escorted by *Vindictive* alone. On the night of the 7th/8th the ten thousand that remained embarked in *Oronsay*, *Ormonde*, *Arandora Star*, *Royal Ulsterman*, *Ulster Prince*, *Ulster Monarch* and *Duchess of York*. On the same night a slow convoy of eight storeships left Harstad, escorted by *Stork*, *Arrow* and ten trawlers. The following night the second groups of troopships left—with them the cruisers *Southampton*, flying the Earl of Cork's flag for the last time, and *Coventry* with the destroyers *Havelock*, *Fame*, *Firedrake*, *Beagle*, and *Delight*. They were joined at sea by *Ark Royal* and three destroyers. There were thus three main groups of ships at sea, two of them carrying an enormous body of troops and only one of them with anything even approaching the scale of a proper naval escort. All were in ignorance of the approach of 'the bloody battleships'. There was a further small group on the way from Tromsö on the 6th, by far the most important of which was the cruiser *Devonshire* carrying King Haakon, his government and his precious gold, together with the British ambassador and his staff and the advance parties of troops who had been preparing the base at Tromsö. There were a few isolated small groups which included a few tankers, the two empty troopships and the hospital ship *Atlantis*. Nothing was left behind that could float or be of any use. Disabled trawlers were sunk and after attempts to tow them away the five remaining landing craft, which had given so much trouble but served so well, were also scuttled. The few anti-aircraft guns which remained to the last were left for General Ruge for what brief use he could make of them. On the French front at least remained great dumps of food which Theodore Broch saw the Lapps looting.

The last naval vessel to be in action in the base area was a highly irregular one—H.M.S. *Raven*, formerly the Norwegian coastal vessel *Ranen*, in charge of Commander Sir Geoffrey Congreve and manned by a somewhat piratical crew of naval ratings and soldiers. Armed with an Oerlikon, a Bofors and some machine-guns, she was officially described as a decoy ship: since the evacuation from Bodö she had been engaged in some peculiar operations which included the harassing of German forces crossing from Rösvik on their way north, cutting telephone cables and sundry similar exploits. She was allotted the task of destroying the oil tanks at Svolvaer, and having done so, encountered a small, enemy vessel somewhat of her own kind, whose appearance and disappearance is something of a mystery. What Lord Cork calls a 'spirited engagement' proved inconclusive: Congreve thereupon set out for Scapa, and arrived there safely.

The last Army personnel to embark are officially said to have been detachments of the Military Police and Royal Engineers in charge of the piers. There are two other possible claimants— a pair of Scots Guardsmen who presented themselves to Wing-Commander Atcherley as he himself was about to board *Southampton*. They were complete with rifles and personal equipment and declared that they had reached Bodö an hour too late to be taken off in the last vessel out of there. Somehow or other they had made their way to Harstad: they demanded that their arrival be signalled to their unit as soon as possible, otherwise they were afraid they might be posted as deserters.

The last personnel of all were Atcherley and the R.A.F. ground staff from Bardufoss, who had done a magnificent job and long since wiped out the memory of their unfortunate fellows at Lesjaskog. Their final and melancholy task had been to detonate the charges which blew more than a hundred holes in the precious runway that had been constructed with such meticulous care and such colossal labour and had stood up so well under the continuous take-offs and landings, in spite of the thaw and everything else. Just before this the remaining Gladiators and Hurricanes had taken off for the last time, and this is a story all of its own.

Since 2nd June *Ark Royal* and *Glorious* had been off the coast: their fighters had given welcome help to the hard-pressed pilots of the R.A.F. and their torpedo bombers had attacked German troops and communications. They were now to carry the R.A.F. machines away, and the few days' lull that the weather had caused in the middle of the evacuation gave a welcome chance of organizing this operation. Given reasonable skill and care and reasonable weather, it presented relatively few difficulties for the Gladiators with their slower landing speed, though they had no arrester hooks; but the Hurricanes were quite a different matter. They had been hoisted aboard from barges on the outward voyage and had never carried out a deck landing before. The experts, in fact, considered such a feat quite impossible, and the first orders had been that they were to be destroyed on the ground. Later there had been a suggestion that they should be flown north to Tromsö, dismantled and put aboard a freighter which 'might be there'—a lengthy and unsatisfactory operation. Cross and his pilots were all too well aware of the shortage of these precious machines at home. They were also aware of the invasion threat that hung over Britain and the fact that massed air attacks would precede and accompany it; and they were determined to save the machines that remained serviceable. They therefore begged for the chance to fly them on, and Wing Commander Moore granted it. And though the machines and all but two of the pilots were, after all, later lost in the sinking of *Glorious*, their achievement remained, for it established the fact that fast, efficient fighters of this type could be carrier-borne. The lesson was not overlooked.

Cross himself went out in a Walrus amphibian to experiment and prepare. *Ark Royal*, as before, would have been the obvious choice because of her longer flight deck, but there was still the insoluble difficulty that the Hurricanes could not be got below without breaking their wings, because of the narrow lifts. He therefore determined to try *Glorious*. A twenty-pound sandbag in the tail of each machine might help the brakes to do their work better, and they could pray for a good head-wind: if the deck proved too short, the pilots would open up, take off again and land on *Ark*, where their wings would be cut with oxy-acetylene torches so they could be got on the lifts.

The morning of the 8th, the last in Norway, brought clear weather and with it the Luftwaffe in strength—still not wise to the evacuation but intent on destroying the airfield and the base which was no longer there. Shortly after four o'clock they came straight in on Bardufoss with the obvious intention of repeating the tactics that had finally put paid to the little Gladiator base at

Bodö. The R.A.F. were not asleep. Cross remembers seeing the Germans diving for the airfield as he took off, thinks he got a Heinkel but never claimed it. In the next moment he was enveloped by a stinging hail of bullets from a Heinkel's rear gunner and immediately there was oil all over the place, with the pressure gauge dropping to zero and the engine temperature soaring. He got down before his engine finally seized up, and took off in another machine. For the whole of that day he and the pilots of both squadrons fought a continuous battle. It was nearly midnight—best part of twenty solid hours—before the attacks petered out and the exhausted pilots could well have looked forward to refreshment and rest. There could be neither; now they must collect their tired wits and hold on to their concentration for the most exacting task of all—the landing on *Glorious*. They refuelled, took off: they had had so many hours of tension that perhaps tension could become no greater. Ahead of them as guide went a naval Swordfish—'string bag' indeed, bumbling along at a steady eighty knots, so that the Hurricanes had to keep their airscrews in fine pitch for the whole of the long slog out to the carrier. They found her, steaming once more at full speed into the good head-wind which everyone had prayed for. Triumphantly, Hurricane after Hurricane—the whole surviving ten—came down, landed, streaked along the deck with squealing brakes, and stopped. There were minor mishaps of no consequence which might have happened anywhere—Cross himself, for instance, bounced his tail and broke the pinion of his tail wheel—but against all chances and all predictions, here were the Hurricanes safe on the deck, ten priceless machines saved for the Battle of Britain and an achievement that made the dead-beat pilots forget their weariness. The naval pilots and airmen were jubilant and d'Oyley-Hughes himself, forgetting all his lectures about impudent young men, greeted them with as much enthusiasm as anyone else. Alas, through error of judgement, through a chance wrongly assessed and wrongly taken—call it what you will—he was about to destroy them, together with his ship and himself.

Out of all the speculation about events on *Glorious* (and speculation most of it must remain for ever, because there were so few survivors from the ship) some few things are definite and certain. *Glorious* was due to rendezvous and proceed with the second convoy group—*Southampton,* the troopships and the rest. D'Oyley-Hughes, however, reported that he was short of fuel and received permission to make for home waters on his own, escorted by his two destroyers, *Acasta,* commanded by Commander C. E. Glasfurd, and *Ardent.* He thus created an additional small and highly vulnerable group, although presumably aircraft reconnaisance would give him protection. Now the fact is that d'Oyley-Hughes was an intrepid and headstrong character—why shirk the fact that brave men, now dead, may have had their vices as well as their virtues?—and he was well known in the service for swanning off on his own whenever he got the chance: so much so in fact that his ship had earned the nickname of Carter Paterson. It is difficult to see what relation his reported shortage of fuel can have had to his being allowed to proceed alone. Churchill, in observing that if he had fuel to steam at a speed which put him two hundred miles ahead of the main convoy (this being what he did) he had enough fuel to proceed at convoy speed, misses the point. What presumably d'Oyley-Hughes lacked fuel for was the high-speed steaming required for aircraft take-offs and landings; and this much is established—that *Glorious* was not flying the normal anti-submarine patrols which routine demanded should be in the air, although she is said to have had aircraft at readiness. The only other explanation for her not flying patrols would be slackness of some kind or false security induced by the fact that there had been so little submarine action against British naval units in this campaign—both of which would be unthinkable in the case of so experienced and so strict an officer. Captain Roskill, the naval historian, and Dr. Derry, the official historian of the Norwegian campaign, both take it for granted that the presence of the Gladiators and Hurricanes aboard interrupted the carrier's flying routine or congested her so much that her own fighters were in some way not available. This cannot have been so, for during her outward voyage with the Hurricanes aboard normal patrols had been flown, normal routine had been carried out and the R.A.F. personnel were quite confident that no embarrassment was caused by them. On this home voyage she was carrying eight Gladiators and ten Hurricanes—the whole of the surviving serviceable machines of 263 and 46 Squadrons—and this by an odd coincidence was precisely equal to the number of Hurricanes in the squadron she had carried out: the only difference being that the Gladiators took up less room below because of their shorter wings. Certainly the R.A.F. themselves were not anything like large enough in number to disorganize the establishment of so big a ship and in any case they were out for the count. But if— through lack of fuel for high-speed steaming or any other reason— she could not fly her normal protective patrols, would she not have been better with the convoy? The mystery must remain.

It was only after landing their machines that the tension broke and the pilots realized how tired they were after as near twenty-four hours in the air as makes no difference, the greater part of it in the intense concentration of combat. They went below to drink hot cocoa and slept. Cross had fixed a conference for 46 Squadron for nine a.m., but both he and his pilots slept long beyond that time, and though he himself managed to get up for lunch, most of the others were still sleeping the deep sleep of the exhausted.

Admiral Marschall with his two battle cruisers, heavy cruiser and destroyers was still as unaware as the rest of the Germans that the Allies had evacuated Norway and that the whole of the evacuation convoys were in the path of his ships, either defence-less or defended by units which he could out-gun. He had timed his attack on Harstad for 9th June. At midday on the 6th he was well out to sea something north of the latitude of Trond-heim and although 'the bloody battleships' had been reported neither the validity nor the significance of the report had been recognized. The course he was steaming now lay dead across the course of each of the convoys' routes in turn and of the smaller groups proceeding independently. The first group—the fifteen thousand men in troopships escorted only by *Valiant*—passed well ahead of him without any inkling of their peril: at one o'clock on the morning of the 8th they were met by destroyers and escorted safely home. The second group and the slow storeship convoy actually passed astern of him, for before they left their rendezvous and starting-point he had crossed their bows and was roughly in the latitude of Narvik, although still farther out to sea than he had been before. At 4 p.m. on the 8th, however, he was within eighty miles of what was, perhaps, politically the richest prize of all, the cruiser *Devonshire*, carrying King Haakon and the

Free Norwegian Government. *Devonshire*, none the less, and the ships with her were also destined by this narrow margin to go unnoticed and escape.

Only a few hours previously the second convoy had been spotted by a German reconnaissance plane: the Germans still did not grasp the significance or purpose and assumed for the moment that these were merely ships returning empty from an outward voyage to Harstad. Presently, however, the aircraft spotted other groups of ships. This information—by the sort of process people got into the habit of regarding as peculiar to our own intelligence at that stage of the war although, in fact, the Germans also were liable to these lapses of still imperfect machinery—did not reach Admiral Marschall until quite late that evening. Marschall decided that the reports indicated 'a noticeable westward movement' and he hazarded a guess that the westward movement might be the evacuation of Norway, although there had so far been not the slightest evidence that such an evacuation was likely to take place. He was in a dilemma because his orders, as we have already seen, were very firm and did not allow the latitude essential in naval operations to the commander on the spot. He therefore informed his headquarters that he proposed to turn westward and attack the convoys instead of attacking Harstad—and promptly had his proposal countermanded: the naval Chief of Staff intervened to let him have his way, but it was in the end to cost him his command. It is worth relating this bit of history in detail because it was too readily assumed at the time and has been too often assumed since that the German Command was not prone to these kind of errors.

Almost immediately afterwards, as though to confirm the German Admiral's proposal and intention, he came upon one of the little scattered groups which were sailing independently of the main convoys. In quick succession he sank the tanker *Oil Pioneer* and the trawler *Juniper* before they could so much as give the briefest of alarms by radio. His next victim was the empty troopship *Orama*, who did get off an S O S, but this was jammed so promptly by the Germans that it was never received: she likewise was sent to the bottom. The hospital ship *Atlantis*, which was with the group, obeyed the international convention and made no signal, and Marschall allowed her to go on her way. It was now near midday on the 8th and his course, unknown to him, was converging with both *Devonshire* and *Glorious*. It had now, however, taken him south of the latitude of Narvik and he doubted, correctly, if there was any further prey to be had by continuing in this direction, so, since the endurance of *Hipper* and the destroyers was less than that of the battle cruisers, he sent them off to Trondheim to refuel (although he had been forbidden to touch that point before his first mission was completed) and himself turned north at speed with *Scharnhorst* and *Gneisenau*, to seek what he could find. Before long he was in a position where, if *Glorious* had been flying her anti-submarine patrol, the scouting aircraft would undoubtedly have spotted the superior enemy in time, the more especially as the two great ships, hurrying in search of their prey, were making smoke when they were first spotted.

Caught out and for all practical purposes defenceless with her 4·7-inch guns hopelessly outranged by the eleven-inch guns of the battle cruisers, *Glorious* turned away and increased speed, but full speed was not for the moment available: the two destroyers laid a smoke screen. She flashed a sighting report on her radio, but it was not received: a second message, making reference to the earlier one, was received in garbled form by *Devonshire*—which could not relay it because, with her precious cargo aboard, the presence of the German ships made radio silence even more imperative than before. At half-past four *Scharnhorst*—'making undisturbed target practice' in Captain MacIntyre's words—opened fire at twenty-eight thousand yards and found the range at her second salvo: a direct hit from one of her tremendous shells devastated the forward upper hangar, and immediately everything in it, including the precious Hurricanes which had been so triumphantly saved, was furiously ablaze. The fire spread rapidly and destroyed in minutes any hope there might have been of getting torpedo-carrying Swordfish into the air.

Squadron Leader Cross, having had his sleep out, was on deck when the first sighting was made—had seen the smudge of smoke on the horizon. Now he was to have further evidence that for the time being, at any rate, his name was, in service language, 'not on it'. He went to his station, irrelevantly bothered by the fact that he was carrying £180, the squadron's mess funds. A shell from the second salvo landed fair and square in the deck not far from him: it made a great hole, but did not explode. Instinct, however, decided him to keep moving, so he walked forward, around the front of the bridge and back down the other side of the ship. He had barely reached the quarter-deck when another shell ripped into the bridge, killing the captain and putting the carrier out of control. It was only half an hour since the first shots had been fired, and now she was a sitting target. Before very long more accurate gunfire had holed her aft and she clearly had not long to live: at 5.20 the order to abandon ship was given. Cross went over the side with the others, and was able to get on to a Carley float.

She was still, however, afloat a few minutes later, when the little *Ardent* came steaming furiously out of the smoke screen at top speed in a desperate effort to launch the only weapons with which she could equal the enemy in striking power—her torpedoes. She got two four-tube salvoes off, accurately enough for the battle cruisers to have to change course to comb them; but before she could reload she was literally blasted to pieces by the accurate salvo which answered her attack. Shortly afterwards, at 5.40, the mangled aircraft carrier herself disappeared beneath the waters. Now only *Acasta* was left to dispute the passage of the seas: beyond *Acasta* the convoys, *Devonshire*, and not a single ship to protect them with more than six-inch guns. Her hour had come: to Glasfurd, her commander, and his men had come the same call as had come to Broadmead-Roope and the crew of *Glowworm*, Warburton-Lee and the men of *Hardy* and to destroyer men time and time again in the bloody seas of two world wars.

The call was answered. Momentarily she turned away into the smoke to prepare herself, as *Glowworm* had turned away before her onslaught on *Hipper*. In those brief minutes Glasfurd made his dispositions, told his men what required to be done. Then out she came again with her turbines driving her as fast as she would go, guns ablazing, torpedo tubes trained. The range was now only thirteen thousand yards: with a great cheer her doomed men saw a brilliant yellow flash from *Scharnhorst*, a huge eruption of water and smoke. The torpedo killed two officers and forty-six men, put the battle cruiser's after turret out of action and sent water pouring into her hull, so that before long her centre and starboard main engines had to be stopped. Then vengeance descended

The damaged railway at Narvik.

Narvik pier and buildings shelled by the Royal Navy.

The lucky ones—troops from Norway land at Greenock.

upon the destroyer: almost immediately she was overwhelmed by a tornado of shell that turned her into a sinking wreck. At eight minutes past six a final salvo sent her to the bottom: of her entire complement one man only, Able Seaman Carter, survived to pass on the account of those last minutes of triumph and sacrifice.

For in those minutes the convoys were saved. The crippled *Scharnhorst* turned away for Trondheim, *Gneisenau* with her. In that port the following day, the 9th, Marschall got news of the British evacuation and was ordered to sea again with *Gneisenau* and *Hipper*, but the chance was gone. The main convoys were already beyond his reach. Moreover *Atlantis*, meeting *Valiant*, which had delivered the first convoy and was now steaming back to the support of the second, gave the news of the German raiders, which was shortly afterwards confirmed by *Devonshire*; and Admiral Forbes went into the hunt with every available ship, including those which had now returned from their phantom-chase to the north. *Ark Royal* attacked the damaged *Scharnhorst* in harbour and scored one hit—but the bomb did not explode and eight Skuas were lost in the attack. Presently *Scharnhorst* was able to limp home, but later in the month the submarine *Clyde* found *Hipper* and *Gnesisenau* and scored a hit that put the latter, too, out of action for six months. Admiral Marschall—unjustly, most people now think, for he had used his initiative and acted to meet a situation not envisaged in his orders—was removed from his command and replaced by Admiral Lutjens. It was a personal disaster with compensations, for it was Lutjens who, the following year, took the brand-new *Bismarck* to sea and met his end in a hunt that ranged from the Arctic mists, down the North Atlantic and almost to the coast of France.

But Britain had lost another of her only four aircraft carriers afloat, all the Hurricanes that had been saved from Norway and all the fighter pilots save two, of whom one was Squadron Leader Cross. The loss of life from the carrier and the destroyers was very heavy, for the fleeing battle cruisers picked up no survivors. After three days in the water, thirty-five survivors from *Glorious* and Able Seaman Carter from *Acasta* were picked up by the little Norwegian vessel *Borgund*, which was on her way from Tromsö and landed them in the Faeröes; five survivors of *Glorious* were picked up by another small steamer and two of *Ardent*'s crew by a

German seaplane—both these little groups were taken to Norway and captivity. All the remainder, more than one thousand five hundred in all, perished.

So for Britain the Norwegian campaign ended as it had begun —at sea, with heroic destroyer action against impossible odds. The tale of vacillations, shortcomings and improvisations was over—so was the tale of high endeavour and personal courage which redeems the follies of the leaderhip that could not match these qualities. Norway was now an alien coast, a part of Occupied Europe; and even the precious iron ore was lost.

But it is to the Norwegians that the last word must go. After all, it was—or had been—their country in which the campaign was waged, and they were left to wind it up as conveniently as they might when their allies had left them still fighting and, on the Arctic front, within sight of victory.

First of all Narvik—liberated, as we know, only to be given up. It had become increasingly a ghost town. In the few days after the Germans left the evacuation plans went so swiftly that only men and unmarried or childless women were left. It was as well, for on 2nd June, the same day that the intensive air attack on the Allied base started, the air raids on the town were stepped up to a pitch which showed that the Germans were determined to destroy it, as they had destroyed Bodö. In a two-hour continuous attack, they showered down incendiaries as well as high explosive, so that the entire lower part of the town—the business quarter—was consumed in so fierce a conflagration that even brick buildings burned, and only dynamiting saved the upper part from going as well. The planes, having loosed their bombs, machine-gunned the fire-fighters and anyone about in the streets. There was no panic, but the people were tiring. Young men were leaving to join Fleischer's forces, and more of those who could be spared were got out.

The days of low cloud and mist which followed gave a little respite, but were filled with foreboding: though the news from the mountains was still good, the flight of the Allied troops from Bodö brought the menace from the south still nearer, while the radio bulletins of events in Belgium and France gave a clear picture of the Nazis in triumph over the whole of Western Europe. Then other strange rumours began to seep in—that the

Allied troops were withdrawing from the mountains, that stores and men were being re-embarked at Harstad. It seemed incredible with victory beyond the fiord so near, and a valiant effort was made to put the rumours aside; but Allied staff officers began to arrive on strange missions and ask strange questions, and things began to add up in a way that could no longer be shrugged aside. At last, on 6th June, the Norwegian liaison officer with the Foreign Legion came in and quietly gave the mayor the news: shortly afterwards the naval lieutenant in charge of the evacuation boats—a young man to whom the Norwegians had taken a great liking—broke the news that he had called his little fleet back, and that the next day would be the last.

It was true. Next day the Foreign Legionnaires, who had remained camped outside the town because of the air raids, marched in and embarked from the quay. There was nothing for the Norwegians to do but leave the town and follow suit. Taking what they could—food, the city records and some few things more—the citizens sadly embarked in the puffers that were making their last trip, leaving only the wounded in the hospital, such staff as were needed to cope with them and all the hopes and aspirations that had made the young and thriving port a happy and rewarding place in which to live. They arrived at Harstad as the last of the ships were weighing anchor and there, their fishing-boats bobbing in the wash, they watched their allies go. Then they went ashore, to wander forlornly for a little around the remains of the base and presently to debate the problem of organizing their lives anew. Under what conditions they would live they could only guess, but already there had been grim hints. The Poles had warned them: so far, they said, the Germans had behaved like angels—but if they ever came back. . . . Back they were coming, and many of those around Mayor Broch were already marked men for the way they had faced up to the 'protectors' in the uneasy weeks of the first occupation. Their names, their faces were known: their deeds were already catalogued and awaiting retribution.

Yet even harder than it had been for these was the way the end came to the men in the mountains—the men whose exhaustion had forced them to pause after the third week in June to gather strength for the final push that was to crown all their efforts and justify all their sufferings. They alone had been in the field from the very first day of the invasion until now. Unaided at all times except for some sporadic attachments of snowbound Guards and some help from the Chasseurs on their seaward flank in the latter stages of the long weeks, they had fought what almost seemed a private war, out of touch not merely with their allies, but with the rest of the battle in Norway. As to events on the Western Front, these might have been on the other side of the world for all they knew of them. What followed, therefore, came to them completely out of the blue.

It will be remembered that the Norwegian government had begged just a few days' more delay to enable these men, at least, to fulfil their task and their hopes; but the Allies could wait no longer. On 7th June everything was ready for the preliminary attack; the men were keyed up and their hopes ran high. But with the morning of the 8th came not the awaited order to go into action and drive the Germans out of Norway and over the Swedish border, but an order to retire to the north instead. Puzzled and resentful, they obeyed. The afternoon brought them a further message. It told them, briefly, that the Allies had withdrawn, and that the troops remaining under arms in northern Norway were to demobilize.

'When the orders became known,' wrote Colonel Munthe-Kaas afterwards, 'it was as though the units had been paralysed. Profound grief and anger filled men's minds. Some wept. . . . All the fighting and all the tough endurance, all the victorious combats had been of no avail. They were standing before the very fulfilment of the goal: to see the long German retreat end in Swedish internment. The border was within easy sight, only a few kilometres away. Beyond the border were Swedish units ready to take the Germans in hand. Indicative of the situation was the fact that the Swedes were then engaged in marking the border with flags. . . .

'. . . Freedom seemed lost, even the right to fight and die for freedom.'

Presently a German major appeared to parley—demanding, under threat of dive-bombing, that they should lay down their weapons and come into Björnfjell as prisoners. It was a bluff, and the Norwegians suspected it: after much argument it was agreed that both sides should remain in their positions and await further orders. So there was an uneasy pause, which dragged out to an inordinate length—until first fear and then certainty dawned on the Norwegians that the Germans were creeping round them. They could make no contact with Tromsö on the telephone. Then mist and snow—once enemies, now friends—came down on the mountains where it is for ever winter, and under the cloak of these they quietly climbed over the plateau and withdrew. The Germans, they found, had indeed used the interval to establish themselves strongly on the watershed; but by then orders had come through that they were to be allowed to pass through unmolested.

Only then did they learn that their government had left the country on 7th June. On the 11th they were demobilized and sent home.

From a point near the Swedish border some few days later, Theodor Broch looked his last on the mountains of the land he loved. Not many years since, a young lawyer, he had come from the south with his wife to make a home and a future in the sturdy and thriving northcountry. He had found it a beautiful country and a good life: the tough, independent folk had taken to him, he had prospered, become their youthful mayor. Now it was over. If any man was marked by the Germans, it was he: like so many others he must leave everyone and everything dear to him and go forth alone to continue the fight from alien lands against the unforeseeable time when his country could again be free.

'Before going on,' he wrote, 'I looked for a long time on what I could yet see of Norway. The ocean was no longer visible. Mountains stretched out on all sides with snow and green moss scattered between. Mountain streams shone like silver ribbons. The lakes were open, but ice bordered their shores. The wild heather had already coloured its small, dark flowers, and but for them the dominating tone was grey.

'It was a harsh land we had had, but never had it been so delightful, so desirable as now. Our leading men had already been driven abroad. Our ships had been sunk or sailed away. All along the border were young men like myself. Thousands more would follow. We had to leave to learn the one craft we had neglected.

'We had built good homes in the mountains, but we had neglected to fence them properly. Now strangers had taken over our land. They would loot it and pluck it clean before we returned. But the country itself they could not spoil. The sea and the fiords and the mountains—to these we alone could give life. We were coming back. The mountains would wait for us.'

It is a matter of history that they did.

EPILOGUE

O N the platform of a windswept and grimy wayside station in the bleak moors of industrial Lancashire stands a grey-haired parson. He wears a clerical hat and an old raincoat, into the pocket of which his hands are thrust deeply in a characteristic attitude. There is a small, bitter wind with a dampness to it—the dampness that brought the cotton mills to these parts: the landscape is a vista of colliery workings, ancient factory buildings and all the litter of the first Industrial Revolution. The railway climbs so steeply that the track plunges out of sight over the top of the gradient beyond the station; and up it a couple of great loco-motives labour tender-first with hoarse, slow blasts, dragging an immense rake of loaded coal-wagons behind them. Lieutenant-Colonel the Reverend E. J. King-Salter, sometime professional soldier, British Military Attaché in Norway and now Vicar of Atherton, watches them keenly: they and the people concerned with them are part of his world, the great industrial parish to which he is now as wholly devoted as, long ago and far away, he was devoted to the business of soldiering.

The smart new diesel car from Manchester runs easily up the gradient with a blast of trumpets, after the manner of its kind, and stops in the station. It seems out of place in these sur-roundings of an earlier railway age—as also, perhaps, does your author, who steps on to the platform, straight from London and feeling a little self-conscious in bowler hat and town overcoat.

In the station yard stands the vast and rusty hulk of an Arm-strong-Siddeley sports saloon, vintage 1935 and indeed a relic of the padré's former days as a smart young staff officer. A pierc-ing draught blows under the doors as we lumber away; and presently we are negotiating the pedestrian crossings of the town's main street, while King-Salter manipulates with his left hand, steering-wheel, preselector gearbox and hand throttle (a necessity with his artificial foot) while with his right he raises his hat to members of his congregation.

Some people would call the vicarage shabby—others might find it cold. For my part, I would call it much used rather than shabby, and I find it warm with a happy family life and the web of human relationships of which this place is the active and enthusiastic centre. Children's toys on the passage floor, an extra length of string on the lavatory pull for little tots—all these things speak. Piled everywhere in the old-fashioned study is the paraphernalia of the parish's Christian Stewardship campaign, which has just finished; upon it and upon us, as we make ourselves comfortable, photographs of an impeccably-uniformed young military gentleman look down in barely credible contrast from mantelpiece and walls.

So we live again for a little in the Gudbrandsdal, Ruge's headquarters and the gorge at Tretten where King-Salter's mission and his military career came to an end. Documents and photographs come out, to be pored over—facts, policies and personalities are discussed. The parson slips back easily into the vocabulary and precise definition of the staff college. Detail is razor-sharp in his memory: circumstances, actions and consequences are crystal clear. It is obvious that his convictions on matters of military necessity and the requisites for military action are as strong as ever they were, that he has no regrets about actions he took or decisions he helped to form.

Over family lunch before a blazing fire in the wide, light dining-room of the rambling house, talk covers the days since the flight over the mountains after Tretten and comes back to the present. We hear of his days in hospital and as a prisoner, his exchange in 1942, the desk job at the War Office he could have kept, his entry into the Church which had always been his other interest, his parish and his busy life. For this strong, clear-minded man it has been an easy transition into this other world, so different from the world of his younger life that the contrast still nags at the imagination. To King-Salter there is no contrast. He was happy in his old life—he is happy in his present one. In both he has been effective, fulfilled and knows the taste of achievement. The qualities that make him a parish priest are the same qualities that made him a staff officer, won him the confidence of Ruge and his Norwegians and the British staffs, and led him to play for a brief space, though but a half-colonel, a major part in a war.

Then the talk moves away altogether—to children and their schooling, the maintenance of elderly motor-cars, the problems of bells in a church tower undermined by colliery workings, the reinstatement of land after opencast mining and a dozen other things. Whole people do not spend their lives looking backwards, and Norway is a long time ago.

A long time ago, indeed. The Norwegians live at peace again in the country which they regained without a blow—fit reward for their courage in defence and steadfastness in resistance: out of all the occupied countries, theirs was the only one in which the German C.-in-C., in full uniform and medals, made his surrender to a civilian. The rest of the world, too, is at peace—albeit an uneasy peace, under a greater shadow even than the shadow of Nazi Germany. It is a changed world, for the chain-reactions of the upheaval that started in the seas around southern Norway on an April day in 1940 and put an end to the Phoney War have spread to its farthest corners and are still going on, so that no man yet can tell the shape of things to come. Britain in particular is no longer a great power to whom small nations turn for succour in distress; for though she, too, had her awakening in the days after Dunkirk—when Churchill, with a whole nation behind him, thundered defiance across the Channel at the victorious powers of darkness—and so briefly became again the centre of the world, old men and nerveless leadership had led her into folly for the last time: in the years of struggle that followed her resources were squandered and her place among the nations lost.

There can never be another campaign like the Norwegian campaign of 1940. In this different world, war is a different matter: it cannot be waged by trial and error, nor is there time for courage to make good grievous mistakes. Figures like Carton de Wiart and the Earl of Cork are become figures of legend, and a whole regiment of Hibberts is of no avail against a single nuclear bomb.

Norway was not only the end of the Phoney War. It was the beginning of the end of wars as men since the Stone Age have known them.

TABLE OF EVENTS

1940	Ruperforce Narvik-Harstad	Scissorsforce Mosjöen-Bodö	Maurieforce North of Trondheim	Sickleforce South of Trondheim	1940
April 9	Germans at Oslo, Kristiansand, Egersund, Trondheim, Narvik, Bergen; Norwegian army mobilized				April 9
10	Norwegian government at Hamar				10
13	British destroyers attack, Narvik *Warspite* attacks, Narvik				13
14			Naval party at Namsos		14
15	24 Bde. lands at Harstad; Allied build-up begins				15
16			146 Bde. lands at Namsos		16
17				Naval party at Aandalsnes	17
18			146 Bde. deployed: East to Grong South to Verdal Namsos heavily bombed	148 Bde. lands at Aandalsnes	18
20					20
21				148 Bde. in line near Lillehammer	21
22			Vist area lost	Germans take Balbergkamp	22
23			Steinkjer abandoned	Germans take Tretten; 15 Bde. lands, move to Gudbrandsdal	23

Date	Order to evacuate from Aandalsnes	Order to evacuate from Namsos				Date
28	Order to evacuate from Aandalsnes	Order to evacuate from Namsos				28
30			Scots Guards Company at Bodö		Norwegian government leaves Molde for Tromsö	30
May 2	Evacuation completed					May 2
3		Evacuation completed				3
4			1 Ind. Coy. at Mo			4
8			4,5 Ind. Coys. at Mosjöen			8
9			3 Ind. Coy. at Bodö	Allied build-up completed		9
10			Germans take Hemnesberget; Scots Guards (3 Coys.) Mo			10
13			2 Ind. Coy. at Bodö. Action at Stien; Mo evacuated	Bjerkvik captured		13
17			Germans take Krokstrand			17
21				Evacuation order received		21
25				Bardufoss airfield ready		25
26			Germans take Pothus; Evacuation order received			26
28				Narvik captured		28
31			Evacuation completed			31
June 8				Evacuation completed	Norwegian government leaves Tromsö in *Devonshire*	June 8
10					Norwegian army demobilized. Resignation of Mr. Chamberlain	10

A SHORT BIBLIOGRAPHY

Operations in Central Norway, 1940 : Dispatches by Lieutenant-General H. R. S. Massy, 13th May 1940, published as a Supplement to the *London Gazette,* No. 37584, 29th May 1946 (H.M.S.O.).

The First and Second Battles of Narvik: Dispatches by Rear-Admiral R. H. C. Hallifax and Vice-Admiral W. J. Whitworth, 25th April 1940, published as a Supplement to the *London Gazette,* No. 38005, 3rd July 1947 (H.M.S.O.).

The Norway Campaign, 1940 : Dispatches by Admiral of the Fleet the Earl of Cork and Orrery, 17th July 1940; Major-General P. J. Mackesy, 15th May 1940; Lieutenant-General C. J. E. Auchinleck, 19th June 1940—all published as a Supplement to the *London Gazette,* No. 38011, 10th July 1947 (H.M.S.O.).

The Campaign in Norway: T. K. Derry (*History of the Second World War,* U.K. Military Series, H.M.S.O. 1952). This scholarly and carefully-compiled volume (referred to in the text as the Official History) is considered by many whose opinion carries weight to be the best of the Second World War historical series: it is a thousand pities that, at the time of writing, it is out of print.

The War at Sea, Vol. I: Captain S. W. Roskill (*History of the Second World War,* U.K. Military Series, H.M.S.O.). A balanced account by the foremost naval historian of our time—which, however, deals less fully with some aspects of Norwegian campaign naval operations than Dr. Derry's book, to which it refers.

The Gathering Storm (*The Second World War, Vol. I*): Winston S. Churchill (Cassell, 1948). Indispensable reading, but suffering from imperfect recollection and imperfect checking back of facts—has been particularly criticized by Captain Roskill.

The Fight at Odds (*Royal Air Force, 1939-45,* Vol. I, H.M.S.O.). Deals but briefly with air operations in Norway.

Narvik: Captain D. F. W. Macintyre (Evans, 1959). Oddly titled, because it deals with naval operations off the whole of Norway. Contains much valuable information not published elsewhere but also, regrettably, out of print at the time of writing.

The Mountains Wait: Theodor Broch (Michael Joseph, 1943). A moving contemporary account of Narvik from the inside, seen through Norwegian eyes.

I Saw It Happen in Norway: Carl J. Hambro (Hodder and Stoughton, 1940). Another valuable contemporary Norwegian account of the early phases.

'Problems of the Norwegian Campaign, 1940,: W. Hubatsch (*Journal of the Royal United Services Institution,* 1958). A German assessment.

The Campaign in Northern Norway: Colonel O. Munthe-Kaas (U.S. official publication, 1944). The story of General Fleischer's 6th Norwegian Division.

Happy Odyssey: Lieutenant-General Sir A. Carton de Wiart (Cape, 1950). A delightful book in its own right, full of pungent understatements.

With the Foreign Legion at Narvik: Captain P. O. Lapie (Murray, 1941). An infuriating but revealing book.

Adventurous Life: Admiral Lord Mountevans (Hutchinson, 1946). He did, indeed, deserve a better mission.

Norway, the Commandos, Dieppe: Christopher Buckley (1951). The author was among the best war correspondents.

Regimental Histories of the following regiments:
      The Scots Guards
      The Irish Guards
      The Royal Leicestershire Regiment
      The King's Own Yorkshire Light Infantry (K.O.Y.L.I.)
      The Royal Lincolnshire Regiment
      The Sherwood Foresters
      The York and Lancaster Regiment
      The South Wales Borderers
      The Green Howards

The above list is not exhaustive, but is limited to what, in the author's view, are the most authoritative or important publications in our own language. For German readers a meticulously detailed official history has now been published under the title, *Weserübung.* For Norwegian readers there are books by many of the protagonists in the campaign: the Norwegian War Historical Department (Forsvarets Krigshistoriske Avdeling) has already published twelve volumes on operations at sea or on land and has another five in preparation.

INDEX

Aalesund, 23, 101, 209

Aandalsnes, 2, 58, 139, 189, 196, 202; landings at, 115, 125, 126, 127, 136, 138, 141, 162, 164, 168, 185–6, 203; air raids on, 145, 179, 186, 187, 190, 204, 210, 245, 274, 291; evacuation of, 209, 210, 213, 235, 245, 270, 272, 293

Aasmarka, 143, 162

Acasta, H.M.S., 12, 304, 308, 309

Achilles, H.M.S., 12

Afridi, H.M.S., 215

air cover, German, 28, 35, 117, 195; Allied lack at Namsos, 133–4; and in Operation Hammer, 161; disastrous attempt at, 176–9, 191; for 15 Brigade, 189, 191

AIR FORCES

BRITISH, 12, 57, 60, 71–2, 115, 128, 204, 215; lack of aircraft, 8, 10, 78, 103, 176, 225–7; few long-range bombers, 8, 64; unable to cover Namsos, 133–4; scratch landing-grounds, 176–8, 256; ground staffs, 178–9; during evacuation, 263–5, 296–7, 301–5; communication aids, 264; and violation of Swedish border, 264–5; at Pothus, 273–4

SQUADRONS

46 Hurricane, 179, 226, 262–3, 270, 271, 279–83, 304–5; 263 Gladiator, 176–9, 226–7, 256, 262–3, 271, 273–4, 281, 304

GERMAN, superiority over Allies, 8, 60, 103; and troop movement, 43, 47, 53, 71, 234, 241; Allies underestimate, 56; hampers Royal Navy, 63–5, 103, 112, 155; towns destroyed by, 83–4, 118, 133, 186–7, 204, 275, 310; attacks landings, 120–1, 135, 155; regularity of attacks, 148, 190, 264, 286–7; increasing pressure, 187, 190, 200–1, 221, 234, 296, 299; ignorant of evacuation, 296–7, 302–3

NORWEGIAN, 34, 47, 55, 227

airborne troops, take Oslo, 46, 53; take Stavanger, 47; in Trondheim, 48; build-up of, 71; near Dombaas, 126

aircraft carriers, 64, 72, 161, 204, 255, 270; shortage of, 94, 110; in final evacuation, 293, 301–5, 309

airfields, shortage of, 24, 60, 225–6; Germans in control of, 64, 70, 94, 98; possible sites, 231, 234, 242, 245; preparation of, 245, 253, 256, 262

Ajax, H.M.S., 12